# HOW TO PROMOTE, PUBLICIZE, AND ADVERTISE YOUR GROWING BUSINESS

## Getting the Word Out without Spending a Fortune

Kim Baker
Sunny Baker

John Wiley & Sons, Inc.
New York · Chichester · Brisbane · Toronto · Singapore

**Library of Congress Cataloging-in-Publication Data**

Baker, Kim; 1955–
    How to promote, publicize, and advertise your growing business : getting the word out without spending a fortune / by Kim Baker & Sunny Baker.
      p.  cm.
    Includes bibliographical references and index.
    ISBN 0-471-55194-5.—ISBN 0-471-55193-7 (pbk.)
    1. Advertising. 2. Marketing. 3. Public relations. I. Baker, Sunny. II. Title.
HF5823.B24   1992
659—dc20                         91-29669

10 9 8 7 6 5 4

# Acknowledgments

We gratefully acknowledge the many marketing, communications, and advertising people we have worked with over the years. They unknowingly supplied us with the ideas and techniques we have adapted, borrowed, and sometimes rejected. And many thanks to our clients, who always taught us something and usually paid our fees.

Special thanks go to Roger Wincek, one of advertising's great copywriters, whom we are lucky enough to have living in Phoenix so we can pick his brains. And to Lucy, Rachel, and the rest of the family at Hollywood Alley, who not only kept us fed while we were writing the book, but also kept us smiling. We are indebted to Joe Taylor and Jan Katayama who were always there to answer our obscure technical questions and even took us to lunch on occasion. To our agent, Mike Snell, thanks for getting the word out for us. Finally, we appreciate the support of John B. Mahaney, our editor, and the staff at John Wiley & Sons who helped bring this project to fruition. Of course, for any errors, omissions, and failures to communicate, we take full responsibility.

Kim Baker
Sunny Baker

# Contents

# Introduction: Everyone in Business Needs to Get the Word Out

This book has been written for all the people in business who must promote, publicize, advertise, make presentations, attend tradeshows, or otherwise get the word out about their products and services. And that is just about everyone at one time or another. Even if marketing isn't your primary responsibility, it's almost guaranteed that someday you will be asked to produce an advertisement, create a newsletter, attend a tradeshow, or help develop a brochure. You may be asked to coordinate a special fund-raising event or to put on a training seminar. You may own a small company and have only a limited promotional budget and need to become your own advertising agency. Or you may be a student who needs to hit the ground running in your first management job and want a more practical point of view about promotion and advertising than was provided in your courses. If you are already in a marketing job or a corporate communications department, perhaps you have experience creating strategies, but lack direct implementation skills in producing advertising, publicity, or one of the other marketing communications tools. This book is for all of you.

Every person with a product or a cause to promote is faced with the challenges of increasing market visibility, developing an image, and implementing the promotional steps required to meet financial goals. Every corporation, business, and not-for-profit organization must communicate with the world at large through marketing communications—including ads, brochures, public relations, packaging, tradeshows, and more. Politician, not-for-profit foundation, small manufacturer, massive conglomerate, retail store—every business and organization must attract attention or perish. And someone in every organization must manage the process of getting marketing communications produced. Although the specific promotional tactics may vary between a corner grocery store and a Fortune 500 corporation, the issues, obstacles, and personalities involved are very similar.

Deceptively, managing marketing communications projects looks easy, perhaps even entertaining. Because the projects are visually oriented and most people have two eyes—it would appear that anyone can do a good job at them. Why then are so many companies constantly switching advertising agencies? Why do marketing communications projects so often finish late and go over budget? Why do some managers feel they get little value for the precious capital spent for promotions and advertising? Why is so much money wasted?

Based on our own experiences, we estimate that typical companies misspend fifty cents or more of every communications dollar for one reason or another. They misspend because they let their agencies do the thinking and make the choices for them, because they create communications without a clear message, because they use the wrong media, and because they don't know the difference between substantive changes and costly ones. They also misspend because unscrupulous vendors take advantage of their lack of production knowledge. The list goes on and on.

## THE MARKETING COMMUNICATIONS PROBLEMS FACING EVERY BUSINESS

Simplified, the problem with producing effective marketing communications is threefold. First, although sometimes perceived as an "anyone-can-do-it" field, the production of effective marketing communications in fact involves tremendous technology and complexity. From the press room humidity that shifts color, to the choice of words and the texture of paper—everything affects the audience's perception and ultimately the value of communications projects. Murphy's Law does not adequately describe the problems that even a simple communications project encounters as it moves through myriad steps to completion. And to make things worse, the technical and artistic jargon of the advertising world makes computer terminology pale by comparison.

Second, even the best manager falters when faced with the intense, egotistical, and mercurial personalities that abound in the communications field. Coincidentally, the most talented creative people are frequently the most difficult to decipher and control.

Third, limited dollars must be effectively spread out and carefully divided among essential projects. Unfortunately, it's just as easy to spend money on improperly chosen projects and inappropriate creative talent than on the right ones.

To deal with these problems, managers responsible for implementing and controlling creative projects need to know how to plan marketing communications projects, budget them, specify them, and hire vendors and agencies to carry them out. You do not need a degree in advertising or marketing to produce effective marketing communications for your business, but you do need a practical understanding of the steps, technologies, and decisions that must be made.

We have worked on the creative side in agencies and have managed communications departments from within corporations for more than 15 years. This book attempts to synthesize our experiences into succinct guidelines, step-by-step checklists, and easy-to-use charts that can help you answer everyday marketing communications questions such as

- How do I get my product or service noticed?
- Which communications tools will best meet my promotional objectives?
- What are the steps to create an annual report, an ad, or a brochure?
- Who should I hire and how should I supervise them?
- How do I manage a communications project and control costs?
- How should I measure and evaluate what I get for my money?
- Are there shortcuts I can use to get the word out faster?

This book guides you through the creation and production considerations for almost every kind of marketing communications project. So the surprises are minimal and the results are positive. In addition, this book is filled with money-saving tips for budgets of all sizes. Real-world stories are included to demonstrate the concepts in action. Perhaps most importantly, we have attempted to explain the principles of marketing communications without delving into complex and incomprehensible theory. Using the steps and guidelines provided in the book and your own natural communication abilities and intuitive insights, you will be able to develop marketing communications that get the word out with impact and hopefully have some fun in the process.

# 1 | Marketing Communications: Creating Your Company's Voice to the World

Businesses, not-for-profit organizations, clubs, Fortune 500 megacorporations, and political groups all use marketing communications every day. That's because any organization with goods or services to sell, votes to influence, donations to request, or an axe to grind must attempt to make its products salable and desirable. And marketing communications are the means of getting the word out about your products, company, and activities. (In the rest of the book the word product is used in place of goods, services, votes, and donations for simplicity—but the information and techniques apply to all of these "products.")

The marketing of all products is based on the four Ps: Product, Price, Place, and Promotion. *Product* is what you have to sell, *price* is what you sell it for, *place* is where your product is available (also called distribution), and *promotion* is how you make people aware of the product so they choose to buy it. So where do marketing communications fit in?

Of course, all promotional activities are marketing communications—but marketing communications encompass more than the promotion of products. Marketing communications include almost every form of communication a company presents to the outside world.

For example, if you own a small carpet cleaning business, the *product* might consist of a "dry" method of cleaning that causes less damage to carpets than older systems. *Price* is the amount you charge customers for the cleaning service. The price must be fair and competitive, but must also include enough profit for the company to prosper. When considering price, you might decide to price your superior technology close to the competitor's price for older technology because this gives you a competitive advantage. The *place* component of marketing would involve determining that in the household carpet cleaning business the customers cannot come to you. As a result, you will need to purchase and equip a suitable truck for distributing the service. You'll also have to decide where to concentrate your sales efforts, and provide the service in neighborhoods where consumers are most likely to need and purchase carpet cleaning services. The consumers in these neighborhoods must have both the resources and the motivation to get their carpets cleaned. *Promotion* for your business might consist of taking out a series of small ads in local newspapers or placing flyers on the doorknobs of houses in a selected area.

The ads and flyers are part of marketing communications. But the marketing communications required for the company also include a logo for the business, the business cards and letterhead, the sign for the truck, and a brochure explaining the advantages of the cleaning process with a price list of services available.

Let's look at another illustration of the Four Ps and marketing communications in a larger corporation. A large company typically spends months in research to better understand how to tailor their products, pricing, promotion, and distribution to the marketplace. After the research is done, the *product* may be a new line of hand-held cellular telephones. When determining *price,* the company decides to produce a budget line of phones because the market for expensive phones is overcrowded with high-end products. *Place* involves distributing the telephones through the company's existing retail and wholesale distribution channels. *Promotion* requires a major ad campaign developed by a large advertising agency, coupled with public relations efforts and a targeted direct mail program. A series of brochures for dealers and attractive packaging to give the phones "shelf appeal" are also required.

In addition to the promotions, the marketing communications for this company again include the company's logo and stationery, as they did for the small carpet cleaning company. Other marketing communications include the articles in trade magazines and newspapers, the booth and materials used in the tradeshows, the seminars given around the country for new distributors, and the presentation used at the stockholders' meeting. Even the choice of new company uniforms for the service and delivery personnel is a marketing communications project because the uniforms reflect the company's image. In fact, the marketing communications include everything that presents the company and the products to the public at large.

These two examples illustrate the line between marketing and marketing communications. *Marketing* is concerned with how to make a product salable to the market and *marketing communications* are the vehicles for persuading the market that it is the right product from the right company. Marketing communications are the company's voice to the world.

Of course, the ultimate goal of marketing and marketing communications is always sales. And if both the marketing and marketing communications efforts have been appropriately executed, the sales process goes smoothly and enjoys greater success.

## THE MOST DANGEROUS COMPUTER IN THE WORLD: MARKETING COMMUNICATIONS THAT WORKED EVEN WHEN THE PRODUCT DIDN'T

Even though effective marketing communications efforts are vitally important to a company's success in the marketplace, you can't expect communications alone to make a company successful. Consider the fate of Gavilan Computer Corporation, for example. The industry darling of the early 1980s, with a tagline, "The Most Dangerous Computer in the World," Gavilan Computer sought to build and market the world's first laptop computer. Introducing the computer in a handsome booth at the COMDEX tradeshow in Las Vegas (the most important tradeshow in the computer industry), the press and public were ecstatic with the news that at last a fully-functional, battery-powered computer, small enough for use on an airplane, was coming to market.

Because of excellent press coverage, Gavilan's powerful advertising, and a well-trained sales team, Gavilan signed hundreds of dealers almost overnight. Major corporations placed hundreds of advance orders for the neat little machines for their executives and sales teams. The marketing communications, including the ads, the tradeshow booth, and the brochures, even won awards from major industry associations.

So where is Gavilan today? Even with the brilliant efforts of the marketing communications department, Gavilan sunk without a trace after squandering more than $30 million in venture capital. Why? Because they couldn't get the promised machines to work before they ran out of money. This is a classic example of a marketing communications success and company failure.

Oddly enough, small groups of former Gavilan employees, most of whom purchased large blocks of now worthless stock, still get together for parties and try to collectively figure out just what it was that went wrong . . .

## INTRODUCING THE TOOLS OF THE TRADE

> It used to be that people needed products to survive. Now products need people to survive.
>
> Nicholas Johnson

In the last 50 years the categories of marketing communications tools have not changed that much, but the number of channels available for getting the word out has grown immensely. Although there are fewer newspapers for advertising and press coverage, there are far more magazines, television channels, on-line shopping services, and AM and FM radio stations. There are also many more products available to consumers than any time in history. Not only must today's companies contend with local competition, but imports and exports have reached a global scale bringing voracious new competitors into most markets.

There are marketing communications tools for meeting competitive challenges of all kinds and a number of choices to make when putting a communications program together. In most cases a combination of tools should be used to meet objectives for promotion and sales development. The combination of tools used by a company to get the word out is often referred to as the *marketing communications mix* or *promotional mix*.

The basic marketing communications "tools of the trade" include *advertising, public relations and publicity, direct mail, collateral materials, tradeshows, image and identity development, packaging and merchandising, special promotions and special events,* and *giveaways and gee-gaws*. An in-depth chapter or section is included in the book for each of these tools explaining how to use them and how they work. Worksheets and step-by-step procedures are presented to help you develop effective marketing communications, either on your own or with the help of outside agencies or communications professionals employed by your company.

Keep in mind as you read the next sections that one tool may overlap into another tool's territory, depending on how it is used. A brochure may be used in a direct mail program. An ad may be reprinted as a sales handout. News releases, originally intended for the trade press, may be sent to customers as promotional materials. The creative mixing of marketing communications tools often saves money. If you are on a tight budget, it's advisable to look for alternative or multiple uses for the communications you produce whenever possible.

## Advertising

Advertising is the most familiar marketing communications tool because it is everywhere—in newspapers, magazines, TV, radio, billboards, even written in the sky in smoke by airplanes. By definition, *advertising* is the persuasive promotion of a commodity, idea, or service communicated through media and paid for by a named, interested party.

All advertising consists of two parts—the advertisement and the medium. The major media are print, television, and radio. There are also miscellaneous media including billboards, bus displays, kiosks, and on-line computer services. If an ad is destined for print, it may consist of several pieces of film, ready for the newspaper or magazine printer. If it's to air on radio or TV, it will most likely be on tape. Newspapers and magazines sell *space* by size, print complexity, and frequency (the number of times the ad will run). TV and radio sell *airtime* by length, time of day, day of week, programming content, and frequency. Billboard and transit ads are sold as *showings*.

All advertising placements, regardless of media used, are purchased (or occasionally donated for charity purposes). The charges for purchas-

| Tool | Strengths | Weaknesses |
|---|---|---|
| Advertising | Offers tight control of the message as well as control of the look & feel of the ad.<br><br>Can reach a large number of customers very quickly.<br><br>Many creative options and media choices. | Expensive.<br><br>May not be cost-effective for products with a small market that is difficult to reach<br><br>Requires professionals to produce quality ad materials. |
| Public Relations | Can be inexpensive when compared to advertising.<br><br>Can be highly influential in many markets.<br><br>Simple PR can often be produced "in-house." | Offers little control of the message because editors screen and interpret PR and sometimes trash materials without reading.<br><br>A positive message can be changed to a negative message by an editor. |
| Direct Mail | Can reach a targeted prospect directly.<br><br>Can be inexpensive.<br><br>Tight control of the message. | Very competitive with many companies overusing this tool.<br><br>Useless if a suitable and up-to-date mailing list cannot be identified. |
| Collateral Materials | Tight control of message and image.<br><br>Many creative options.<br><br>Flexible document length means that message can be tailored to a wide range of uses.<br><br>Can be used as direct mail piece in a pinch.<br><br>Long life compared to other tools. | Useless without a delivery channel (i.e., salesforce, tradeshow, retail store).<br><br>Little control of how it's used in some environments. Retailers are fond of stacking important product literature in unsightly piles in the back room. |
| Tradeshows | Immediate influence of interested people.<br><br>Industry presence.<br><br>Direct feedback from customers. | Can be expensive and time-consuming.<br><br>No control of volume or quality of show attendees. |
| Packaging & Merchandising | For products where it can be employed, attractive packaging and merchandising can be compelling selling tools. | Can be very expensive in some markets.<br><br>A poor choice can sink some consumer products. |
| Special Events | Compelling selling and interest-generating tools. | Not useful or too expensive in some markets. |
| Special Promotion Items (Gee-Gaws) | A good choice may have a long life on a client's desk or in his home. | A poor choice or obviously "budget" item may offend some customers. |
| * Note that the category Image is not included because it is composed of too many sub-categories. | | |

Figure 1.1. A comparison of marketing communications tools.

ing *media* are based on the number of potential readers or viewers for that media. For example, a full-page ad in a small town newspaper is much cheaper than a one-eighth-page ad in the *New York Times*. Airtime on late night *Gomer Pyle* reruns on a UHF channel is far less costly than on *World News Tonight* or *The Cosby Show*. Generally the cost to produce an ad is actually less than the media charges to run it, although megacorporations may spend millions of dollars producing a single ad. You don't think that Michael Jackson sang about Pepsi for free do you?

To show how persuasive commercial advertising can be, a survey in the 1970s disclosed that by the middle of the decade more American children knew who Ronald McDonald was than Santa Claus! Advertising is the most expensive tool for promoting products, but is highly effective when used properly. According to research done by England's global news-weekly, *The Economist,* Coca Cola is currently the most recognized corporate name in the world followed a few steps behind by Japan's Sony Corporation. Coke is promoted primarily with *very* expensive advertising and with obviously impressive results.

Advertising's strength is that a product's message can be tightly controlled, along with the look and feel of the ad, be it in print, on TV, or elsewhere. Depending on the product, it can also influence a great number of people very quickly. Advertising's weakness is that even with the most careful choice of *placement* (which newspapers, radio stations, magazines, or television networks run the ad), there is no guarantee that the intended market will see it or pay any attention to it.

Some kinds of advertising are more difficult to identify than the obvious ads in magazines and on TV. For example, a trend that started in American movies during the late 1980s was to showcase consumer products for a fee as an integral part of the movie. Tom Cruise in *Top Gun* was frequently seen quaffing an ice-cold Pepsi with relish, transforming this movie into a two-hour Pepsi commercial! Or how about the Reese's Pieces eaten by the adorable alien in *ET: The Extraterrestrial?* A relatively unknown product was a hit almost overnight. (Reportedly, Mars, the manufacturers of M & Ms, turned this opportunity down.) Music videos are another example: they are really song-length commercials for a band and album.

## Public Relations and Publicity

Advertising is even more effective when combined with other tools of the trade. One of the most important tools to combine with advertising is a complete publicity and public relations program. By definition, public relations is self-generated information on a commodity, idea, or service to be used as news, education, or for general interest. Publicity is one aspect of public relations—the free mention of your products or company by the media.

Public relations is usually referred to as *PR.* PR uses the press, including magazines, newspapers, trade journals, and broadcast media, to explain and promote products. PR also includes special events sponsored by your company, such as educational seminars, customer parties, and charity events.

PR is also an excellent tool for what is known in the communications industry as *damage control*. When the Exxon Valdez soiled Prince William Sound in Alaska in 1989, Exxon immediately mounted a major PR program to show what they were doing to clean up the mess.

Companies (or their public relations agencies) write news releases describing a product, event, or something of interest and then submit the materials to a targeted list of editors and industry VIPs. Photos, videos, and other promotional items may accompany a news release. Editors pick and choose the best material and publish it as news and feature articles or air it as news on TV and radio. Besides press releases, PR tools include news conferences, events for the media (a factory tour, for example), self-serving magazine articles, books, media kits, and more.

Unfortunately, one of PR's weaknesses is that PR materials are open for interpretation and screening by editors. Unlike advertising, where the message can be tightly controlled, editors can use PR material at their discretion. During the Valdez incident, some of Exxon's PR was turned around to show a negligent attitude on the part of the company. When the company pronounced the cleanup complete, the press used this opportunity to show that much work still remained. The press made it appear as if the company was trying to put the incident behind it without finishing the costly cleanup process.

On the other side, public relations is often viewed as more objective and accurate than advertising. PR also has other advantages over advertising—it can be almost as effective in getting the word out and, in most cases, it costs considerably less.

## Direct Mail

Direct mail is another powerful communications tool that does a great job of getting the word out. It typically consists of a brochure, letter, flyer, price list, or catalog mailed to a list of prospective customers. Everyone who has ever opened a mailbox knows what direct mail is ("You may already be a winner!"). Newsletters are another kind of direct mail tool that have recently become very popular (and overused in many markets).

In markets in which customers can be identified by address, direct mail can be a powerful vehicle for building awareness and gaining sales. Mailing lists can be accumulated from customer records or rented from magazine subscription lists and a variety of research organizations. For example, a wildlife conservation group soliciting donations might choose a list of subscribers to a nature magazine. The assumption in this promotion is that if the magazine's readers enjoy learning about nature, they will want to do something (donate) to protect it.

The strength of direct mail is that it can be a less expensive, more targeted alternative to advertising. Its major weakness is overuse. There are so many direct mail pieces hitting mailboxes that unless the *mailer* is particularly unique or compelling, it will hit the trash unread along with the rest of the day's *junk mail.* Also, if a product is targeted to a large or broad group of customers, it will be difficult to identify a suitable mailing list. Still, many companies get great results from well-executed direct mail programs.

## Collateral Materials

Collateral materials are the printed materials used to communicate or reinforce a company's message or facilitate the sales process. Collateral materials include brochures, annual reports, catalogs, and datasheets— printed matter that is handed out to prospective customers and investors. A visit to any new car showroom will disclose a rack of fancy color brochures for each model. Technical products rely on datasheets to extol their features and specifications. Major retailers supplement their operations with catalogs of wares for consumers unable to visit distant stores.

Collateral can be as expensive and complicated as an eight-color, sixteen-page brochure costing over $100,000 for writing, design, production, and printing, or it may be a simple price list photocopied for 4¢ per page.

The strengths and weaknesses of collateral programs depend on how they are used in conjunction with other marketing communications tools. In some markets, strong (expensive) collateral is a must; in other markets, collateral plays a relatively minor role and simple, inexpensive materials work just as well.

## Tradeshows

Many organizations use tradeshows to promote their products and present their image to the world. A tradeshow, by definition, is an event where purveyors of related commodities, services, or ideas assemble to showcase their products to other interested parties with a common interest in the trade.

Tradeshows involve a group of companies or organizations using a shared exhibit location to attract prospective customers, the press, and industry analysts. Tradeshows vary considerably in format, size, and presentation. Most cities have car and boat shows put on by local dealers and the industry to sell cars and boats. Many industries have booths in shows catering to customers in one particular field such as computers, machine tools, or the construction industry. Political parties stage massive party conventions and psychics and mediums have fortune-telling fairs.

In some industries tradeshows are a critical component of the marketing communications program; in other markets they are unimportant. Tradeshows can be expensive and time-consuming to attend as an exhibitor, but for industries with limited press coverage, they can be an important resource for identifying prospective customers. Attending a large tradeshow with a huge booth is also a standard tactic for demonstrating corporate prowess and product success to one's competitors while communicating industry presence and dominance.

Another kind of tradeshow idea that has waxed and waned during the 1980s and 1990s is a permanent or semipermanent tradeshow often called an *expo* or *industry mart*. Expos house exhibitors with related product lines to showcase their wares on an on-going basis. They work best for industries with a high-dollar volume and fast-changing product lines such as clothing, electronics, and computers.

## Image and Identity Development

Image is the most all-encompassing aspect of marketing communications involving the perception of a company and its products by customers, analysts, the community, and the press. An organization's image is created through the cumulative effect of all its communications materials, and involves other internal and external factors such as news coverage and community standing. Almost everything a company does contributes to its image, either positively or negatively.

From a marketing communication's perspective, image starts with a logo or symbol depicting the company. (Some professionals such as attorneys and accountants use a simple typeset of their name rather than a logo. This is to give them an image of being honest and trustworthy. Used this way, it becomes their logo.) The logo is used on all communications materials including business cards, letterhead, signs, and ads.

Other aspects of corporate image may include company colors, office location and furniture, and even the appearance of the salesforce. IBM, for example, is known by the nickname, "big blue." Why? Because the company's logo is blue, they are fond of building products with blue cases, and, for years, IBM's salesforce wore similar pin-striped blue suits.

Image is designed to position a company correctly in the mind of its customers. A computer company might choose a very modern look to convey an image of technological prowess. A bank may rely on a very careful, conservative look to connote dependability and stability.

Image is pervasive and insidious in its affect on customers. For example, you would probably have second thoughts about visiting a dentist who hands out business cards on fluorescent paper, makes you wait hours in a messy waiting room, and practices in his pajamas. It wouldn't matter that his professional credentials are impeccable—you would still have a bad feeling about him because of his image. Thus, image is affected by everything you do that makes contact with your customers and the outside world. You should always consider your image when communicating in any form.

## Packaging and Merchandising

Almost every tangible product is "packaged" in one way or another. *Packaging* is used to ship a product or make it suitable for display and purchase. Packaging is also used to attract attention and compel customers to purchase one product over another. For example, the right packaging can make one kind of breakfast cereal catch the eye better than another. A visit to the laundry soap aisle in the local supermarket demonstrates the results of millions of dollars in packaging research and testing. The brightly packaged brands attempt to "outscream" each other to get your attention.

Packaging can also be used to visually project the quality or price of a product (part of the product's image). The wine industry, for example, differentiates cheap wine from expensive vintages with different labels. Wine labels with a slightly shiny appearance are used for sweet, inexpensive wines. The higher priced varietals are labeled with a matte-finish paper, embossing, and gold inks. In the case of elaborately packaged goods such as expensive cosmetics and perfumes, the cost of the packaging can far exceed the manufacturing cost of the contents.

Packaging includes functional components too. Boxes and custom-made foam are used to protect products during shipping. Many products require packaging that includes multiple elements. Toothpaste, for example, must be packaged in a tube, the tube put in an attractive box, and groups of boxes protected during shipping in a strong corrugated cardboard box.

*Merchandising* is related to packaging in its production, but is different in its purpose. Merchandising refers to any physical element that helps generate awareness and sell a product, but in itself is not a part of the product or packaging. Merchandising tools include displays, signs, racks, and shelving. An example of merchandising is a colorful cardboard display rack for a new product placed at the end of a drugstore or supermarket aisle. Neon beer signs and giant inflatable Pepsi cans are also examples. Merchandising is especially powerful in retail environments and less so in most other markets.

## Special Promotions and Special Events

There are many marketing communications and events that do not fit neatly into one of the categories we have already presented. They encompass a variety of unusual activities and ideas called special promotions. *Special promotions* include contests, discount giveaways, couponing, and special events designed for promoting a company or a product. For example, General Motors designed and built a solar-powered car and raced it in a number of competitions limited to solar-powered vehicles. GM used the car in a powerful advertising and PR program, but not until after the car had won its first important race.

In another example, a small store that specializes in *very* expensive stereo and video systems began holding small, friendly parties four times a year for customers and their friends. The events were run after regular store hours and no sales discussions were initiated by the store's owner or staff. However, each single event typically accounted for more sales than the volume of the entire previous month!

A unique special promotion that may be considered merchandising by some is the Goodyear Blimp. It has nothing to do with Goodyear's primary products—tires—but it certainly gets the company's name remembered the next time someone needs a set of radials.

The underlying goal behind most special promotions is short-term, immediate sales. Special events are used to educate customers or generate awareness. Special events and promotions can be powerful sales development tools for companies of any size, limited only by imagination and budget.

## Giveaways and Gee-Gaws

This final miscellaneous category of marketing communications includes a variety of items known in the trade as *gee-gaws* and other promotional tools that do not fit neatly into one of the standard categories. Many of these tools are related to collateral materials because they are often given away in a sales setting. Examples include pens, pencils, paperclip holders, notepads, and shirt pocket protectors imprinted with your company's name or logo. Many distributors for these gadgets have opened storefront showrooms so clients can look over the variety of items available. National chains such as The Idea Man have sprung up all over the United States selling nothing but these kinds of giveaway items.

Prices for gee-gaws range from 10¢ for a ballpoint pen to over $1,200 for an engraved sterling-silver tea set. Much of the work is custom designed for a particular project. The range of possibilities is striking too. A Phoenix-based software company gave away coffee mugs that stand on two cowboy-booted legs. A northeast-based chicken fastfood restaurant gave away hilarious rubber chickens with their name imprinted on each one. McDonald's is famous for its children's gee-gaws, including hamburger cars and stuffed Ronald McDonald dolls. A few have turned into products because the demand was so great. Like special events, gee-gaws are limited only by budget and ideas.

The basic tools, issues, and concerns in creating marketing communications have been introduced. The next thing to understand before you begin your marketing communications program is how the basic messages are developed, which is covered in the next chapter. Creating the messages is a step shared in producing any marketing communications tool. After the chapter on message development, the other chapters show you how to use and produce each of the basic marketing communications tools with impact.

# 2 | Marketing Messages: Deciding What to Say to Make Things Sell

The power of all marketing communications tools is embodied in how well they communicate their messages. There are two messages at work in all marketing communications—the message the company intends to deliver and the message the audience actually receives. From the consumer's point of view, the messages are the thoughts, ideas, or concepts that are perceived after a tool like an advertisement, a brochure, or direct mail piece is seen or heard. If a tool is doing its job effectively, it delivers the right message to the audience you selected to receive it. If a tool isn't working, it is usually because it is delivering an inappropriate, convoluted, or ambiguous message to the people for whom it was intended (or for reasons covered in other chapters, it is not being seen by the right people).

Marketing communications use three primary methods for delivering messages: written, verbal, and physical representations (also called nonverbal communications). Verbal communication is spoken whereas written communications use printed words. Physical elements in communications include representational elements such as photographs, illustrations, or in media such as radio and TV—body postures, voice intonation, gestures, and sounds.

In essence, everything encompassed in a communications tool is part of the communication and thus part of the message being transmitted—words, pictures, textures, position on a page, tone of voice, background music, choice of models, or whatever. Unfortunately for the marketer, the same tool will communicate different things to different people. Based on their personalities, social status, culture, and other social and psychological factors, people have very different ways of perceiving their world and making judgments about what they see and hear. The challenge in developing marketing communications tools is to consistently have the target audience perceive the underlying message as being close to what you intend the message to be.

It is of little concern if people outside your target audience don't get the message correctly as long as they don't find it offensive or irritating. Keep in mind that today's uninterested observer could become tomorrow's hot prospect as the market shifts or if you introduce new products. For this reason, you don't want to offend anyone.

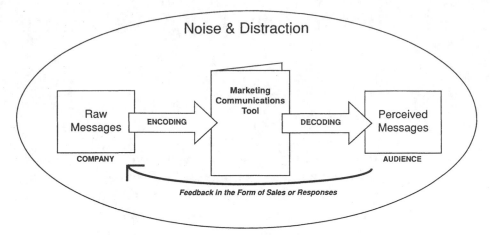

Figure 2.1. The basic communications process.

## THE COMMUNICATION PROCESS IN DELIVERING EFFECTIVE MESSAGES

Understanding how messages are communicated in marketing situations starts with an understanding of the basic communication process. All marketing communications start with a set of basic messages or concepts, which are then translated or encoded through a variety of mechanisms into a marketing communications tool, such as an ad or a brochure. The individual members of the audience then decode the messages delivered by the tool based on their own perceptions and biases. Feedback occurs in the form of inquiry or purchase actions sent to the company by the audience, making the communication process a two-way affair as shown in the diagram.

Using this simple communication model as a guide, consider an athletic shoe company that determines its primary target audience is aspiring professionals who are concerned about their health and fitness. The messages the company decides to deliver include the following: "We make stylish sports shoes that last." "We sell superior sports shoes for a fair price." "Our shoes are the choice of romantic couples who jog together."

The company then encodes or translates these messages into a television commercial for viewing during prime time movies that employs written, visual, and physical channels of communication. The ad agency and company executives review the finished ad and agree on what they want it to say and, with the agency's help, how to say it. The verbal message includes the narrator's delivery of the words—rhythmic pacing and a dynamic, assertive tone of voice. The written channel includes the headlines and copy used to reinforce the verbal message. Even the choices of logo and typeface are conscious decisions to communicate durability and style. The physical elements include the filmed images of the models wearing the shoes in various activities—jogging, walking, playing basketball, even shopping.

More symbolism comes into play with the use of music in the background, the glowing light around the shoes, the expensive sports cars in the background, and images of friends of both sexes running together wearing the company's shoes while staring romantically into each other's eyes. The models used are also symbolic, representing the ideal kinds of people who wear the shoes—young, active, and living in trendy, up-scale surroundings. All these elements combine to form the coded transmission of the desired messages from the company's point of view.

When each person in the television audience sees the advertisement they decode the various elements into a perceived message. For example, an older widow living alone sees the ad and gets the message this is a product for young people and she thinks her granddaughter might like some of these shoes for her birthday. She thinks also how different shoes and life are now than when she was young. A 20-year-old man who jogs each day gets the message that the women in the ads are attractive, but he thinks shoes that can be worn by both men and women might lack the ruggedness required for a serious sports buff such as himself. A young girl likes the way the women look in the ad and decides she wants some of these shoes so she can be like them. A very pregnant woman sees the ad and wishes she were able to jog around like that. Feeling heavy and uncomfortable, she has no interest in the shoes.

However, in one case from the target market at which the message was aimed, a young couple who often jogs together sees the ad and immediately relates to the people shown engaged in activities they enjoy. The decoding tells them this is the shoe for couples who run together and enjoy each other's company. They have been convinced they'll get a good, durable shoe at the right price; in addition, wearing the shoes will make a visible statement about their positive relationship. Next time they buy running shoes, they'll buy the ones in the ad. Assuming that this was the intention of the company making the communication, the message hit its mark without negatively affecting the mass of other people who saw the ad.

In the example, everyone who saw the ad decoded the message in a slightly different way and not everyone decoded it as was intended by the company—though in the case of the couple, it came close. If the message was seen by and decoded successfully by enough people in the target market, feedback will arrive at the company in the form of increased sales or as numerous inquiries about the shoes for couples who jog together.

Ultimately, this feedback is one of the most important elements in the basic communication process. The actions of the audience provide information for the company to use in evaluating the messages, the tools, and the media used to communicate the messages. If enough people from the target audience buy the product, the company assumes that the correct messages are being delivered through the correct media and channels. If customers don't buy—then something is wrong. Unfortunately, it may not be the messages themselves that are at fault. Further research must be completed to discover whether it is something wrong with one of the messages or the implementation of the marketing communications tool. The choice of media may not reach enough people or some other part of the marketing mix may be at fault—such as price, distribution, or even the product itself.

For now, consider only those potential problems associated with the messages. Even in the simplified explanation of communication, there are many possibilities for error in the message development, encoding, and decoding process. The message could be improperly encoded (translated) by an ineffective choice of words or the inappropriate use of symbolism. Peripheral elements used in the communication such as the unintentional use of a background color could communicate messages that are unconscious and unknown. Noise in the communication process, such as a telephone call or other outside distractions, could affect the impact and decoding of the message. And, most importantly, the recipient of the message who decodes it based on a complex array of personal criteria will come up with an entirely unique interpretation of the intent.

Of course, even if you are lucky enough to accomplish reasonably good encoding and decoding of the messages, you may be delivering the wrong messages to the audience. For example, if you correctly deliver the message that your new cereal product is healthy—but your market really doesn't care about healthy food because they are interested in taste and image—then you have delivered the intended message but it does not have the expected result of motivating your audience to purchase your product.

## THE STEPS IN DEVELOPING APPROPRIATE MARKETING COMMUNICATIONS MESSAGES

The example for the athletic shoe company demonstrates that delivering marketing messages successfully involves determining the right message for the right audience, encoding the messages with the right verbal and nonverbal elements, and putting the messages in the right form or media so they are seen by people with a high probability of decoding the messages the way you want them decoded. To accomplish this, the development of marketing communications messages involves the following key steps:

Figure 2.2. The communications message process.

## Step 1. Determine all the relevant facts possible about the products and the company.

The preparation of the basic messages for your marketing communications starts with a complete list of facts relating to your company, the product, the competition, and the market, preferably in your own words or in tandem with your agency. The document you draft should include answers to key questions about the product and company to be used as background material for creating the messages.

The checklist describes the information you should gather, depending on the type of product and company you wish to promote. This assemblage of information will become a crucial source document as you, your agency, and others in the company produce various marketing communications tools.

## Step 2. Determine the key markets and audiences for the messages.

Audience targeting depends on your ability to segment the market into groups of people likely to buy or influence the purchase of your products based on their common geographic, demographic, psychographic, and/or sociopolitical profiles. Target audiences can also be seen as a combination of selected persons from all possible groups of people who have a common want, need, or interest in your products. Breaking your target markets into styles of consumers is also important as you develop messages. Lifestyles, purchasing patterns, family orientation, cultural traits, personality, and other factors can be used to define a target audience.

No single segmentation system or approach for defining target audiences works equally well for all products. The same people may occupy different market segments for different product types. For example, when buying laundry detergent you may be an impulsive shopper who grabs the brightest box of cheap detergent off the shelf with little regard for quality. However, when buying a new car, the fact that you are an aspiring, upwardly mobile professional might dominate your purchase behavior. Unlike choosing a box of laundry soap, where low price and eye appeal were your main purchase motivators, when choosing a new car, status and style might be your main concerns. So instead of choosing a a vehicle that is economy priced and has a reputation for reliability, you select an expensive German import of questionable value and reliability because this make and model has the prestige you seek.

**Product Description and Features**
- ☐ What sizes, models, shapes, styles, and other options are available?
- ☐ Are there multiple names or brands?
- ☐ What is the product? What does it do and what is it for?
- ☐ What is the physical description of the product in 25 words or less?

**Uses for the Product and Benefits**
- ☐ Who uses the product now (customers) and what do they use it for?
- ☐ What are the advantages of using the product?
- ☐ Is the product a necessity, a habit, image-oriented, something negative that people have to have (i.e. medicine), something of entertainment value, or something else?

**Desired and Current Image of the Product**
- ☐ How is the product perceived now? Is this appropriate or are changes in the image desired?
- ☐ Is the product perceived positively or negatively?
- ☐ Is the image one of value, luxury, practicality, fun, style, reliability, or something else?
- ☐ What do people think about the product? Is there research or testimony to back this up?
- ☐ What is the corporation's desired image for the product? What will be happening to affect this change in image?

**Technological Advantages and Performance Statistics**
- ☐ Is there any technology used in the product that makes it unique or superior?
- ☐ Are there any patented features in the product?
- ☐ What are the performance statistics?

**Competitive Positioning and Competitive Messages**
- ☐ Who are the competitors?
- ☐ What are the advantages and disadvantages of competitive products?
- ☐ What messages do the competitors use? Do any of these conflict with messages you may want to use?
- ☐ Do you have clear advantages over the competition? If so, what? If not, why would people buy your products instead of theirs?

Figure 2.3. Checklist of product and marketing information used to create marketing communications messages.

Although there are many theories in consumer behavior and consumer research that advocate different methods for market segmentation, the basics are quite simple if you work around the jargon. If you are interested in learning more about formal market segmentation systems, pick up a textbook in consumer behavior or advanced marketing in any major library. However, if you don't have time to become a consumer behavior expert, there are easier ways to effectively segment your marketplace for the purpose of targeting your marketing messages.

**Manufacturing Advantages**
- ☐ How is the product made or produced?
- ☐ Is there anything special about the manufacturing or production process?
- ☐ How many people are involved?
- ☐ Where is the product made?
- ☐ What are the key components or ingredients in manufacturing? Is there anything unique or special about the ingredients or components?

Service Advantages
- ☐ Are there any special services you provide?
- ☐ Are there any unique advantages your employees have, including training education or experience, that makes the level of service superior?

**Incentives and Special Promotional Features**
- ☐ Are there any special discounts, coupons, or other offers being made that customers should know about?
- ☐ Does the product work well with other products that customers use regularly? Is a joint promotion with this other company's product planned?

**Credibility Factors Unique to the Company or Product**
- ☐ How long has the company been in business?
- ☐ Are the company locations significant? If so, why and where are they?
- ☐ Are there any customers of significance?
- ☐ What are the highlights of the company history that may be of interest to potential customers?
- ☐ Are there executives or other employees with significant backgrounds and experiences that lend credibility to the company?
- ☐ Are there specific warranties and guarantees offered?
- ☐ Are testimonials available from important customers, celebrities or organizations? If so, do you have permission to use them?
- ☐ Is there any research that has substantiated the product's performance or company's claims?

**Weaknesses**
- ☐ Are there any weaknesses in the product, services, or company you definitely need to improve or minimize? List all you can think of and be excruciatingly honest about it.

Figure 2.3. *continued.*

If you work in a large company, there are research firms and databases available to help you define your target market. There are databases for both consumer and industrial products. Your advertising agency or public relations firm should know about the commercial databases most appropriate for your business. There are even inexpensive computer programs for mapping the census and demographic information down to the street level in cities across the United States. These databases and computerized mapping systems and can help identify both markets and locations for your business.

If you work in a small company, you can determine the attributes most important in defining your target audiences by answering the fundamental questions below. Not all of these questions are appropriate for all businesses, but they will give you a good idea of where to start:

- What kinds of people buy my products?
- Who are the best prospects for buying this product? What is it that makes these prospects similar in some way?
- What are the differences between the people who buy my products, use my products, and those who influence purchase decisions regarding my products, if any?
- Where do my customers live?
- Where do my customers work?
- What kinds of jobs do they have? Is there a pattern? Do they work specific hours that would affect their ability to purchase my product?
- Is there an age range into which most of my customers fall?
- Do my customers have children? What age ranges?
- Is there an educational level that most of my customers have attained?
- Is there an income level common to most of my customers?
- Why would people want to buy my products?
- How far would my customers come to buy my products?
- What do my customers do in general in their spare time?
- What do my customers consider most important about the products or the company (i.e., quality, image, prestige, durability, service, choices, etc.)?

When answering the questions, you may find that you actually have more than one target market. For example, a small restaurant serving Thai food may appeal to one type of customer who can be classified as a "wealthy gourmand," another kind of customer that includes students from a local university who consider eating Thai food an adventure, and a third general type of customer, such as the family with teenage children, who occasionally have Thai food for a special night out. Each of these customer types is a different target market with different buying patterns and needs profiles.

✎    # TIP: NAME YOUR AUDIENCE SEGMENTS
# FOR EASY REFERENCE

You may find it useful to identify your market segments and audiences with specific names customized to your own marketplace. For consumer products give the market segments names such as Baby Makers, Aspiring Young Professionals, Empty Nesters, Active Grayhairs, Health Nuts, Trendy Preteens, or whatever makes sense for your product and company. Be creative if you want or just be descriptive. The names should help you recall key aspects of the segment—age, demographics, values, motivations, or needs.

For industrial or commercial products, you might want to classify your markets by company size and type, giving them names such as Fortune 500 Manufacturer, Small-Time Entrepreneur, or High-Tech Megacompany.

Names help you keep the needs and buying profiles of each market segment separate in your mind and also make it easier to refer to specific market segments when you are working with other people. Be sure you detail the specific attributes of the named audiences, however. What is young to one may be middle-aged to another. What you defined as a large company may only be a small potato to someone else.

The trick in defining the target audiences or target markets for each product is to specify those elements common to as many purchasers and influencers as possible that define them as a unique market segment with a need for your product. Thus, a *market segment* is a general group of people that can be defined by shared criteria. Males working in blue collar jobs and living in Philadelphia might be a segment. Families who watch *Jeopardy* nightly and try to guess the answers while they eat dinner might be another. The segments you define will depend on your product and company.

To discover the market segments relevant to your company, list all the types of people who will potentially want or need to buy your product. Then, break your audiences into target markets with specific needs profiles related to your product. For each target audience, specify the desires, image, generalized personality profiles, and key lifestyle elements that affect a purchase decision related to your product. For industrial or commercial products, specify the decision makers involved in the buying process, detail the motivations these decision makers use to make their choices, and specify the general types of companies that will buy your products.

The bottom line is to profile the generalized behaviors that are relevant to definable groups and types of people (or companies) who will be involved in the purchase decisions for your products. As you develop different marketing communications tools, you will target them to these specific audiences. Why? Because the format and delivery of your messages will differ for different market segments and audience profiles. They read different magazines, watch different television shows, have different motivations, are concerned about different aspects of society, buy products from different stores and outlets, and, most importantly, have unique ways of decoding the messages you deliver.

The sample *Audience Segmentation Worksheet* provided here can be used to help specify the audiences for your own marketplace. Fill in one sheet for each of your product's major market segments.

**Step 3. Match the facts about the products and company to the key buying motivations of your target audiences.**   After you have identified the primary target audiences for your messages, you can determine the facts from your list most likely to influence each audience. The better you have done the job of specifying the needs, wants, desires, financial position, lifestyle, decision-making processes, and general expectations of each intended audience, the better you should be at determining the facts that are most appropriate for selling your products to these types of people.

Pretend for a moment that you are the marketing manager responsible for selling a new personal computer. After considerable thought and research, you have divided your market into three primary audiences and profiled each audience segment on an Audience Segmentation Worksheet. The three audiences are the purchasing agents of large companies who need to buy personal computers but are concerned about price and service more than technology; the obsessed technology buffs who want the whizziest, most advanced system they can afford—but who are unwilling to pay a premium for name or style; and education-conscious families who are mostly interested in computers as an educational tool for the kids, though they may also use it for financial applications in the home.

The facts that concern the commercial audience include specific competitive price–performance advantages, compatibility with other office systems, and the availability of on-site service. The facts that appeal to the technology buff include the speed of the central processing unit and other advanced technical specifications, the number of expansion slots for adding peripheral devices, and the test results compared to other similar computers. The facts that appeal to the young education-conscious family include ease of use, the large number of educational programs available, and the proven long-term investment value. Some of the key facts that appeal to all of the audiences include reliability, the superior reputation of the company, and the extended warranty. These

(Complete One Form for Each Audience)

Audience Name: ——————————————————— Date: ———————————————

Product: ———————————————————————————————————

Size of This Audience: —————————————— % of Overall Market ——————————

Priority of This Audience:  ☐ Primary    ☐ Secondary

Age Range: — to —  Sex: ————————— Location(s) ——————————————

Type of Jobs:

Education Levels:

Family Structure:

Significant Lifestyle Attributes:


Leisure Time Activities:


Values:


Needs for This Product:


Decision Process for Choosing This Product:


Financial Motivation:


People Who Influence Buying Decision:



Other Significant Audience Attributes Related to This Product:

Figure 2.4.  Audience segmentation worksheet.

facts matched to the target audiences will become the raw material for developing specific marketing communications tools.

**Step 4. Determine the message styles and appeals that are appropriate for each audience.**  After determining the facts that are most likely to influence each of your target audiences, you need to determine the style and tone that are appropriate for each audience. Specific appeals and styles will help you deliver the facts in the correct context for the audience. List any specific images or words you believe can be used in the marketing communications to help reinforce the facts. For example, if you sell volleyball equipment, a dynamic photo of young adults voraciously pursuing a frantic game using your equipment on the beach is probably an appealing image to a market segment of active young adults. A static picture of the equipment sitting in a pile in an empty room probably isn't.

Types of appeals usually go along with audience motivations, images, and lifestyles. There are rational appeals to meet the practical, physical needs an audience has for your product and there are emotional appeals that seduce, tantalize, and otherwise bring the psychological, social, and emotional needs of consumers into play.

The style for a message is defined with words such as upbeat, humorous, conservative, straightforward, academic, trendy, exciting, and stylish. This information will be used to help the people working on your marketing communications do a better job of translating raw message material into specific words, images, and designs. Though the style of the messages and images should be matched with the target audiences, it is also important to consider the overall image you want to portray as a company. Never adopt a style for a specific audience that will be in conflict with your overall corporate image goals.

**Step 5. If in doubt, test the message elements with people from your target audience.**   If you are not sure how people will react to the facts, images, and style you select for your messages, do a little testing to see how people really interpret the elements you intend to use to communicate your messages. There are research firms and agencies that can help you do this—usually at considerable cost. If, however, your advertising and communications budget is large, message research can save a bundle before you say the wrong things and drive potential customers to the competition.

If you don't have the budget for a research firm or agency to do the testing, complete observations and questionnaires on your own. Ask potential customers who represent each of your target markets to tell you what they feel and think when they read your headlines, see your images, and hear your words. Sometimes co-workers are a good source of feedback. Ask them what they think of the colors you have chosen. Just because you think red represents power, for example, doesn't mean your audience does. They may think it represents danger or fear. Ask people what they think are the most important aspects of your product—and compare their answers to your own list. If you find that you are really off base, more detailed analysis and more formal testing are probably required. Of course, the other way to test messages is to complete the marketing communications tools and see if they work. In reality, this is always the ultimate test. Even the best research firms are wrong sometimes about what will work and what will not.

**Step 6. Summarize the raw messages for easy reference.** After you are satisfied you have identified the markets, facts, and appeals for your products, one form for summarizing messages that has worked well is the *Message Grid Form* shown here. To complete the grid, just follow the steps as documented above. Complete your list of facts first, on a separate sheet. List the primary audiences from your Audience Segmentation Worksheet on the top of the form as shown. Then prioritize the key facts that appeal to each audience under the appropriate column. Notice that there is a column provided for "All Audiences." The facts that appeal to everyone should go there. After matching the facts to the audience, list the style, key images, and appeals for each audience in the space provided.

When you have completed the Message Grid Form you have outlined your raw messages. This form can be given to your agency or to a creative person who can use it to develop a concept or copy platform for your marketing communications. Ultimately, these raw messages will be translated (encoded) into specific marketing communications tools using words, visuals, imagery, and other elements to communicate the underlying messages.

## USING THE AIDA FORMULA FOR TRANSLATING RAW MESSAGES INTO POWERFUL COMMUNICATIONS

All of your raw messages will be translated (encoded) into specific implementations of marketing communications tools. Though it is beyond the scope of this book to go into all the possibilities for doing this, one approach—the AIDA formula—is useful in almost any situation. The *AIDA formula*, which stands for *attention, interest, desire,* and *action,* is a classic guideline used by many copywriters and marketing communications professionals to translate raw messages into media representations that will communicate the intended message to the appropriate audience.

| Audience Names | (FILL IN) | (FILL IN) | (FILL IN) | All Audiences |
|---|---|---|---|---|
| Key Facts | | | | |
| Key Motivations for Buying This Product | | | | |
| Appeals | | | | |
| Styles for Messages | | | | |
| Possible Images to Use | | | | |

Figure 2.5.  Message grid form.

The basics of the AIDA approach include the following:

**1. Get their attention.**   Stop them with a headline or visual. Use visuals to show them the message and support the words—or to intrigue them into reading or viewing the rest of the communication.

**2. Hold their interest.**   The body copy or narrative that follows the atten-tion-getting headline or visual should reinforce the interest you created. Tell them something they want to hear. Appeal to the emotions, needs, fantasies, and self-image of your customers. When talking to your cus-tomers in marketing communications, talk to them one-on-one. Use honest, precise words that convey clear-cut facts. Paint clear pictures of the product's benefits, but never boast or generalize. Make your words convincing. Some of the most convincing elements used in good mar-keting communications include:

- Unique product features.
- Sales leadership.
- Repeat purchases and satisfied customers.
- Testimonials from current users.
- Quality and performance guarantees and histories.
- Positive, dramatic results of formal tests.

**3. Create or satisfy a desire.**   Satisfy specific needs the customers have relating to your products. Solve problems. Fulfill as many needs as pos-sible at as many levels as possible, using your list of raw messages as source material. Your words should clarify specific benefits that relate to the customer's own situation. Each benefit should heighten a desire because it is matched to a specific real or perceived need. Provide examples that prove what your product will produce or the needs it will satisfy. Your audience descriptions are especially important to know what to say to accomplish this.

**4. Motivate an action to purchase the product.**   Almost every marketing communications tool, whether ad, brochure, or direct mail flyer, should ask customers to take some action. Give them easy instructions and clear opportunities for taking the next step in the purchasing decision. Call. Write. Mail in the card. Go to the store. Give me your phone number and I'll call you next week. Make it simple and make it direct. Avoid wimpy closes such as "Awaiting your response." Instead use urgent, compelling closes such as "Call our toll-free number today!"

Beyond the basic AIDA guidelines, there is one more device that can help you get your messages across in almost any situation and that is CREDIBILITY. Your customers are sophisticated. They are smart enough to know that not all advertisers are trustworthy. They want proof of your credibility and product performance, not just flowery words or unbelievable claims. Honesty is always the best policy—a trite adage that still has meaning in marketing communications. Don't insult your audience with wild claims and overly superlative language that can't be substantiated.

---

## THE GREAT ONES SPEAK

Many of the most notable experts in advertising and marketing communications started out as copywriters. Copywriters are the people in agencies who translate raw messages into memorable concepts, jingles, headlines, and images. They are often lovingly referred to as *wordsmiths*. As an insight to the process of message translation, here are some quotes, both entertaining and profound, on their craft from a few of these advertising gurus, based on interviews with David Higgins reported in the book, *The Art of Writing Advertising: Conversations with the Masters of the Craft* (NTC Business Books, 1987):

> Many people—and I think I am one of them—are more productive when they've had a little to drink. I find if I drink two or three brandies, I'm far better able to write.
>
> (David Ogilvy)

> We're all concerned about the facts we get, and not enough concerned about how provocative we make those facts to the consumers.
>
> (William Bernbach)

> On some types of products—drug products, for example . . . experience is highly desirable—knowing what's worked and what hasn't worked, and knowing some of the scientific facts involved. . . . But that knowledge and experience aren't nearly as important as [a writer's] expressiveness, his ability to think and to marshal his thoughts into persuasive English.
>
> (Leo Burnett)

> I think central to good writing on advertising, or anything else, is a person who has developed an understanding of people, an insight into them, a sympathy toward them.
>
> (George Gribbin)

> Only advertising men hold seminars and judge advertising. The public doesn't. . . . The public either acts or it doesn't act.
>
> (Rosser Reeves)

---

## A BRIEF WORD ON DEVELOPING INTERNATIONAL AND ETHNIC MESSAGES

International and ethnic-specific business has become more important to American companies in the last few years, even small ones, so many companies find they have to develop marketing communications and messages targeted to specific countries, ethnic backgrounds, or subcultures. Though the steps for developing the communications and messages are the same as the ones already detailed, the social attributes, motivations, and market segments are not. Some messages and images can be used in multicultural or global promotions, but you have to plan for it in advance. You cannot assume that people in Mexico or Germany are motivated by the same needs and desires as people in California. And don't be surprised if the images that you find humorous or tantalizing may be viewed as offensive, odd, or obscene to other nationalities.

Developing communications for specific cultures and countries requires specific expertise in the culture and language specific to that market. Within cultures there are many subcultures and market segments that also need to be considered as you target your international messages. If you aren't well versed in the culture, language, rituals, beliefs, and values of the people who constitute your market, hire someone who is. There are agencies that specialize in international and ethnic advertising. There are even international agency networks that can work hand-in-hand with your domestic agency. Be sure the agency or consulting firm you choose for your international marketing efforts is familiar with the specific media, marketing structures, and distribution channels of the country, as well as the customs and the language.

## MATCHING MESSAGES TO THE MARKETING COMMUNICATIONS TOOL

From your list of target markets, each marketing communications tool will have one or more intended target audiences from your list of possible audiences. Sometimes marketing communications tools will be used to communicate to more than one of your audience segments. If this is the case, the messages will need to encompass shared needs and interests. The emphasis on the messages you use in a specific marketing communications tool will also depend on the way the tool will be used in the sales cycle and the promotional objectives of the tool. If the tool is an ad used to gain initial interest, you will likely use strong emotional appeals and interest-catching visuals. On the other hand, if you are creating a brochure to provide additional information to people who have already expressed an interest in the product, your brochure will emphasize benefits and features of the product and reinforce some of the specific applications of the product.

In the next chapters we will explain the best uses for each of the marketing communications tools and how to produce them effectively. However, to get maximum benefit from any of the marketing communications tools, you always need to start with the messages and the audiences as we have described them here.

# 3 | Advertising: Making It from Message to Media without a Migraine

> Advertising may be described as the science of arresting the human intelligence long enough to get money from it.
>
> (Stephen Leacock)

The business of selling products is often referred to as a war—a war to beat the competition to market, a war for limited consumer dollars, a war with increased sales and profit as the victory. In the battleground of business, advertising is the key tactical weapon. The right ad seen by the right people can change a company's position in the sales war almost overnight. That's why companies continue to spend more and more on advertising. Yet advertising is a battle in itself—a battle for recognition and response and a clash of creative concepts and creative minds.

Advertising was defined earlier as a *persuasive, nonpersonal communication paid for by a company or sponsor to be published, displayed, or broadcast with the purpose of promoting a product.* This means that when you advertise you pay to get your message across to your marketplace through print, television, radio, or outdoor advertising media.

Advertising can be used to educate, inform, motivate action, and reinforce or change an image. Advertising is generally regarded as the single most powerful tool for getting the word out. While often the most costly form of marketing communications, with some advertisers spending more on ad placements than any other single line item in their budget, the expense of a strong advertising program can result in substantial returns.

All advertising must meet three basic criteria if it is going to do its job in the sales struggle:

1. It must be seen or heard by the target customers.
2. It must deliver its message effectively.
3. It must be seen or heard often enough to have impact and be remembered in a world crowded with advertising.
4. It must stand out from ads for competing products.

A successful ad not only catches the attention of its viewer or listener, it keeps it long enough to get its message across. If your ad works, people will take action and buy your product or remember you the next time they need what you have to sell. The resulting income is used by the business to build more products and buy more advertising in an on-going cycle. Effective advertising can profoundly affect a market in short order—turning an unknown product into a major profit center within a few days.

# THE GROWTH OF ADVERTISING

> Promise, large promise is the soul of advertisement.
> (Samuel Johnson)

Advertising has been around since the dawn of man. (Wags might argue it was an invention of Neanderthals and that's why it so often appeals to a low level of intelligence.) Some of the first documented evidence of early advertising is a crude inscription on a wall in excavated Pompeii announcing a contest between two gladiators complete with the names of the participants and date for the event.

Modern advertising began to take shape as a way to sell patent medicine in the early nineteenth century. These early advertisements earnestly extoled the "benefits" of medicinal products. Most of these remedies used a large nip of alcohol (for use in social circles where liquor was frowned on) or addictive opium and similar "cures." The best pitches for these "medicines" were remarkably similar to today's advertising approaches, but because most advertising during this period was for dubious potions and devices, "respectable" magazines and other publications refused to accept ads of any kind. Likewise, advertising practitioners were regarded as being of questionable moral fiber. No proper gentleman would approve of his daughter seeing or marrying an advertising man.

But the reputation and effectiveness of advertising changed radically during the period of the late nineteenth and early twentieth centuries. Although advertising agencies began to hang out shingles as early as 1850, the first agencies with significant parallels to modern ones weren't established until after 1900. Agencies initially focused on advertising that was pretty to look at but said little. Soon it was recognized that good copywriting and concept-driven ads were the most effective way to sell products—and at that point advertising came into its own.

Flowering into a substantial business after the end of World War I, advertising became a major channel of influence as printing techniques improved and more "respectable" magazines were willing to accept a larger share of advertising. Then technology opened entirely new channels of promotion and persuasion—first with radio, and later with the most persuasive medium of all, television.

Today, because of the acceptance and power of advertising, large sums of money are available for purchasing advertising media. Money and media go hand in hand—one reason there are an ever-expanding number of channels for promoting products. Advertising single-handedly supports the very existence of all radio and television stations and networks with the exception of not-for-profit religious stations, PBS, and National Public Radio. Almost every magazine and newspaper is fully dependent on advertisers. Subscription and newsstand revenues barely pay for paper and printing used to produce most publications—it's advertising revenue that keeps them alive and well.

The growth in specialty magazines and newspapers was and is completely fueled by advertisers looking for better ways to reach an audience and market with specific needs, interests, and tastes. There has been equally phenomenal growth in trade-specific publications. Where once a handful of magazines such as *The Ladies' Home Journal* and *Saturday Evening Post* dominated the market, today's publications can be pretty esoteric. Trade magazine titles include *Llamas Magazine—The International Camelid Journal, Your Virginia State Trooper Magazine,* and, who could forget, the *Mid-Continent Bottler,* which, according to *Writer's Market,* is dedicated to "soft drink bottlers in the 20-state Midwestern area." Everyone from mortuary owners to automobile glass installers has his own specialty trade publication.

Media expansion and targeting are also taking place in television. The cable-only channel, *Lifetime,* runs shows and ads targeted at doctors and the health conscious. The *Travel Channel* runs travel videos that are really long TV commercials to attract tourists. *ESPN* provides full-time sports coverage and the sports-oriented ads to go with it. Other new cable entries include one for science fiction, two for humor, and one for gourmet cooking. The trend toward targeted programs and channels is just getting started on television and we can expect more specialized programming as the cable companies scramble to add channel capacity.

This expansion of media and advertising is both a blessing and a curse to advertisers—a blessing because many companies can buy advertising space in magazines or media that clearly appeal to people with specific interests; a curse because companies that sell products to a very broad market without clearly differentiating traits (such as toothpaste and soft drinks) must use very expensive space and airtime in popular media such as network television and major news magazines to reach enough people.

## THE FUNCTIONS AND CLASSIFICATIONS OF ADVERTISING

Today there are four general classifications of advertising: (1) image advertising, (2) consumer product advertising, (3) trade and professional business advertising, and (4) retail advertising. Each of these classifications has specific functions and market appeal.

## Image Advertising

To ensure a positive reception and confidence in the communities and markets they serve, large corporations develop *image ads*. The primary function of an *image ad* is to build corporate awareness and positive associations in a broad marketplace. Sales development is a long-term, peripheral goal of image ads. These ads rarely focus on specific products, but instead highlight a recent corporate success or innovative new program. Image ads are also used by large, faceless corporations to establish a corporate presence in the mind of the public. Transamerica Corporation, for example, is a financial services company that was publicly invisible before building their now-famous pyramid-shaped office building in downtown San Francisco and spending a fortune on image ads showing the pyramid. Sometimes groups or organizations (The Beef Council, The American Gas Association) use image advertising to jointly promote a cause or interest. Many examples of image ads can be found in upscale business-oriented magazines such as *Forbes, Fortune,* and *The Economist.*

## Consumer Product Advertising

Consumer advertising is designed to reach and influence the mass market. Consumer ads have the function of making the public at large aware of products used in everyday life. The bulk of television advertising and the ads in widely read popular magazines are consumer advertising. Although often placed by the same companies that do institutional and corporate image advertising, these ads focus on a specific product or product line and are intended to persuade you to buy the product. A reverse consumer products ad is one that solicits donations for charities and not-for-profits. Examples of consumer product ads can be found in magazines such as *Cosmopolitan, Sports Illustrated,* and *Time.*

## Trade and Professional and Business Advertising

For products sold directly by one business to another or products that are used only in a specific occupation or profession, it would be a waste of money to advertise in mass media because only a small percentage of readers, viewers, or listeners would have any interest in the product. So, a business selling products aimed at another business or profession uses specialty publications and media that appeal directly to their market. The goal of this category of advertising is to be highly focused and well targeted. These ads are often more educational in approach, with more detail on product features and benefits than normally found in consumer advertising. Examples of these ads are found in trade or business-specific magazines and newspapers.

### Retail Advertising

Retailers, including department stores, specialty shops, markets, and malls, must also advertise to attract customers. Retail ads may emphasize specific product specials ("Iceberg lettuce 59¢ this week only!") or may instead announce a big sale or promote a special event at the store. Retail advertising primarily uses local media to get its messages across. The purpose of this kind of advertising is to make consumers aware of the store's existence and range of products and to motivate them to buy. Retail ads are the most common type of advertising found in local newspapers.

---

## MERA BANK: THE LITTLE SAVINGS AND LOAN THAT COULDN'T

Image ads are often used by organizations that have been through a major scandal or upheaval. In an attempt to convince the public or market that the organization is now well managed and that positive changes have been made, they run image ads to build up confidence.

Mera Bank, a Phoenix, Arizona-based savings and loan, went through massive losses during the savings and loan crisis of the late 1980s. After allegations of poor lending judgment and other well-publicized problems, Mera Bank decided that an aggressive image campaign might be the right approach to convince skittish depositors that the savings and loan still had a bright future. A massive billboard and television campaign ensued with the positive message, "We've been there, we'll be here!" The billboard dramatically displayed a collage of former American presidents, the Space Shuttle, and other historic, patriotic images.

While the numerous billboard ads were still in place, Bank of America bought the bank that had finally been declared insolvent. Bank of America closed many of the former Mera Bank branches and changed the ones in good locations to Bank of America branches. So much for "We've been there, we'll be here!"

---

## THE PROCESS OF DEVELOPING AN ADVERTISING PROGRAM

The same basic process is used to develop all advertising, regardless of media employed. The process starts with defining marketing messages and goals and finishes with the published or broadcast advertisement. The step-by-step path illustrated here should be followed, whether you're developing a small, simple ad for a local newspaper or assembling a major advertising *blitz* involving multiple media and formats.

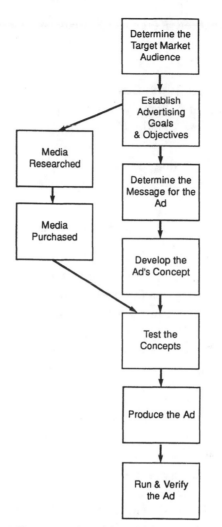

Figure 3.1. The advertising process.

From setting a goal for an advertising program to implementation and measuring results, everything should be tracked and thoroughly thought out. A worksheet has been provided to help you make the right decisions as you plan your ads. Let's review the general steps first, and then cover media selection and the specifics of print, television, and radio advertising in more detail.

**Step 1. Define the target audience for your ad.** All advertising programs must be based on an in-depth understanding of who your customers are. For consumer and retail-oriented companies you need to know what attributes your customers share as a group (if any), where they live, work, and play, and on what they spend their money. For business to business ads you need to know how many companies need your product or service, where they are located, their financial profiles, and how they are structured. We covered options for defining your target audiences in the last chapter. Refer to the material again, because an in-depth under-standing of your audiences is central to effective advertising.

**Step 2. Establish the advertising goals and objectives.**   Once you get a handle on your target markets, you need to establish goals for your advertising and decide who will develop the ads if you don't already have an agency or in-house staff to work with. (There is more on working with an advertising agency later in this chapter and Chapter 9 provides detailed advice for selecting freelancers and agencies.)

There are two fundamental goals, common to all advertising:

- First, your primary message must be delivered successfully to the target audience. An ad that fails to deliver its primary message is either poorly executed or placed in media ignored by the intended target market.
- Second, good advertising strives to get the maximum response from prospective customers for the least amount of cost.

In addition to these underlying goals, there are objectives that need to be established for measuring advertising effectiveness. These objectives are the specific results you expect to achieve with individual ads and advertising programs. Objective-driven advertising is more likely to be effective than placing an ad without a clearly defined payoff in mind. A measurable objective helps clarify thinking concerning all aspects of the process from media selection to concept to final design and production. There are several standard types of measurable objectives for ads:

- **Sell a specified amount of product within a set time period or collect a specified amount of contributions within a set period of time.**   Almost all advertising has some sort of sales goal attached to it, whether tangible or intangible.

- **Position a product within a market.**   *Positioning* as a marketing term means defining a place for your product in relationship to the competition. For example, if your company manufactures big-screen televisions with a brighter picture and a higher price than the competitor's less-capable sets, you would position your product as worth the extra price because of superior technology that produces a better picture. The competitor would probably position his TVs as capable products of good value for less money.

- **Educate a market on a product so people see a need that they did not recognize before.** The personal care products market uses this approach to *educate* the public on major health risks that they did not know existed such as plaque build-up on teeth that leads to gingivitis. Through this education process, markets are created for both new and existing products.

- **Change or improve the image for a product or company.** For example, you might want to change the public's conception of your company from one of providing conservative, expensive products to one that delivers innovative, value-packed merchandise.

- **Gain a specific number of responses in the form of business reply cards, new customers, or telephone calls.** In the case of new companies or new products, it may be difficult to come up with a specific sales goal, so product awareness and interest can be used as a success indicator instead.

In addition to the primary objective, an ad may have one or two secondary objectives that can be accommodated, as long as the primary objective is the ad's focus. For example, a retailer of fine men's clothing may have a once-a-year 50% off sale with the objective of moving $10,000 worth of inventory. However, a secondary objective of "continue to position the store as a purveyor of fine-quality, expensive men's clothes" can still be accommodated in the ad's copy. Or a television commercial for a radical new electric toothbrush with an objective of "position our product as technologically superior to the competition" might have a secondary objective of changing the company's image from a maker of home-care products to a provider of health-oriented products.

If you decide to work with an advertising agency, giving them objectives will help focus their efforts and, as a result, enable them to make better decisions on your behalf. Most agencies will help you develop and specify objectives. Realistic objectives are a powerful yardstick for measuring and improving the effectiveness of your advertising and your agency.

**Step 3. Determine the marketing message for the ad.** In addition to having measurable objectives, strong advertising is based on a clearly defined message. In the last chapter we discussed how to define and refine a marketing message for use in ads and other communications tools, so we won't cover the process again here. Remember that a crisp message is key to all of your marketing communications efforts, especially advertising.

### Step 4. Choose the media placement for the ad.

After you have determined your target audience, the objectives for your ad, and the message you want to convey, you need to determine which medium will best meet your objectives. The standard classifications of media include print, television, radio, and outdoor.

Newspapers and magazines sell *space* for ads. Radio and television stations sell *airtime*. Outdoor advertising companies sell *placements* or *showings* for billboards on highways and posters on buses and in stations. It is the choice of medium, more than any other decision, that will determine who will see or hear your ad—and thus determine the overall effectiveness of your advertising effort. A great ad running in the wrong medium is a waste of time and money.

Your choice of medium should be based on the following question: "What is the best time and place for this ad(s) to run in order to meet the advertising objectives?" The steps and considerations in media selection are covered in detail later and topic-specific aspects of media selection are covered in the media-specific sections in this chapter for print, radio, television, and outdoor advertising.

### Step 5. Customize the ad concept for the target media.

To convey your message, a concept or idea is developed that (1) gets the ad noticed, (2) delivers the message with as much impact as possible, and (3) is appropriate for the selected advertising media. A good concept is what makes an ad interesting to read, see, or hear. Many advertising people refer to the concept as the *big idea*. Rosser Reeves of the Ted Bates advertising agency defines one kind of concept as the *USP* or *Unique Selling Proposition*—the idea that every product has something unique about it and that this USP differentiates the product from its competitors. Behind every *big idea* or concept in advertising is always the message. Remember that *delivering the message* is the primary focus and purpose of all ads. The following illustrates a sample message and concept for an ad:

> *Message:* The Big Black Tire Company is now open nights to better accommodate the schedules of busy, working customers.
> *Concept:* "We're open evenings so you can spend your Saturday with the kids instead of at the tire shop." The associated visual concept, appropriate for both print and television ads, is that of a professional-looking young women wearing business dress watching as a (smiling) burly tire technician tightens up the last lug nut on a wheel with an obviously new tire. It's after dark and the moon shows clearly outside the shop's open bay door.

Notice that the raw message is very ordinary and would make dull advertising copy. That's why a concept is invented to make the message interesting and compelling. A *concept* is thus an idea that translates an ordinary message into a provocative ad. Creating a concept requires imaginative thinking. If you are not an "idea person" yourself, a talented creative director or freelance writer is a good source for coming up with interesting concepts for an ad. Creating a unique, impactful, and communicative concept for an ad is the most difficult aspect of advertising. For this reason many ads have little or no concept behind them, instead relying on flashy graphics or film effects and a laundry list of features to sell a product.

## The "No-Gimmick" Concept or the Straightforward Sell

Can't think of a snappy idea for an ad? Don't want to hire an expensive writer or an advertising agency? There is an alternative to developing a brilliantly creative concept that works for almost any product. It's the straightforward sell or *SFS* for short. SFS ads are best suited to print advertising, though they can be used in other media with good results. To create an SFS-based ad, you need only come up with a simple headline that states your message clearly and then match a strong visual to the headline.

The headline should be a strong description of the product, one that almost single handedly states the ad's message. Examples of SFS headlines include the following:

- The Merril Timesweep is simply the most accurate watch you can buy.
- Shop at Salles today and save 50% on everything in the store!
- Help us feed the hungry children of the third world.
- We give you unlimited mileage when you rent a mid-size car for $49 per day!

Match the simple SFS headline to an eye-catching visual. Add a little "straightforward copy" and you've got yourself an ad. If you handle it correctly, your ad will have as much impact as ads based on strong creative concepts. For some products, including technical or business equipment, health-care products, and overadvertised consumer goods, an SFS ad can work even better than strong creative concept ads because the message is clear, concise, and gimmick free—providing an image of credibility and honesty.

**Step 6. Test the concepts with preadvertising research.** Advertising agencies and large corporations spend considerable money and time researching the potential impact of advertising concepts before the ads are placed in the media. The basic kinds of research used for evaluating advertising and promotional programs include the following:

- **Focus groups.**   Focus groups involve assembling a group of customers or potential customers in a group meeting, showing them alternative ad concepts or other marketing materials, and then having them discuss their reactions to each of the choices. The group is moderated by a focus group specialist. A trained observer takes notes on the reactions or the group is videotaped and the observations are documented later. Focus groups don't provide conclusive evidence, but they are excellent tools for evaluating the impact of alternative choices among ad concepts or other marketing communications tools, such as packaging, product names, or corporate image programs.

- **Consumer surveys.**   Surveys can range from simple to complex and have a wide range of applications. They can be used to test messages, concepts, and attitudes and to define the market demographics. Survey methodology involves using a well-designed survey instrument (the questionnaire) and mailing it or otherwise distributing it to an appropriate list of customers or potential customers. For new consumer products, surveys are often conducted in malls, supermarkets, or door-to-door. In-store surveys include informal surveys at the point of sale that are initiated by the sales clerk or brief questionnaires at the check-out stand or on the back of an invoice.

- **In-store tests.**   In-store research programs are used by large consumer product companies inside stores in controlled market areas. Consumers are provided with a variety of test products and merchandising choices. Observations are then recorded about the consumer's behavior. This type of research can also be completed by small companies to test reactions to sales displays and the mix of products on the shelves. Other common research techniques include comprehensive market analyses, consumer panels, purchase monitoring programs, and special trade studies. Most of these are suited for large companies and are best handled by agencies or research firms that specialize in promotional and marketing research.

The reality is that most research is less accurate than it could be. It may be incomplete, poorly executed, ask the wrong questions, or present contrived responses to artificial questions. Another reason research can have limited value is because the statistics are often used to reinforce a political point of view within a company or advertising agency.

---

✎                    **TIP: INSTANT RESEARCH**

While sitting across a desk from a co-worker unfamiliar with a new print ad, place it face down without letting him see it. Now ask him to look at the ad and try to remember what he saw. Flip it over, show it to him for exactly three seconds, and then immediately place it face down on the desk again. In that period he should have received the basic message of the ad. If not, then the ad is either too complex or its message is garbled.

---

Still, most companies with large advertising budgets like the security a research campaign provides. And, in many cases, it can point out not-so-obvious flaws in an ad before it runs. Think of preadvertising research as optional in the case of small campaigns and necessary, yet open to scrutiny, when used with larger ones.

**Step 7. Produce the ad.**   Equal in importance to the proper media selection is the production of the ad. Even with the right media selection and a good concept, a poorly executed ad or commercial will not work. In severe cases, it may work against you. Proper execution is critical to the impact of an ad campaign—for large and small programs alike.

The production of each kind of advertising is a process in itself. A section for print, radio, television, and outdoor advertising follows with step-by-step descriptions of the process and the choices required to produce quality ads.

**Step 8. Run and verify the ad.**   After your ad is produced, it will run in the media you have purchased. Wherever possible, check your ad to make sure it ran properly. Listen to the announcer read your ad on the radio, watch it on TV, check out newspapers, and flip through the magazines. In the case of ads running in remote cities, ask a friend or associate living there to make sure the ad ran correctly. Mistakes are common, particularly in print advertising. Ads may not run when scheduled or there may be a serious flaw on the part of the media supplier—such as incorrect placement or the wrong use of colors. A television soap commercial caught our attention one day because while the video for the soap commercial was displayed, the audio was from the Humphrey Bogart movie we had been watching before the commercial break.

If anything is wrong, i.e., poor printing, muddled transmission quality, placement at the wrong time of day, or whatever—complain immediately to the media supplier. Complain verbally first, and if you are not satisfied with the media supplier's response, write a letter documenting the problem. You should, depending on the severity of the problem, get a free placement or a percentage discounted from your bill. The contract between you and the media works two ways—they promise to print or broadcast your ad as specified and then you agree to pay the bill. If they don't deliver as promised, you deserve an equitable adjustment.

**Step 9. Conduct postadvertising research to find out what works.**   To measure your success in meeting advertising objectives, you must do postadvertising research. Again, this can be simple or complex depending on your company's information requirements. By far the most effective kind of advertising research is done after the fact. And this is one kind of research every company should and can do effectively, at a relatively low cost.

*Postadvertising research* involves reviewing the effectiveness of an ad after it is seen or heard. After an ad runs, or on a monthly basis if it is a continuing program, you should track the number of responses you get from the ad. Depending on your product, ask callers or customers where they heard about you, count *bingo* leads and business reply cards from magazine ads, or poll customers walking in the door of a retail store. (*Bingo* leads are the leads generated by circling numbers on a magazine's "reader information card." They are called bingo cards because the rows of numbers resemble game cards from real bingo.) If no one mentions or responds to your ad, then you know it isn't being seen or heard.

*Post purchase research* involves customers who have already purchased your products and is used to determine satisfaction and demographics and is a valuable resource for developing future advertising strategies. For example, restaurants often have short questionnaires querying satisfaction with the price, food, service, and environment on the back of the bill. By adding a question or two about customer demographics and customer media preferences, a restaurant can use this information to improve its advertising effectiveness. The customer warranty cards inside consumer products are often postpurchase research in disguise. They may ask many questions about where a product was purchased, what other products the person has, what media the person subscribes to, and more.

If your postadvertising or postpurchase research discloses a trend in the customer base—for example, all your customers live within a certain radius of the store or they are all over 50 years old or they all have children who watch Sesame Street—you can better target your advertising message to the people most likely to buy your product. Also, if you find that a whole segment of your target market is not represented, you know that your promotional efforts to this group are not working. Most likely the media mix for your ads is wrong or the message is not appropriate for the market.

## CHOOSING THE BEST MEDIA MIX FOR YOUR MESSAGE

As one of the primary steps in creating an advertising program, your choice of media will determine if your ads are read, seen, or heard. If you are a small company, you will probably use only local media to run your ads. However, as your company becomes larger or if your product sells to more than one market, you will want to look into expanding the range of media you use. The combination of media used for advertising is called the *media mix*. A media mix may consist of a series of ads placed in several magazines, or it may include ads run in newspapers, magazines, and on radio and TV.

In addition to getting your ad in front of more people, the media mix can be used to reinforce the message to the same people. For example, the people who saw an ad on TV will also see it on a billboard as they drive to work and hear it on the news station they listen to when they commute. Multiple exposures to the same message help keep it in the mind of the consumers.

The goals behind the selection of a media mix are very similar to those for advertising in general:

- Getting noticed by the largest segment of potential customers.
- Using advertising dollars for maximum overall impact. For example, an advertiser might use an expensive media source such as television for only a few placements and then add less expensive print media placements to reinforce the message.
- Covering the key target markets effectively. For a product purchased by more than one kind of customer, the media mix must reach each of the different target groups.
- Coordinating messages across the media for reinforcement and consistency of image.

Professional media planners use specific terms such as *frequency* (number of times an ad is seen by the same person), *reach* (number of different types of people that see the ad), *impressions* (the total of all exposures to the ad by all people), *rating points* (a way of expressing the total audience delivery of a specific media schedule), and other technical media terms to define the objectives of media selection. For example, a media objective written by a professional media planner might be worded as follows:

> Reach at least 75 percent of the primary target audience an average of five times and 40 percent of the secondary audience at least three times in the first month.

If you hire a big advertising agency and do a lot of television or mass market advertising, expect and require them to do this level of planning. But for ordinary media planning purposes, objectives stated in more general terms are sufficient.

After establishing media objectives, the selection process for determining the optimum media mix for advertising your product includes the following basic decisions and processes:

**1. Determine which advertising sources are likely to be seen or heard by the market you want to reach.** All legitimate publications and television and radio stations publish demographic profile charts and tables of their audience. Your task is to match the demographics of your target markets to affordable media with similar demographic profiles. To do this you should start by listing all the media to which your potential customers are likely to come into contact, whether you can afford to advertise in these places or not. The library has references on available magazines and newspapers to get you started.

Identify as many channels and possibilities as you can think of to effectively reach all of your potential customers. Start with broad categories of media such as television, radio, and print and then narrow them down to specific choices. Consider both major and minor media possibilities. For example, you could advertise an amplified telephone on a television show with closed captions for the hearing impaired. And, because many people over 50 years old suffer from hearing loss, you could also promote the product in senior-citizens magazines, such as *Senior Golf Journal* or *Modern Maturity*. Many seniors own RVs, so *Motorhome* magazine and travel programs on television featuring RV life-styles are possibilities. Because a wide range of potential hearing-impaired customers, not just seniors, watch television, you could include an ad in local TV programming guides. The potential list is vast. You will narrow it down later—but for the first step, do not limit your options.

One way to informally determine the media your customers pay attention to is to ask them. Opportunities include having them complete a questionnaire, check boxes on warranty cards, or chat over coffee. If

☑ 1. Which media formats are most likely to reach my customers—TV, radio, magazines, newspapers, etc.?

_____

_____

_____

_____

☐ 2. Which specific media outlets should I consider (station names, magazine titles, etc.)?

_____

_____

_____

_____

_____

_____

_____

_____

☐ 3. Of those listed in #2, which are likely to be the most effective?

_____

_____

_____

_____

☐ 4. Of those listed in #3, which can I afford?

_____

_____

_____

☐ 5. Is there anything realistic and workable listed in number 4?

☐ YES        ☐ NO

(If no, then advertising may not be an effective medium for your needs and you should consider another form of promotion, or ask an ad agency for assistance locating hard-to-find but more cost-effective media.)

Figure 3.2. Media mix selection worksheet.

you take this last approach, it should be done with tact and in an informal conversational setting. Do not tell them you are doing research, just casually ask what they like to do in their spare time or on their job and go on from there. Since most people love to talk about themselves, your problem won't be getting the answers you desire, but getting the people to stop talking.

**2. Get a media kit from each of the media possibilities for your advertising program.**   Media kits are used by media channels to promote the advertising space or time they have to sell. They include the information a prospective advertiser needs before buying and producing ads for a specific publication or station. Media kits vary from poorly photocopied information presented in a wrinkled manilla envelope to flashy folders stuffed with colorful brochures.

---

### ✎   TIP: STUDY THE MEDIA YOUR COMPETITORS USE

When studying media options, find out where your competitors advertise—there's a good possibility that they have already done some of the media homework for you by identifying effective media for their product. Don't make the mistake of limiting yourself to these outlets, however. You may be able to locate media they've ignored and get the word out to a market your competition did not recognize or understand how to reach.

---

Newspapers have the simplest media kits, sometimes consisting of little more than a photocopied rate sheet. A magazine's media kit contains a price list with a description of available formats and positions, a recent sample of the publication, various promotional information, and readership profiles. Many publications also provide an editorial calender. This shows upcoming feature articles or the focus of specific issues during the year. For example, a magazine for backpackers might have an early spring issue featuring articles on camping and camping equipment. Manufacturers of camping equipment may want to use this opportunity to run an ad on their wares because of the issue's specific editorial focus.

TV and radio media kits are similar, providing information on programming schedules, viewer profiles, ratings (how many people were watching at a given time), pricing, a map showing how far their signal reaches, and information on upcoming shows, special features, and special deals. Special and new programming is often featured because stations and networks usually need sponsors for new shows more than established ones.

Outdoor advertising companies also use media kits. These contain rate cards and maps of the target city showing the locations of available billboards, transit stations, and shelters.

Media kits are free and most sales representatives will drop one in the mail to you the same day. Or they will show up with it on your doorstep first thing the next morning if they really need the business.

---

## DEFINITION: DEMOGRAPHICS

Demographics is a word you will hear over and over when defining your target markets and researching and choosing media for your marketing communications. Although an unabridged dictionary defines *demographics* as the science of vital statistics, such as births and deaths, it means something slightly different in advertising. Quite simply a demographic is a personal profile of the kind of reader, listener, or viewer of a media source. For example, a magazine space rep may show you statistics defining his magazine's readers as white males, 35 to 45 years old, making $35,000 to $55,000 a year, and working in management positions. So if your product appeals to this market, the publication has the right *demographics* for your needs.

---

**3. Get to know the advertising representatives or space representatives for your target media.** The people who sell advertising space in newspapers and magazines are called *space reps* in the trade. TV and radio stations have sales or airtime reps. In the case of a small-town radio station, the rep may be the station's owner or general manager. A major television station in Los Angeles may have 20 or more representatives. A good rep will help you get the right placement or airtime for your needs and will negotiate a discount if there are problems. Because reps are commissioned and depend on selling airtime and space to pay the bills, they often attempt to sell you more than you need or can afford. Still, because they are usually knowledgeable and can often provide you with "special deals," it is important to establish good relationships with them.

If your account is a sizable one (in proportion to the publication, network, or station), your rep will probably take you out to lunch on a semiregular basis. Keep in mind that once you contact a rep, he or she will be calling on you regularly to drum up business. Some particularly annoying ones will call you every couple of days for an order or show up unannounced. Your mail volume will also double with information on placement special deals, upcoming editorial opportunities, and a variety of useless promotional items. One publication sends out a bar of nasty smelling soap four times a year with the message, "This is no reflection on your grooming habits, it's just that we clean up in the industry!"

**4. Choose a combination of media with the right impact and price tag for your needs.** Study the readership profile to see how many prospective customers the media will potentially influence versus the cost of the media. Remember that your goal is to identify the *least expensive media channel with the most impact for the dollar.* Don't buy a pricey ad spot on a large, local TV station if a less expensive ad on a local radio station will work almost as well.

**5. Choose media with the right timing.** If you need to get the word out quickly because of a hot new product or a newsworthy event—TV, radio, and daily newspapers work best. Some TV and radio stations will juggle their schedules or cut programming to make way for your paying commercial.

In the case of monthly magazines, it may take as long as three months for the magazine to hit the streets after submitting the ad. Outdoor advertising is also a slow medium when you are in a hurry, with a minimum turnaround time of 45 days for most placements.

Being aware of these timing factors is the key to running ads effectively in multiple media if you want the maximum retention and reinforcement value that media mixing provides. If you want to reinforce the messages, you need to coordinate the production of the ads to accommodate the different media schedules. For example, if you want to run an ad on TV and in a monthly magazine, you have to coordinate when the ad will air and when the magazine hits the streets and mailboxes.

---

### ✎   TIP: START YOUR OWN MEDIA LIBRARY!
### IMPRESS YOUR FRIENDS!

Every advertising agency has a print media library and you can too. To start yours, make a trip to a well-stocked magazine retailer. Look for and collect specialty and trade magazines important to your market. Subscribe to as many of the publications as possible. Subscribing is easy and it doesn't have to cost anything. All it takes is a phone call to the magazine's local advertising rep. (Look in the front section of most newspapers and magazines for the *masthead.* It will provide the locations and phone numbers for sales offices.) When your local rep finds out that you are interested in advertising, he or she can arrange a free subscription for you. Your media library should also contain the media kits from all prospective publications, radio and TV stations, and outdoor advertising sources of possible interest to you.

**6. Choose the appropriate media frequency for maximum exposure.** The more often an ad is run, the better the chance it has to be seen or heard by the target market. This number of times an ad is run in specific media is called *frequency*. Establishing the frequency for advertising placements is an art of sorts and there are no hard or fast rules. There are a few things to know when you make your decisions, however:

- Running an ad on a daily program or in a daily newspaper requires more frequency than running it on a weekly program or in a monthly magazine. That's because something seen or heard only once among myriad other ads in daily media quickly is forgotten. A magazine typically hangs around on the desks longer than a newspaper—so the potential life of the ad is expanded.

- Research indicates that airing or running the same ad at least three times in the same place or publication gives you a significantly better chance of getting noticed and remembered than running it once or twice. And six or nine placements are that much better.

- Running any ad too many times in the same place will bore people and the message loses impact as a result. Optimum frequency is a balance between recognition and overkill. Don't waste money on an overused ad—instead spend a portion of it on a fresh promotion to maintain your market's interest.

**7. Choose the most credible media for the money.** When researching media, it is important to consider the credibility of the media-supplied demographic profiles. Legitimate media are researched or audited by outside reviewing agencies or companies. In the case of television, the Arbitron Company and A.C. Nielson Company audit viewers and stations. In magazines it is Business/Professional Advertising Association (BPAA) and similar auditing organizations. For newspapers the Audit Bureau of Circulation (ABC) is a reliable, independent source of circulation statistics.

A few media channels claim an impressive number of readers, listeners, and viewers based on questionable accounting. Don't accept self-audited numbers at face value. A way to check up on demographic claims is to study the advertisers that already use the media to get an idea of who *they* think reads, watches, or listens to the media source. Paging through a magazine with impressive readership claims and very few ads or watching a commercial-less cable channel should raise a red flag.

As an example of questionable readership statistics, consider a new national magazine launched several years ago. Millions of letters were sent out offering free subscriptions to a supposed limited number of VIPs (we received at least four of these "limited" VIP offers!). To see what the magazine was about, we sent in a reply coupon. And, after looking through the first issue and finding nothing of interest, future issues went from mailbox to trash unopened. Still, this publication was able to claim a large and impressive readership as a result of the free subscriptions.

## DETERMINING WHAT ADVERTISING SHOULD COST

There is no rule on how much advertising should cost or how much you should pay for it, but there are guidelines you can use to get a handle on the price tag in relationship to the effective promotional value of an ad.

First, if the cost to produce an ad is more than the media charges to run it then you are either producing too complicated an ad for the market, not placing the ad in the right media, or not placing it enough times. For example, if your car dealership puts together a one-shot commercial for use on a local TV station and the media charge is $5,000 and you have spent $18,000 getting the ad produced, then you have clearly violated this guideline. You should either air the commercial more frequently or spend your advertising dollars elsewhere.

Another way to look at advertising charges is to calculate how many potential customers will be exposed to your ad through the chosen media. Divide the cost of the ad placement by the total number of people who fit your demographic profile to give you a dollars per "exposure" ratio. This is a handy tool for not only evaluating media but also getting rid of pesky media sales reps. If a single placement costs $22,000, excluding production, and the publication's media kit shows 2,500 readers with the correct profile for your market, then 22,000/2,500 = $8.80 per exposure, a figure that justifies looking for another media source if you are are selling a $20.00 product.

For some products and industries, there is an established optimum percentage of sales and revenue dollars that should be used for advertising. You can get this kind of information from Dun and Bradstreet reports and from advertising research organizations. If you are a retailer, your distribution source or major product line provider can help you by providing ratios that have worked in the past for other companies.

Although grumbling is commonplace when the cost of advertising comes up during a planning and budgeting meeting, advertising still remains the most powerful tool for building companies and increasing revenue. Well-chosen ads placed wisely have helped build most of today's largest corporations and successful charities and established a new wave of up and coming entrepreneurial companies. If you want to stay in business, you have to advertise. If you do it right, the cost is worth it.

# USE OTHER PEOPLE'S MONEY TO PAY FOR YOUR ADVERTISING

**Co-op Advertising.**   Depending on the nature of your company, there may be money available in the form of co-op dollars from your distributors or manufacturers. If you advertise someone's product in an ad or catalog, co-op program dollars work by reimbursing a percentage of the advertising media (and sometimes production) charges to you. All co-op programs are different and some work better than others by paying a higher percentage and having fewer rules and restrictions. (Be sure to follow *all* the rules and observe *all* the guidelines and restrictions carefully.)

One warning—don't count your co-op dollars until they arrive. In most programs, you collect co-op funds after the fact by submitting copies or tapes of the ad, along with copies of placement orders and bills. Some co-op programs pay promptly, knowing you will keep up the good work with reimbursement money in hand. Others take months to cut you a check or waste time quibbling over interpretation of rules and restrictions before paying you. In some markets manufacturers provide co-op dollars as a discount on the next order. Be sure you are clear on the form of repayment before making a commitment.

**Joint-Promotions and Cross-Promotions.**   Sometimes you can use a *joint-promotion* or *cross-promotion* to stretch your budget. For example, a paint manufacturer might join up with a paintbrush manufacturer and a major chain of paint-supply stores to run ads touting paint, paintbrushes, and stores in one ad. This way each company spends only one-third of the cost of going it alone.

Cross-promotions can be used by large companies to advertise more than one product at the same time and save money. For example, if one division of a toy company builds scale model toy trains and another division makes model car and airplane kits, then advertising them together saves money over advertising them separately.

Sometimes joint-promotions and cross-promotions result in ads that are collectively stronger because they provide a more complete solution and/or a stronger message.

We have now covered the general process of developing advertising and choosing media—but a basic understanding of the production process for each kind needs to be covered separately because they are quite different. We will start by introducing the print advertising process with similar sections following on radio, television, and outdoor advertising.

# THE PRINT ADVERTISING PRIMER

Print advertising is the general term used for ads placed in magazines and newspapers. Effective print advertising begins with an awareness of the strengths and weaknesses of both magazine and newspaper media. In understanding the advantages and disadvantages of the media, you can make better advertising decisions—and won't expect unrealistic results.

## Newspaper Advertising's Strengths and Weaknesses

Newspaper media are classified by the size of the paper (standard or tabloid), the frequency of the paper (daily, biweekly, weekly), and publication reach (who gets the paper and where). The general strengths of newspaper advertising include the following:

- Newspapers can quickly influence large markets because newspaper ads can be produced relatively quickly and published almost immediately.
- Newspapers are excellent local and city-specific media.
- Newspapers provide special interest sections that help focus a message to specific target markets.
- Newspapers offer a variety of ad formats and sizes to accommodate budget limitations.

The weaknesses of newspaper advertising are:

- Newspaper ads have a short contact life span.
- Newspapers are a one-shot affair and require frequent or multiple insertions for the ads to get noticed by everyone. A reader who misses the paper one day, will miss your ad.
- Newspapers offer you little control over the placement of ads on a page. You can specify a location in a special interest section, but you cannot usually specify position on the page and this can have a strong influence on the impact of the ad.
- Common to all print advertising, newspapers can relay only static events, so a dramatic television commercial of a new high-technology lawn mower chopping down giant weeds to clear land won't come alive as easily in print.
- Limited print quality dictates the use of simple ads and visuals.

## Magazine Advertising's Strengths and Weaknesses

> Consistency and continuity—that's the secret for magazines if you want to be visible. For us, that's the way to use print. It's a slow-building medium.
>
> (Dick Costello, president and CEO,
> TBWA Advertising Agency,
> as reported in the *Wall Street Journal*)

Magazines are classified by content, geographic reach, and audience appeal. There are consumer, business, local, and special interest magazines. The strengths of magazine advertising include the following:

- Magazines have the longest potential life span of any of the advertising media. In addition to staying around, magazines have a high pass-around or secondary readership in addition to the primary subscribers.
- Magazines are the most selective media for targeting specific demographic profiles. There are many general interest and specialty magazines that offer excellent opportunities for targeting advertising to just about anyone.
- Most magazines provide high-quality printing and support for special treatments such as metallic inks, foldouts, and even microencapsulated fragrances.
- Magazines offer flexible advertising formats (sizes and colors) and usually allow specific placement within a section of the magazine.
- Magazines have a high credibility and authority factor. Therefore they are good for image advertising and complex messages.

The weaknesses of magazine advertising are:

- There is a long lead time before the ad is seen. It can take one to four months to get an ad into print after delivery of the artwork.
- Media costs in well-read national magazines are expensive. A full-color ad in *Better Homes and Gardens* or *National Geographic* costs approximately $100,000 an issue.
- The ad competition in popular magazines is high, making it difficult to stand out from the crowd.
- The frequency is relatively low—typically only once a month. This means that other media need to be used to reinforce the messages if more frequency is desirable.
- Like newspapers, magazines can relay only static events.

To be effective, print ads need to catch the reader's eye long enough to deliver their message and get it remembered. To see what works and what doesn't in print advertising, begin by collecting several newspapers and magazines targeted toward your customers and spend time looking through them to see what grabs your eye. Consciously study the pages to notice ads that don't look good and don't get noticed. Examine the ads to understand why they worked and why they didn't. You may want to buy a notebook or scrapbook with blank pages and start a collection of print media ads. Glue them down with a simple glue stick and make notes on the page margins about each. Collect ads you dislike too and keep them in a separate section of the notebook.

## The Key Elements in Successful Print Ads

When you look at print advertising samples you will notice some similarities among the good ads. The two main elements in an effective print ad usually are a strong visual element and a short, succinct headline. Ads that use a powerful or catchy visual (illustration or photo) coupled with a potent headline are consistently the most noticed and read. There are some type-only ads and other formats that work if done well, but most of the best print ads use the headline-visual combination. Good advertisements also make a complete sale—the ad stands on its own to get the message across and includes all the information necessary to take the next step in the purchase decision.

Avoid cluttering your ad with too many elements that detract from the main photo or illustration. Simple formats work better than complex ones in most media. Keep in mind that your ad is competing with many others in most publications. You have less than half a second to catch a reader's eye. Once you attract a reader's attention with a strong headline and visual, the next task is to get him to read the copy. Keep it short and make it easy to read and interesting. If the reader pauses while reading your copy, because of an ill-chosen word or convoluted sentence, you've lost him. Good copy carries the reader along like a moving sidewalk to the end of the ad.

The other elements that improve the recognition and readership of print ads include

- **Color.** Color is very important to print advertising, especially in magazines. Readership studies show full-color ads get noticed by the most readers, followed by two- and three-color ads, with black and white ads the least noticed. There are some powerful black and white ads around—but they require great concepts and exceptional design to pull as well as a color ad.

- **Size.** Obviously a larger ad gets noticed more than a smaller ad.

- **Position.** Some pages get read more than others, so the effectiveness of an ad varies depending on its location in the publication.

## Selecting and Placing Newspaper Advertising

Newspaper advertising is usually the simplest because it rarely employs complicated color. Newsprint stock seriously limits printing quality, so detailed designs and high-resolution photography are not appropriate. Your local advertising space representative can help you with questions on placements and rates.

Rates for newspaper advertising are based on the following combination of factors:

- **Circulation.** The more people who read the paper, the more the advertising will cost.

- **Size of the ad in pages or column inches.** Some newspapers charge by the *agate lines,* a system for measuring depth that measures 1 1/4 inch deep and one column wide.

- **Color charges.** Ad rates are usually quoted for black and white standard ads. Additional charges for color are then applied to this base rate.

- **Special placement or preferred position charges.** If you want the front of the paper or a location in a special section or a guaranteed placement on the page, you will usually pay an additional charge.

There are often different rates for national and local advertisers. National advertisers usually pay more than local ones. Special reduced rates are often available for frequent advertisers. Advertisers willing to take any position in the paper—called a *run of paper rate* (ROP)—are also provided discounts. Combination rates are available for advertisers who place ads in morning and evening editions or on consecutive days or weekends.

The best place to run ads in a newspaper are (in order of preference):

1. Page 2 or 3 of the news section.
2. The back page of any section (except multisection classified ad sections).
3. The first three pages of any section (except the classified ad section).
4. Pages 4 and up of the news section.
5. Features pages including comics, sports, entertainment, etc. These pages have a higher priority if you are selling a directly related product.

When you decide on the size, color, placement, and frequency of your ad, you will make an *insertion order* to specify the dates and other details.

If you want to do extensive out-of-town advertising, this may be a good time to look up an advertising agency with experience placing out-of-town advertising on a national scale. If you want to do it yourself, locate a bookstore or newsstand that carries major papers from cities across the United States, Canada, and sometimes even Europe. For the name of one look under *Newspapers* in the *Yellow Pages.* The papers contain phone numbers and addresses for you to use to obtain a media kit. If your plans include small town papers out of your area, find the annual *Gale Directory of Publications and Broadcast Media* in your local library's reference section and make a list of the papers you might consider. (Doing this with a detailed map is helpful to understand the size and locations of towns and cities.)

## Guidelines for Placing Newspaper Ads

Here are some guidelines to help you get better placements and better value for your newspaper advertising dollars:

- One opportunity that works well for local services is the TV guide section of the Saturday or Sunday paper. Unlike the bulk of the Sunday paper, which gets trashed, it stays in reader's homes for a week and household members who don't read the paper may still use the TV section.

- Although the price is attractive, avoid running your ad in the regional section of a newspaper that runs midweek. Several different regions or outlying cities will have their own section assembled into the paper and delivered only to that region. These sections usually contain uninteresting news from local organizations and clubs. Many readers do not give this section much more than a cursory flip-through on their way to the comics. So, although the price may be right, you will not get good value for your money.

- If you are advertising a product purchased by both men and women, avoid running the ad in the newspaper's sports or cooking section for obvious reasons.

- Newspapers frequently run *special interest* sections of ads and articles pertaining to a particular product line such as cars, boats, home entertainment, and other consumer goods on an annual basis. Before signing up for one of these sections, study last year's version of the special. If it contains mostly ads and only a limited number of poorly written articles, spend your media dollars more fruitfully elsewhere.

- Adding a second color will get you noticed on a page of black and white ads, but since many newspapers reserve only certain pages for second colors, you may get poor placement or be surrounded by ads with the same second color. Check this out in advance with your space rep.

- Many newspapers will insert your independently printed flyer or catalog into the papers during binding. For some products and markets, especially supermarkets and department stores, this works out well and is less expensive than multiple full-page ads.

## Selecting and Placing Magazine Advertising

If your magazine advertising plans include multiple placements of four-color ads, you may want to consider using an advertising agency or design firm to help produce and place your ads. Remember, if your ad doesn't look good, it won't get noticed. If you have no experience with design and production, pay for the experience of someone who does.

Rates in magazines are based on the same general factors as newspapers—circulation, size of the ad, location in the magazine, number of colors, and frequency of insertion.

Color is more important in magazine advertising than in newspapers. When advertising in a magazine, the largest color ads usually get the first shot at the best pages. Depending on how many color pages the magazine has and how it is assembled, some color ads may end up in the middle or back of the magazine. Your best shot at good placement in a magazine is to request, "a space as close to the front of the magazine as possible surrounded by or across from editorial (articles)." This (hopefully) will buy you a placement away from competing ads and near the front of a magazine, which gets read more than the less important articles in the back. In most publications, the smaller your ad, the less chance you have of getting good placement.

The best locations for ad placement in a magazine are (in order of preference):

1. The inside front cover.
2. The back cover.
3. The first few pages of the magazine.
4. Across from the issue's feature article or cover story.
5. The inside back cover.
6. The first 25% of the magazine's pages.
7. The next 50% of the magazine's pages.
8. The last 25% of the magazine's pages.

Of course, the preference list varies from magazine to magazine and some publications such as *National Geographic* have no advertising in the middle, so the above list doesn't apply.

After you make your choices, you will place an insertion order with your advertising rep, as you would for newspaper advertising, specifying all the details for location, frequency, color, size, and insertion dates.

---

✎ **TIPS FOR PLACING MAGAZINE ADVERTISING**

1. Thoroughly investigate all prospective magazine channels before buying an expensive ad in a general-interest magazine—even if you need to employ an ad agency to help you. There are so many special interest magazines, you may find several that will do an excellent job for your needs at a fraction of the price of a major publication.

2. A tear-away business reply card (BRC) will make the magazine pop open to your ad's page when readers casually flip through it. It may also bring you more leads than just an address and phone number.

3. In some publications, a well-orchestrated one-page ad located across from an important feature story will get more notice than a more expensive two-page spread. Talk to your rep well in advance to secure this kind of placement.

---

### Step-by-Step Print Advertising Production

Print advertising is generally the simplest kind of advertising to implement. As with all ads, the print ad starts with a defined goal and message and selection of the appropriate media. The message is then translated into a concept. If you use an agency, your account representative and the creative director will come up with the initial concepts for approval. After these initial advertising planning stages are completed, print ads go through the steps detailed below.

- A writer drafts headlines or an outline for the copy based on the general concept. Producing headlines will usually give you and the designer a better idea of how the ad will go together than an outline, but some writers prefer one method over the other.

- At the same time the writer is drafting the copy, the designer produces sketches for the ad. These sketches may take the form of simple drawings done on tissue or they may be rendered as *thumbnails*. Thumbnails are miniature renderings of an ad. Depending on the project, budget, and time available, the designer may provide several different versions of the design from which you can choose.

- Once the headlines and thumbnails have been given the go ahead, the writer rewrites the copy until reaching a final draft. Depending on the project and the number of people involved in the approval process, this can be as few as one draft completed or as many as ten or more in the case of an inexperienced writer and/or a large, bureaucratic organization.

- In parallel with the writing, the designer takes the approved sketch and renders a *comp* (for comprehensive). The comp shows the final look of the ad with sketches substituting for photos and illustrations and the headlines drawn in. Since the copy is probably not complete, the text is *greeked*, which means that a block of dummy text is set in the correct style and size to substitute for the actual words so you can see how the text looks in the design. Depending on the designer and the project, the comp will vary from a crude photocopy to a piece that looks almost exactly like a finished ad. You should carefully review the comp and specify in detail any changes you want made.

- If the project requires illustrations or photos, they are usually completed after the comp or occasionally in parallel with it. If a photo session is required, you may want to attend so you can look at the Polaroid test prints of the shots and approve them. In the case of illustrations, ask to review the pencil sketches before the final illustrations are started.

- The designer takes the approved copy and sets the type while preparing a *mechanical* of the ad. The mechanical is the final assembly of the ad, with copy, illustrations, and other elements mounted on a cardboard art board ready for the printer or color separator to process. Once the mechanical is finished, the writer and client proofread it one final time for any errors that may have crept in (common). If you have the opportunity, ask the designer to explain the various elements of the final mechanical, such as the color overlays, art paste-ups, and marked color breaks

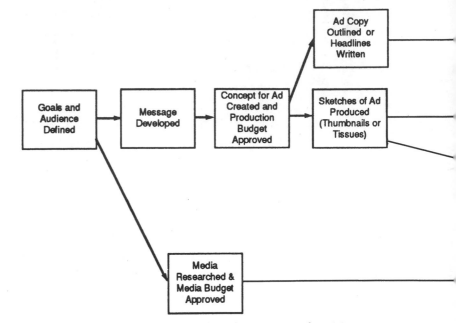

Figure 3.3  The process of producing print advertising.

on the tissues. You should review and approve the mechanical. Even if you don't understand how all the pieces fit together, at least reread the copy and ask questions.

- Depending on the complexity of the ad and the number of publications in which it is to run, duplicates of the ad materials may be necessary. If the ad uses complex color, a *color separator* (an outside service company) will be used to produce final negatives for the publications. If the same ad is to run in multiple publications with different physical requirements, several mechanical adjustments to the final ad may be required.

- In most cases, a *proof* will be produced for your approval before publication. You and the designer (or agency) should review the proof to make sure the publication has not made any errors in assembly.

- When the ad runs in the selected media, the production cycle is complete. After your ad runs, the media should provide you with *tearsheets*—samples of the ad as it ran in the publication.

## THE RADIO ADVERTISING PRIMER

Most radio advertising is local in nature, even on nationally produced programs such as *CBS News*. Radio advertising consists of announcer-read or prerecorded commercials for use on commercial radio stations. Sometimes a radio commercial will also be used as part of the background music programming in modern supermarkets and other stores.

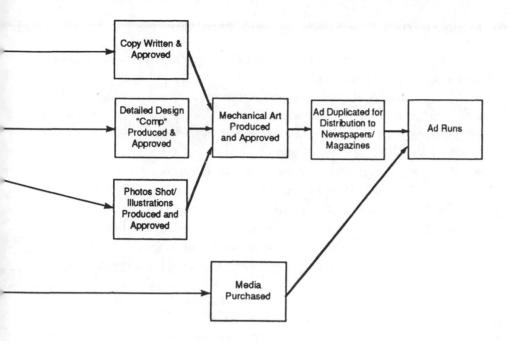

Radio advertising is divided into three categories: local, spot, and network. Local is used by most advertisers and focuses on local advertisers promoting local products and services. Spot advertising is sold to national advertisers who buy airtime on individual stations. Spot time should not be confused with *radio spots,* another term for radio commercials.

## Radio Advertising Strengths and Weaknesses

Be aware of the strengths and weaknesses of radio as a medium for advertising before you begin to produce your ads. The strengths of radio advertising include the following:

- Radio can reach and influence a large audience quickly. There are more radios than there are households—and people have them in cars and take portables with them on vacations and picnics. Radio has the broadest reach of any of the media, meaning it is heard by the widest range of people.
- Radio ads are less expensive to produce and place than TV commercials and, like TV, radio is quite an effective media for promoting a variety of products.
- Radio spots are less expensive than other media. Radio offers the lowest media cost per thousand (CPM) contacts.
- Radio stations have formats that appeal to specific market segments, making it easier to target groups of potential customers.

Radio advertising's weaknesses include the following:

- Unlike print advertising, once the commercial airs, it no longer exists to be referred to.
- The creative options on radio are limited.
- A large number of competing stations can make it difficult for an advertiser to choose among stations and most listeners are loyal to only one kind of station.
- Because radio reaches a very broad range of listeners, many will have no interest in your product.
- The sound quality is difficult to control and some commercials may be only half-heard. Many people use radio for background music, so they don't pay attention to the messages.
- The audience size and composition vary over the period of a day or weeks.

If you don't frequently listen to the radio, now is the time to start before putting together a radio ad. Get your hands on a media log of local stations (usually found somewhere in the Saturday or Sunday paper). This log will give you a list of stations, their place on the dial, and a one- or two-word description of their format (adult contemporary, jazz, rock, easy listening, etc.). Spend time listening to various stations and studying the commercials. Note what kind of companies advertise on each station. This will give you a better idea of the kind of commercial that works with each station. Unlike reading the local newspaper, choosing and regularly listening to a radio station is a very personal matter, so the listener profile for a mainstream country and western station is very different than for a classical music station.

## The Key Elements of Successful Radio Commercials

Your radio advertising must get and keep the interest of a listener frustrated with yet another commercial break in his favorite program or music show. You must hold the undivided attention of listeners until your message has been delivered and remembered. Your audience may be listening on a car radio with handy buttons for changing stations if they don't like your ad. Remember that you are painting a picture in the listener's mind. This requires quality writing and professional delivery and as much creativity as you can muster on the air. Concentrate on getting your message across. If the listener remembers only one thing from your commercial, it should be your message.

Elements that help create a successful radio commercial include the following:

- Interesting, provocative, or unusual sound effects and/or music.
- A story or testimonial.

- Particularly impressive or unusual voice talent.
- Combining elements to tell a story that is interesting and compelling.
- Comedy can be a powerful tool, but tailoring it to make a commercial work well is best left to talented professionals. People's perception of what is funny varies considerably based on age groups, intelligence, and geographic regions. What is hilarious to you may be offensive or simply dumb to your audience and your commercial will get the raspberry.

The common element in all successful radio advertising is a compelling conversation, joke, debate, a story, or the now largely obsolete commercial-length radio jingle. The narrative must appeal to the audience you want to reach.

A standard structure for radio commercials, and one that works well if it is properly executed, includes (1) an introduction to get attention, (2) a middle section where the main message is delivered, and (3) a conclusion and/or call to action ("Buy today!"). The use of a simple, provocative sound effect or statement at the beginning of a commercial is an excellent tool for getting a listener's attention. Then immediately deliver your message. Follow up with more detail, ending with a conclusion that reinforces the message one more time and may include a call to action. Music can be used in the background to provide continuity.

## Selecting and Placing Radio Advertising

When you receive a radio station's media kit it will specify the demographics of the listening audience and the reach of the station. Now is the time to decide whether you want an advertising agency to assist you in creating and placing a commercial. Choosing radio media is usually easier than selecting TV media, but expertise is required for producing and placing the commercial, so you may need to employ an experienced agency or production firm.

There are two basic steps for matching a radio station to your target market:

1. Determine when your audience is most likely to be listening. If you are selling a cure for insomnia, late night and early morning hours are obvious times when those receptive to your message will be tuned in.
2. Match your product to the station's programming and listener profile. For example, if your commercial promotes luxury cars, running a radio spot during a popular show on investing money is a good shot.

A fairly high level of frequency is required for radio spots to have much effect. Unlike print media, which is usually subscribed to or purchased by people interested in reading it, radio is more "scattershot" in its success in attracting and keeping regular listeners. Running the same commercial on several stations, several times a day is the best way to ensure that a large audience has heard it.

Buying radio time is based on the *dayparts* (time of day), average quarter-hour audiences, and cumulative audience measurements *(cumes)*. These are radio terms used for setting the rates for particular times of day. The frequency of your advertising commitment will also affect your rates. Obviously, the more people listening to the station at a particular time as audited by the station and independent auditors, the more money you will pay for the spot. Advertisers can also buy reduced-rate spots on a *run of station* (ROS) basis. These are aired at the station's discretion (much like ROP ads in newspapers).The best times to run radio ads include:

1. During drive time. The drive time is the morning and evening commute, when many people are stuck in traffic listening to their car radios for entertainment and diversion.
2. Saturday and Sunday mornings. Many radio stations have special programming on weekend mornings that avid radio listeners listen to while enjoying coffee and making a half-hearted attempt to look through the newspaper.

---

### ✎   TIPS FOR PLACING RADIO ADVERTISING

1. Running a commercial frequently over a period of a couple of weeks is more effective than running less frequent spots over a period of months.

2. Many stations run several commercials sequentially. If you must settle for this arrangement, ask to be the first commercial aired in the sequence so that the audience is still paying attention. People tend to tune out during commercials and if yours follows a particularly obnoxious one, it will have less chance of getting heard.

3. Commercials running in the middle of a show often work better than at the end or start of a show. This is particularly true in the case of radio specialty programming. For example, a popular talk show on politics may command a very specific audience who listens to the station only during the show. Your commercial at the end of the show may air after this listenership has turned the radio off.

4. Radio fans quickly tire of the same commercial airing over and over, so it is important to produce fresh commercials on a regular basis.

5. An inexpensive and common practice for radio commercials is for the announcer to read the commercial live. Before agreeing to this practice, listen to the announcer(s) who will be handling your commercial. If he or she sounds bored, insincere, or mumbles, pass on this opportunity.

---

3. During work hours for certain kinds of radio stations. "Light" radio stations that play popular music are used as background music by stores and companies. Some classical music and jazz stations are also used this way.

4. During a specialty show that applies to your product. For example, the *Gardening Today* show is an obvious possibility if you run ads for a nursery or gardening products.

If you intend to run radio spots in multiple cities, spot selection is more complex and should probably be left to an advertising agency experienced with national radio media placement. If you must do it yourself, you can get station names and addresses from the annual *Gale Directory of Publications and Broadcast Media* and/or *The Broadcast Yearbook* from The Associated Press. National network advertising is somewhat easier than individual local spot placements because it offers one-stop shopping for the entire country.

## Step-by-Step Radio Commercial Production

Many radio stations offer two kinds of commercial formats: announcer-read and taped. An announcer-read commercial is one in which the announcer or disc jockey reads the commercial on the air from a script. In some stations the announcer does a personal testimony describing how wonderful the product is and claims that he or she personally uses it. (If you've never heard one of these, count yourself lucky.) Announcer-read commercials are pretty straightforward because they rarely employ special effects or background music and require no recording sessions or voice talent. All you need is a good script.

The second format is a recorded commercial produced in a studio and distributed on perpetual loop tapes called *carts* (short for cartridges). To use these, the announcer puts them in a machine with several others and touches a button to start the tape rolling at the appropriate time. When the commercial is finished the tape automatically stops, ready for the next use.

Even if you write the script yourself, other people will be involved in developing your radio advertising. Radio spots use actors and actresses to provide the voice talent or use announcers and disc jockeys to read every commercial. Complex radio ads require the services of an experienced producer to create and edit the voices, supply the music and various special effects, and then effectively assemble the pieces into a finished commercial.

Again, every radio commercial starts with an objective, message, media selection, and concept. After a writer or creative director comes

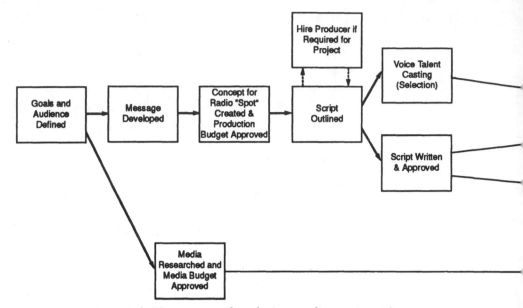

Figure 3.4. The process of producing a radio commercial.

up with the concept, the steps in producing a radio commercial include the following:

- The script is outlined by a writer and a producer is hired if one is required. The script outline demonstrates how the commercial will be structured. A production budget is also produced for your approval.
- The writer and producer develop a final version of the script for your review, possibly revising the production budget again if necessary.
- In tandem with the final script development, actors and/or actresses are hired as the voice talent to read the script. These people are usually found through an agency that handles a wide variety of talent, or freelancers may be used. (If the script requires the voice of a famous personality, this is negotiated well before the script is written.)
- The voice talent rehearses for the part after studying the script. Most radio spots require little rehearsal unless the reader is not a professional actor, i.e., the owner of a company talking about his firm.
- Special effects and music are chosen from an existing library or arrangements are made to record them. Many large libraries of sound and music are available, so it isn't often necessary to record new sounds unless a big budget is available for production. You should approve the choices in advance of final mixing.

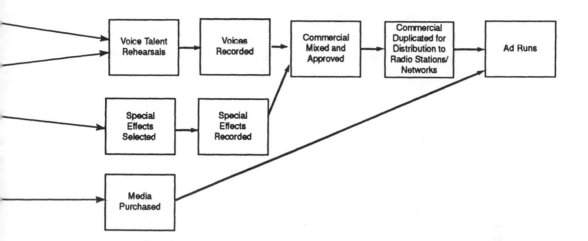

- Next the voice talent (and often the producer and you, if it is an expensive ad) make a trip to the sound studio to complete the recording. The narrators or actors read their lines onto tape, completing several *takes* if a line is flubbed. Some professional voice actors have their own in-home sound studios, but most of the time an independent studio or the radio station's facilities will be used.
- Special sound effects (or SFX as they're known in the trade) and music are recorded if required. This may require the hiring of professional studio musicians.

---

✎    TIP: BE AWARE OF THE TECHNICAL DIFFERENCES
            BETWEEN AM AND FM RADIO

AM radio is less clear and more subject to noise and interference than FM radio. AM radio tuners are far more limited in sound capability than their FM counterparts. AM stations do have a longer range than FM transmitters, with some *clear channel* AM stations having ranges of hundreds of miles. Stations also vary in transmitting power, and the presence of natural barriers (hills and mountains) can seriously affect the clear transmission of a given station's programming.

---

- After all the separate sounds and voices are recorded and approved, the radio spot is mixed to a *master tape*. A recording technician or sound engineer edits and mixes all of the individual sound elements together while adjusting the volume levels. In some cases the sound engineer may also manipulate the sound quality through equalization and other sound processing systems. You should carefully review the finished master before it is duplicated. Note that major changes at this point may be expensive, so avoid making them unless absolutely necessary.

- The master tape is duplicated for distribution to radio stations and the finished commercial runs according to the media contract.

## THE TELEVISION ADVERTISING PRIMER

When most people think of advertising, they think of television commercials. Television is the most pervasive and persuasive modern medium for advertising. Television advertising has grown faster than any of the other media and continues to grow and develop its influence and reach.

Not all the news about television advertising is good, however. The *Wall Street Journal* recently reported a study by Video Storyboard Tests Inc., a company that tracks advertising popularity among consumers, that showed that the percentage of people who can name an outstanding TV advertising campaign has been plummeting recently. In 1986, 64% of the people polled could, unaided, cite favorite campaigns—a measurement that came in at only 48% in 1990. The reasons may be because there are more channels and more ads. It may also be because ads are of such relatively high production quality that they do not stand out from the crowd any more. It may also be that the ads lack ideas. In the same *Wall Street Journal* report, Martin Puris, president and CEO of ad agency Ammirati & Puris, was reported to state, "It's hard to find a really badly executed piece of [TV] advertising any more, but it's very easy to find a lot of irrelevant, rotten ideas."

At the same time that television advertising's memorability seems to be waning, print advertising's memorability has consistently hovered in the 26–31% range. Even though many consider print advertising a stable medium and a relative bargain for this reason, print remains a tough sell to national, consumer-oriented companies. Television is still too glitzy and alluring to ignore.

Like radio, most television advertising is classified as either network, spot, or local, except that the placements (commercial time) are orders of magnitude more expensive, especially on the networks.

Most television advertising is regional or national because nearly all of it consists of ads for consumer products or nationally distributed products. Ads are also run for local restaurants, appliance retailers, car dealers, attorneys, and private schools and colleges, but they make up the minority of commercial programming in terms of media dollars and are mostly found on less expensive nonnetwork stations.

Another kind of commercial option that has evolved primarily on cable channels is the program-length commercial also known as an *infomercial*. Often consisting of an expensive production, complete with professional acting talent and a large and endlessly enthusiastic studio audience, infomercials are used to promote weight loss programs, life improvement tapes, make-up kits, skin care products, and "magic" cleaners—the list goes on and on. Debate continues on regulating the infomercials because the best ones look misleadingly like regular programming. Some stations and cable networks run them with the word *Advertisement* prominently displayed at the bottom of the screen during the entire program.

Since most people watch a fair amount of TV, you may not need much additional study of the medium or its commercial formats to become familiar with the advertising options. However, if you rarely watch TV, or spend evenings with the local PBS station, study the format and ads of the commercial channels one by one.

If your foray into television advertising includes cable-only channels, it's time to install cable if you don't already have it. Many of the cable channels such as *The Discovery Channel* and *The Nashville Network* are viable media, but their ads and advertisers are somewhat different than on familiar local and network channels. Unlike radio, where listeners primarily tune into only one station or kind of station, most television viewers watch any channel offering something they wish to see and change channels frequently. The advent of remote control TV and 50-station cable has exacerbated this effect.

## Television Advertising Strengths and Weaknesses

Though television is by far the most powerful of the media in getting its messages across to a wide range of viewers, like all media, television has its strengths and weaknesses. Its strengths are as follows:

- Television can reach and influence a larger audience more quickly than any other media.
- It can persuasively demonstrate a variety of action-oriented products and processes.
- Unlike radio advertising, which depends solely on hearing, and print advertising, which relies on sight to deliver a message, television uses both sight and sound, making it a potentially more persuasive medium than either print or radio.
- Whereas large segments of the population do not read magazines or newspapers, and another segment rarely turns on a radio, almost everyone in the United States watches television on a regular basis.

- A wide range of creative options are available, allowing advertisers to create strong image and brand identification.
- A strong empathy with the television actors can be created, which causes people to quickly identify with a particular product.

The weaknesses of using television advertising include the following:

- It is very expensive, both to produce commercial spots and for media charges. The cost of television advertising is prohibitive for many small businesses and organizations.
- It takes considerable time, money, and experience to produce and place effective television ads.
- Unlike print media, once a television commercial airs, it is gone forever unless videotaped by a viewer along with a program or movie.
- It requires a high level of frequency to reinforce a message.

## The Key Elements of Successful Television Commercials

To produce effective television commercials, you must create an ad that is at least as interesting as the program during which it airs. Because most Americans watch a lot of TV, they have become connoisseurs of the medium and subconsciously know when a commercial is not up to snuff for any reason.

Elements that help a television commercial get noticed include the following:

- Dazzling, provocative, or unusual visuals, sound effects, and music.
- A complete story line. Television is a visual medium that lends itself to storytelling formats.
- A high human interest factor. You know how popular the human interest shows are; the same principles apply to advertising.
- Action and movement in the ad to keep people's attention.
- Advanced computer-based animation. Though currently very expensive, animations can be spellbinding. They will become increasingly commonplace and less effective as prices for computer animations fall.
- Famous acting talent can get people's attention. Not all people are swayed by this trick and some actors and actresses do so many commercials and promotions that audiences respond negatively to their image (and your message).
- Comedy can be a powerful tool, but tailoring it to make a commercial work well is a job for professional comedy writers with

experience writing commercials. Comedy can also be a big flop, so it is usually risky to use humor without substantial pretesting first.

Many television spots are structured much the same way as a good radio spot: (1) an introduction to get attention, (2) a middle section where the main message is delivered, and (3) a conclusion and/or call to action. Instead of a simple, provocative sound effect or statement at the beginning of a commercial, as used in radio, a television commercial may use a stunning visual image for the same purpose. This may deliver the commercial's message or it may immediately follow. The middle section of the commercial provides more detail on the product to reinforce the message. The ending reaffirms the primary message and may include a call to action.

Not all commercials stick to this format. Television ads may be structured any way the writer and director see fit and many deliberately "break the rules" to get noticed among the peas and carrots of television commercialdom.

## Selecting and Placing Television Advertising

Normally, your advertising agency should make the television media recommendations for you. They will know how to negotiate the rates and choose the best frequencies and placement. Consider purchasing television media on your own only if you will be using local stations. It's not that choosing television media is necessarily more difficult than buying media for print or radio, it's just that television is so pricey that even one mistake is costly.

There are three ways a television advertiser can purchase television airtime for advertising:

1. Companies can sponsor an entire program and secure all the advertising spots associated with the program. For many programs, sponsoring a network program or special requires paying for the program production and the media charges, so it is prohibitive for all but the largest corporations.
2. It is less expensive and almost as impactful to buy advertising on a participating basis with a group of advertisers buying a number of national 30- and 60-second spots within the same program.
3. The least expensive form of advertising is spot advertising—which can be purchased nationally or locally. Here the advertiser can request various commercial lengths, frequencies, and time periods for each station.

You may not always be able to secure the spots you want for local commercials because some advertisers purchase time far in advance. When you contact your television media reps, they will research the spots that are available (called *requesting avails*).

The actual rates for television advertising are based on the size of the audience, the rating of the programs, and the length and frequency of the advertising commitment. Most television advertisers compare advertising costs in terms of cost per thousand viewers.

Before you place your ads you will need to match the television stations or networks and programming to your target market. Here are two guidelines:

- Determine when your audience is most likely to be watching. If you are promoting a college that trains unskilled high-school graduates in new careers, the weekday daytime hours are a likely time when the unemployed will be watching and receptive.
- Match your product to the programming and to the station itself. For example, if you advertise disposable diapers during prime time, a show such as *The Simpsons* is a better choice of media than reruns of *The Lawrence Welk Show*.

You may be offered airtime as a package of commercial spots. Study alternatives carefully to identify the package that gives you the best coverage for your product at the best price.

If you are planning on running your commercial on local stations not affiliated with a network or national cable channel, you will have your work cut out picking and choosing compatible stations and programming for your message. If you are considering a major campaign on out-of-area channels, it requires a lot of research and thinking to get your message under the noses of the target market. Who knows whether a suitably large percentage of Duluth viewers tune into *60 Minutes* on a weekly basis and whether or not female Bostonians between the ages of 35 and 55 and working in senior management watch reruns of *Gilligan's Island*. This is definitely advertising agency territory unless you have a lot of spare time to research such pertinent issues and/or a lot of money to waste.

If you do decide to place the ads in remote cities yourself, you can get a list of stations, along with their ratings from the library in the *Gale Directory of Publications and Broadcast Media* and/or *The Broadcast Yearbook* from The Associated Press. However, unlike print media where you can get a copy of the publication for inspection along with a request for a media kit, you'll be left in the dark on the look and feel of remote stations and viewer idiosyncrasies.

The best times to run television commercials include the following:

1. During *prime time* programming—the period beginning at 7:00 P.M. and running until 10:00 or 11:00 P.M.

2. During news programs, particularly during the early evening and late evening news.

3. During sporting events such as *Monday Night Football,* but *not* the local bowling championship unless you sell bowling balls.

4. On news channels during times of crisis (obviously hard to predict).

5. During movies with commercial breaks of no more than three spots in a row.

6. During specialty shows that pertain to your product. If you are soliciting donations for hungry third-world children, a documentary on poverty in the third-world is a potentially good place for an ad.

7. During soap operas and daytime programming. Although not appropriate for every product, household cleaning and baby care products work well during this period.

Like radio, frequency in TV advertising gives your commercial a better chance of being seen by a larger share of the target market. Running and rerunning your ad is the best way to ensure that a maximum number of prospective customers have seen it. Also like radio, television is scattershot; although an enormous number of people may see your ad, it is unlikely that more than a minority of viewers will be immediately interested in your product.

---

✎  **TIPS FOR PLACING TV COMMERCIALS**

1. As with radio, running a TV commercial frequently over a period of a couple of weeks is more effective than running the same number of placements over several months.

2. Many stations group four or more commercials together, and that gives the audience time to get up and grab a snack or head for the bathroom. Attempt to avoid these kinds of placements.

3. If your product appeals to a very up-scale audience (i.e., educated, high income), statistics show that these people watch a lot of movies. In many cases, a well-chosen local-channel movie can be an inexpensive place for your ad, but choose *Casablanca* over *Conan the Barbarian.*

4. Commercials running in the middle of a show often work better than at the end of one show and the start of the next.

5. Viewers quickly tire of seeing the same commercial over and over. Do three or four different commercials or variations on one and rotate them to keep the message and the look fresh.

6. It is important to get noticed, but particularly loud or brash commercials send TV viewers for the mute button. Use common sense and discretion.

### Step-by-Step Television Commercial Production

Television ads are the most complex marketing communications to execute because there are so many elements that must work together in harmony to make an ad effective. Television advertising is not something you should do on your own. Instead you will need to hire an advertising agency or a professional commercial production house. Don't write your own script and have the station produce it, unless you want your ad to look like the frequently laughable late-night commercials on local UHF channels.

It is important for you to understand the basic principles and steps in producing television advertising, because it will help you work with your agency more effectively. As in radio, television once had two forms of commercials: taped and announcer-read. Because television programming and commercials have become increasingly sophisticated, the announcer-read commercial is now rarely seen except in third-world countries. However, the *product endorsement* variety of an announcer-read commercial is still around on stations serving small markets and on game and talk shows.

To be effective, television advertising must grab and hold the viewer's eyes, ears, and brain. This consists of more than just keeping the audience's eyes glued to the set. Research shows that when watching television, people have brainwave patterns similar to people sitting around and watching a campfire, i.e., a state of quasiunconsciousness. At one time stunning film sequences could effectively break the monotony, but today almost every commercial includes vibrant visuals and seamless production techniques. For this reason, you should hire the best talent you can afford to produce your commercial.

Producing television commercials requires expertise, experience, and a practiced eye that takes years to fine tune. If you are interested in learning more about television commercials than covered here, a good overview on television commercials and production is *How to Produce Effective TV Commercials* by Hooper White (NTC Business Books, 1986).

Television advertising again is a complex process involving a variety of skillsets to carry out the writing, preproduction, filming, and postproduction tasks. Depending on the nature of your commercial, as many as 50 people can be involved in assembling a complex commercial from start to finish. Only the major steps and primary personnel in television production are listed here.

## TIP: DO NOT USE TV STATION TALENT
## TO PRODUCE YOUR TELEVISION COMMERCIAL
## UNLESS YOU HAVE TO

Unless you are running a commercial in a very small market where competing ads are not produced professionally, avoid using the station's production staff to put your commercial together. Although the price and convenience is there, the talent is not. Occasionally you will find a creative gem, but this is the exception. Most people working inside a station specialize in getting things done fast and cheap—but have little concern for your image or your message. If you are competing for the eye of viewers already accustomed to watching commercials that cost $100,000+ to produce, yours will look cheap and incompetent in comparison.

Television advertising starts with the advertising objective, message, and concepts. Concepts are particularly important in television advertising for highly competitive products—so advertising agencies get paid a lot for their creative services. The format for the ad must also be determined—is it a 60- or 30-second spot or will it be designed to be run in multiple formats?

Once the agency and client agree on the concept, the production begins. Here are the steps all television ads go through before they air. Refer to the diagram, as many of the steps must be completed in parallel to get the commercial completed in a timely manner:

- A writer assigned to the project by the agency will produce a script and *storyboard* for your approval. The storyboard is a sequence of small, captioned drawings that illustrate the flow of the commercial.
- The storyboard and script are sent out to bid at production companies interested in producing the commercial. If you are working with an ad agency, before the production company is hired, the agency will produce a semifinal script and storyboards and send the ad out to bid at several production companies. Most agencies hire outside production companies and their directors to work on the commercials—the agencies provide the management and creative input to the process.
- A production company is selected based on bid responses and experience. Talent is usually more important than price, so it is not always the cheapest company that gets the project. A "rough cut" production budget is also produced at this point for your approval.

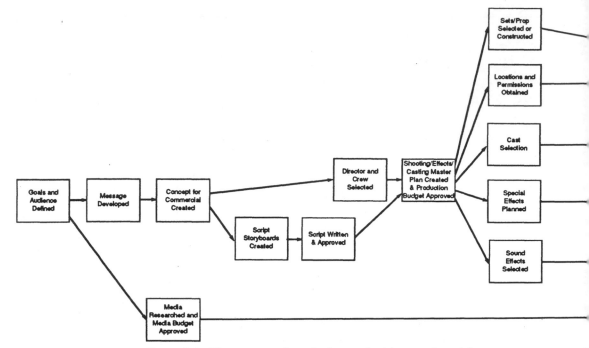

Figure 3.5. The process of producing a television commercial.

- The script, in theory, was finalized before being sent out to bid, but in practice changes are often needed for a variety of reasons. The writer and director may go over it and fine tune it where necessary. At this point, usually in tandem with the next step, the final budget and script are worked out among you, the agency, and the production crew. Because commercial production is expensive, sometimes even minor changes to a script can substantially impact the production budget.

- The commercial is *master-planned* in a *preproduction* meeting and a shooting schedule is established. Depending on the complexity of the commercial, several meetings may be required to iron out the details with various *production units* involved. For example, if 50% of your commercial is shot in the studio and 50% shot on location in Europe, several preproduction meetings will take place.

- Sets, if required, are constructed and props are rented or built. All studio shots require set construction because most studios consist of little more than a big room with a concrete floor. Props are rented from prop companies that maintain large inventories of both ordinary and unusual items.

- If the filming is to be done on location (not in a controlled studio environment), suitable locations must be identified and permissions sought to use the sites. Sets and props may also be required for location shots.

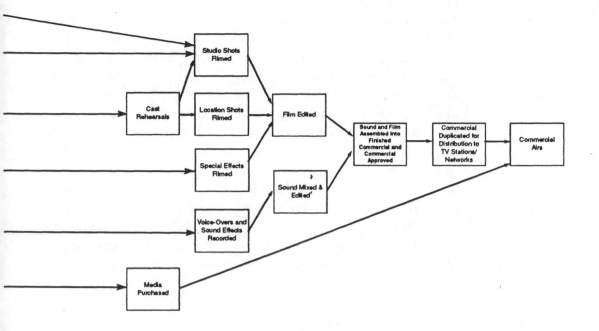

- In parallel with establishing the locations, sets, and props, a cast for the commercial is selected, usually through a talent agency with a wide variety of actors and actresses from whom to choose.
- While all the other preparations are being made, the special effects and music are planned. These include titles, speeding cars, animated sequences, special video treatments, and more. The commercial's music may come from a library of available music, or in the case of a big budget production, it is performed by professional musicians. If special music or jingles need to be written, then a song writer must also be screened and hired through an appropriate agency.
- All of the planning and preparation steps need to be reviewed prior to the final shooting of the commercial. Typically there are several review meetings between the agency and the client to go over the progress in completing a commercial.
- Once the script is "cast in concrete" and most of the preparations are well underway, the cast rehearses their parts and costumes are prepared for them. Because few commercials show an actor on stage for more than 60 seconds, rehearsals rarely require more than an hour or two.
- Finally, the filming takes place. Studio shots are completed. Location shots are filmed. Special effects are filmed. Voiceovers, sound effects, and music are recorded. The results of these separate filming and recording sessions will be reviewed and approved

by the advertising agency, though the client will not see them until the next step.

- The film *rushes* for the commercial (the results of the individual filming sessions) are roughly edited and put into sequence. The rushes are a rough approximation of the commercial, not yet edited for final production. You should review the rushes, although it takes experience to understand how the pieces will look once assembled into the finished commercial.

- After the sequencing is complete, the sound is mixed and assembled into its final form as a master soundtrack, ready for incorporation into the master tape.

- Both sound and video images are integrated, edited, and combined on one tape or film master. You should carefully review and approve the commercial before the final edit and duplication. Note that changes become more expensive the further along in the process they are made. Make them at this point only if absolutely necessary. Prior to final duplication, the finished commercial may be tested on an audience to make sure it delivers its message as planned.

- Finally, the finished commercial is duplicated and ready for distribution to the television stations.

## THE OUTDOOR ADVERTISING PRIMER

Outdoor advertising, or just *outdoor* as it is known in the trade, is a very specialized field. Outdoor includes billboards, signs painted on buildings, and transit posters (both inside and outside busses and trains). Major advertising agencies often have complete divisions dedicated solely to outdoor. If you don't use an agency, outdoor advertising suppliers can be located in the telephone book under *Advertising, Outdoor,* although some listings may be for ad agencies that handle outdoor rather than direct suppliers. Outdoor advertisers will gladly send you their media kits, which include location maps, viewer statistics, and rates.

Your outdoor advertising objective is to place an ad where it will be seen by the largest possible number of people in your target market—catching and holding their attention long enough to get your message understood and remembered.

A drive around most cities reveals a variety of billboard and transit ads. Study them to see which ones grab your eye and why. Notice also how some outdoor ads are placed in better locations than others in terms of being easy to notice and read.

### The Key Elements of Successful Outdoor Advertising

For billboards, where your ad may get only a brief glance—a short, large headline and a strong visual are important to getting the ad seen. Billboards that work are never cluttered. The design must be crisp and clear. Billboard readers passing in cars simply do not have time to sort out the message from the clutter of visuals along a highway or street. In the case of transit posters, simplicity is also important. Outdoor advertising should have very little copy because people passing by at 55 MPH will not be able to read many words.

A highly effective approach to billboard and transit ad design is the "T" principle. The headline represents the top of the T and the visual represents the perpendicular line that meets the top of the T. Easy-to-read outdoor ads usually look like a T with the visual moving off to the left or right in some instances. This is a very easy format for a glancing reader to digest in a fraction of a second. The T can be used upside down, with the headline on the bottom and the visual above it.

## Outdoor Advertising Strengths and Weaknesses

Most outdoor campaigns are used to reinforce other communications or to build broad awareness for a new product or service.

The strengths of outdoor advertising include:

- It can reach and influence a large, broad audience very quickly.
- It has a potentially long life span.
- It quickly builds name and product recognition for mass-market products.
- It can be used to target very specific geographic locations even better than newspaper advertising.
- It offers one of the lowest "cost per message" rates of any of the major media.

Outdoor advertising's primary weaknesses are the following:

- Though the reach is broad (encompassing many kinds of people), outdoor advertising is geographically limited. This can be both an advantage and a disadvantage, depending on your product.
- Outdoor campaigns are time-consuming to produce and must be produced eight weeks or more in advance of placement.

## Selecting and Placing Outdoor Advertising

Purchasing outdoor advertising normally requires the expertise of an agency familiar with the issues of location, demographics, and visibility. If your outdoor media plans include only your own city or town, you can avoid the agency expense by taking advantage of the knowledge of the reps who sell outdoor media. A good rep knows what works and what does not when it comes to locations. If your outdoor media plans include multiple cities, use an agency experienced with outdoor advertising on a national scale.

Local transit advertising is easier to manage on your own than billboard media. The transit companies can provide you with statistics on readership and package prices for various options. A ride on the bus (correct change only please) or a drive around the city will give you a good indication of the package you should choose.

Billboard media are usually purchased as a package of more than one installation called *showings.* There are several sizes of billboards and transit ads available, the largest and most "seen" being the most expensive. Billboards and transit shelters with lights for night viewing are more expensive than ones without. Most outdoor media providers offer rotation programs where your ad can be moved to different areas of a city so more people will see it.

Billboard media rates are based on the length of the commitment and the number of placements or showings. The rates are also based on the size of the display, demographics, and location. The best outdoor ads are located where a maximum number of people will see and have time to read them and these "ideal" locations are priced accordingly.

The best placements for billboard ads are:

1. Along major arterials and near major intersections.
2. Along heavily commuted freeway routes, preferably with few other competing billboards.
3. In cities with limited public transit options that force people to drive their cars (Los Angeles, for example).
4. During warm weather, when people are out walking and driving.
5. Painted on walls in districts with no competing billboards.

Transit media consists of poster ads placed in transit shelters, stations, in transit vehicles, and on the outside of vehicles. Ads can be purchased for showings inside or outside the vehicles or in the stations or in some combination of showings. Like billboard media, transit ads are purchased by number of showings, size, location, and time commitment. A full-showing means that there is one ad on each vehicle in a fleet. There are also package rates known as a run rate or service rate.

The best places for transit ads are:

1. Inside or on the outside of transit vehicles in cities with a significant public transit ridership. The frequently bored riders read every one, even the ugly ones.

2.  In lighted shelters located on major arterials if the ad can be clearly seen by approaching motorists.
3.  At the end of station corridors, stairs, and escalators where approaching pedestrians walk toward the ad.
4.  In airport walkways, especially if you offer products and services to travelers and business people.

## Producing Outdoor Advertising

Because outdoor ads are frequently used to reinforce advertising in other media, their production rarely requires more than a redesign of a print ad used in a magazine. In most cases the steps for producing an outdoor ad are virtually identical to those used to assemble a print ad. The only exceptions are that the writing process is considerably shortened and some billboard ads are painted (not printed) by either a billboard painter or more recently by a computer. Of course, you should use vendors who specialize in outdoor media to supply the production services.

# THE ADVERTISING PLAN

Before you place or produce any ads, an annual advertising plan should be created as part of the total marketing communications plan we discuss in more detail in Chapter 10. The plan should detail the advertising production schedules, budgets, and media placements. Because advertising can be expensive, it is important that the plan shows not only the "event" calendar but also cashflow requirements to support the plan.

If you are working with an ad agency, they will provide this kind of planning for you. When presented with an agency plan, spend time away from the agency personnel to study it. Most agency plans have elements that can be hacked out while still accomplishing your objectives. The worst of these efforts are more like an agency wish list of ads and media they would like to sell you rather than a working document— so you will benefit from knowing your own priorities, markets, and media choices.

Once your advertising plan is complete, you can begin the execution of the ads according to the steps already presented. Of course, as powerful as advertising is, it is only one of the marketing communications tools you will use to get the word out about your product or company. Read on to find out about the others.

# 4 | Publicity: Making News and Getting Noticed by the Media

Have you hired someone important for your company? Do you have a new product to announce? Have you invented an innovative technology or process? Are you making a special discount offer to senior citizens? Have you made a contribution to an arts group or local charity? Does your volunteer organization need donations for a worthy cause? Are you moving to larger headquarters or opening a new office? All of these and many more are opportunities for *free* publicity.

As explained in the first chapter, publicity is one aspect of a broader communications category called public relations. *Publicity* is defined for the purpose of this book as free news coverage by the media. *Public relations,* on the other hand, is a more expansive term, encompassing not only media coverage but self-generated events and activities that promote your company or products without involving paid advertising. Public relations events include seminars, special promotional events, articles in magazines, and more. This chapter concentrates on publicity, the mainstay of any public relations program. The next chapter focuses on special events and other public relations activities you can use to generate interest and awareness in your business and products.

Publicity efforts are generally used along with other communications tools as one part of a complete program, but some small companies that are very adept at managing their publicity programs can survive almost totally on their publicity and other public relations efforts to develop sales.

In small companies publicity can be handled by a single person, usually the owner or a senior manager. Publicity is one area of marketing communications most managers can handle on their own if they know how, though most large companies work with an in-house publicist, public relations department, or public relations agency. Some companies use both an in-house department for regular media contact and a public relations agency for planning, strategy, and special events.

## PUBLICITY IS CHEAP, POWERFUL, AND CREDIBLE

Publicity is a way to get your message out to the world without the expense of advertising. In fact, publicity is one of the least expensive forms of promotion, taking only paper, envelopes, stamps, and a telephone to get started. It does, however, take time, organization, and persistence.

Many companies, especially small ones, fail to realize the potential power and influence of the press for their business—believing that only the big guys or big stories will get mentioned. This is not the case. Any organization, from a restaurant with a new menu to a not-for-profit agency announcing a fund-raising event to a giant corporation with a major product roll-out can use publicity to get the word out about their products and events.

Unlike advertising, which is obviously self-serving, if a write-up about your company appears in credible news media, people feel that the editorial opinion and articles are independent and objective. Thus, publicity can be used to add credence to your advertising messages.

If you have to pay for a write-up or an article in a magazine or newspaper this is not publicity in its true form—this is just a disguised form of advertising, called *advertorial* in the trade. However, in some industries buying an ad also buys placement of your news release. And don't be surprised if you get more publicity in a magazine or newspaper in which you advertise frequently. This is more true of trade and industry publications than the major media. Though there may be "ethical" issues concerning the independence and objectivity of the press, remember that magazines and newspapers are businesses. You can't expect them to ignore their customers any more than you ignore yours. In most cases you can get adequate press coverage without paying for it, but you will need to know how to make yourself, your products, and your events newsworthy.

There are many benefits to actively developing a publicity program for your company or products:

1.  Publicity can reinforce other communications.
2.  It can reach a relatively large audience for a low cost.
3.  It develops positive relationships with the community at large.
4.  "News" is more believable than ads.

Because of these strengths, companies of all sizes should take advantage of every opportunity to use publicity.

## HOW PUBLICITY WORKS

Publicity works by making editors, reporters, journalists, or writers in the media aware of your news so they will write about you in their publications or mention you on the air. Although this sounds easy, there are many companies and products trying to get the attention of the same people, so part of the publicity process is to get the media's attention. Only if the press people are interested in what you have to say will they print or broadcast your announcement.

Why do some companies get written up in the business press so frequently, whereas other similar companies are rarely mentioned? Because companies that get the publicity make themselves available to the press and they make their everyday events sound like news. Another new line of canned goods may not sound exciting, but if the announcement goes along with the right photos and explains how the new brand employs a new can technology with environmental advantages, then it's news.

When implementing a publicity program you always need to think in terms of *news value*. Who would want to know about it? What do they want to know? When should they know about it? With which media do the interested people come into contact? Which media would be interested in telling the news? And, most importantly, what can you do to make your news interesting, or better still, exciting?

Almost any event has news value to someone. For example, people in business are always interested in who gets promoted or hired into new positions and read the new employee announcements even if they don't know the individuals involved. It is a good opportunity to get your name and the name of your company in print. A list of other possible publicity opportunities is provided in this chapter to get you thinking.

---

- New Product Announcements
- Product Pricing Changes
- Product Innovations
- Key Personnel Changes, Additions, Promotions, and Retirements
- New Members Joining an Organization
- Large Contract with a Government Agency
- Joint Venture with Another Company
- Change in Operating Hours
- Addition of Another Distribution Channel
- Company Reorganization
- New Office or Sales Location or Remodeling of Current Facilities
- Awards Received
- Major Charitable Donations or Fund-Raising Activities
- Product Purchase by a Major Customer
- Visit by a Famous or Important Person
- Innovative Personnel Programs
- Sales Performance and Financial Results
- New Advertising Campaign or New Packaging Scheme
- A Special Promotion or Contest
- Start of a Community Service Project or Fund-Raising Activity
- A Unique Way the Company Promotes Ecological Concerns
- A New Investor or Partner

---

Figure 4.1. Some publicity possibilities.

Remember that publicity is best when it is used to

1. Develop name recognition, industry presence, image, and positive associations with the customers and public in general.
2. Support advertising programs, promotional efforts, and other communications tools.

Don't expect publicity to do all your promotion and selling. Stories of public relations successes that made companies rich overnight are very much the exception rather than the rule.

The goal behind a publicity program is frequent mention of your company and your products or services in media with which your customers are likely to come in contact. The idea is to keep your name in front of the people who buy or influence the purchase of your products. Repetition over a long period of time is often more important to successful publicity programs than the one-time headline news event. Everyone wants front-page mention, but don't assume you have to wait for a major event before you begin your publicity program. Send out a news release for everything even vaguely newsworthy.

Publicity requires persistence as you build up *share of mind* on the part of the editors and it may take several news releases before you get noticed. Publicity is less valuable as a one-shot attempt to get your name in print. Sometimes one-time publicity works if you have something spectacular to tell, but advertising or more direct communications tools are usually better for immediate sales development.

## THE STEPS FOR GETTING PUBLICITY

Unless you or your organization is particularly controversial or well known, the media won't know if you have done something newsworthy unless you tell them. Of course, if your organization is a large, influential company, the press may come asking for quotes or opinions about industry trends or news developments. Over time, if you work with the media you will become a source of information, even when you don't send out news releases. But until you become a household name or are recognized as an industry guru, this won't happen without a substantial effort on your part. In most cases, if you want stories, articles, or mention in newspapers, magazines, on radio, or on TV, you must go to the press yourself.

The steps in executing a basic publicity program or campaign are simple and, if handled properly, will get you the publicity you want and need. The steps to managing a successful publicity program include the following:

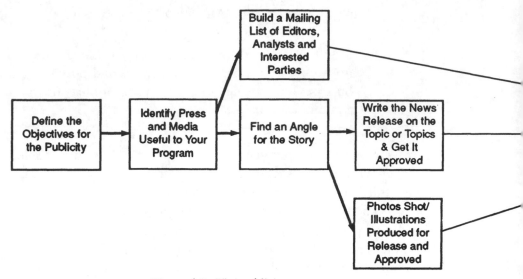

Figure 4.2. The publicity process.

1.  **Define the objectives for your publicity.**   Do you want to create general awareness or announce a specific product? Do you need to support your advertising messages? Do you need to reach a wider audience? The objectives will help you identify the media best suited for your publicity efforts.

2.  **Identify the press and media that will be most useful to your publicity programs.**   Develop positive relationships with the most influential people in your business. Sometimes people set up breakfast meetings or lunches with the press to meet them and let them know what is going on, even when there is no specific news story.

3.  **Clearly state the news you have to tell and develop an angle for presenting it to the target media.**   For your story to be regarded as newsworthy it needs to fill one or more of the basic news criteria: (1) The participants or companies must be significant or recognized. If the people or company are well known, then the story has a better chance of being mentioned. (2) The news must be important in some way. The news needs to be interesting and relevant to the individual readers, even if it is not national or international in scope. (3) The news should have local appeal whenever possible. People want to know about their own communities, events, and local successes. (4) The story must be timely and current. Nobody reads yesterday's newspapers, so they won't want to hear your old news either.

4.  **Write concise, professional news releases or presentations.**   Follow the standard formats accepted in the industry. Schedule news releases on a regular basis. There is more infor-

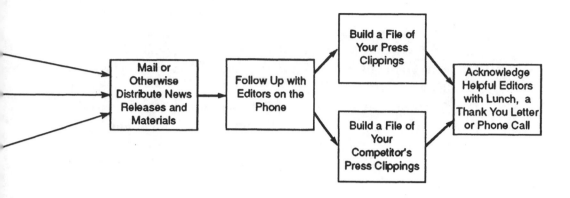

mation on developing news releases and press plans later in the
chapter.

5. **Mail or distribute the news release to the appropriate media
   lists.**   Sources for your media lists are detailed later.

6. **Follow up on your news releases or media proposals to see if
   the editor or writer is interested.**   At one time letters to editors
   and cover letters on press releases were quite common. Today,
   it's better to use the telephone to follow up with the press.

---

### TIP: PERSISTENCE IS IMPORTANT FOR
### MAXIMUM PUBLICITY RESULTS

Because editors are inundated with news releases of all kinds from many organizations, it is important to build and improve press relationships over time. The best
way to build a *news channel* is to maintain a helpful attitude and send out regular
news releases. Once an editor remembers you and your product, even in the busiest
markets, you will find that it becomes easier to get the editorial coverage for your
product. Most importantly, don't forget to say thanks for even the most banal coverage because that keeps the door open for better press coverage next time.

---

7. **Keep a file of all resulting press clippings and articles.**   Use the
   clippings to learn about ways to improve the next round of
   news releases. The clipping file is the traditional, tangible way
   of measuring publicity success because coverage in other media
   is harder to track and capture. Some companies keep logs to
   track television and radio coverage that list the date, station,

and subject of the coverage. If you don't have time to maintain the clipping file, you can hire a clipping service to do it for you (listed under *Clipping Services* in the *Yellow Pages*). Some public relations agencies also provide clipping services.

8. **Keep complete clippings files on your competition.** Compare your competitor's publicity to yours as you develop your publicity efforts.

9. **Acknowledge the press and their support of your company.** A thank you note or phone call and the occasional lunch or dinner when feasible and appropriate can do wonders to build relationships with the media. Don't appear to be bribing them, just treat them with dignity and appreciation.

## THE TOOLS OF PUBLICITY PROFESSIONALS

Every form of marketing communications has a *bag of tricks* that makes it work. Publicity is no different. The following is a list of the tools available for your publicity program with explanations of how each is used by experienced publicists and public relations professionals.

### The News Release

If there is one tool that is most important when trying to get publicity, it is the news release (also called a *press release*). News releases are the primary source of information for editors and journalists creating the stories they publish and broadcast. News releases should be clearly written and should always include the who, what, where, when, and why of the news story. They also need to be produced in a professional, standard format that allows editors to get the *gist* of the story by scanning only the first few lines of the release. A step-by-step process for producing a quality news release is presented later in the chapter.

### Company and Product Backgrounders

Company and product backgrounders provide more information than news releases can about your company and products. They are used to provide general background information for the press, hence the name *backgrounder*. They are often kept by editors in their permanent file on your organization. A backgrounder can be a simple typed narrative on your company or product, or can consist of attractive folders with photos and other marketing communications materials, including brochures or product datasheets.

There are two basic kinds of backgrounders—a company back grounder and a product backgrounder. A company backgrounder typically includes company history, biographies of key employees, company goals and positioning, financial information, and descriptions of key company successes. A product backgrounder includes product features and benefits, design and technology information (where relevant), specifications, pricing, and competitive positioning. A list of key customers, if available, is useful for both kinds of backgrounders. Some companies with only one or two products combine the company and product backgrounders into one document.

Whether you have news to tell or not, a company should always have company and product backgrounders ready to distribute on request. When editors first receive your backgrounders they set up a file on your company. When you send a news release to these editors, the filed backgrounders are used as a source of general information for adding depth to press write-ups. You should periodically send updated backgrounders to the media with which you work.

## Media Kits

*Media kits*, also called *press kits* (not to be confused with the kind of media kits provided by the media to potential advertisers), are an assemblage of current stories and press clippings published about your company, current press releases, and a backgrounder on your company and products. Media kits also include photographs and biographies on your key employees and executives, and may include brochures and information sheets on each of your products. These materials are usually packaged in an attractive folder for easy distribution.

Simple folders for this purpose are available at any office supply store. Because they are a primary tool in presenting the company's image to VIPs in the industry, media kits for large corporations are often elaborate affairs employing custom folders and expensive printing.

If you frequently work with television contacts, you may also want to include videotape clips as part of your media kit. These might consist of a product demonstration video, a plant tour showing off your manufacturing technology, or a brief narrated biography and speeches if you are promoting a political candidate.

Every company, regardless of size, should have media kits ready at all times to hand out to customers, industry and financial analysts, and press people who want more information before completing a story. In addition to being an important tool for informing the press, an attractive, complete media kit can also be an influential tool for persuading a bank or investment firm to make a positive loan or investment decision for your company.

## Interview and Program Proposals for Television and Radio

News programs on network and local television, cable television, and public access channels offer many opportunities for gaining publicity. If you want a television or radio station to do more than just make an announcement on the air, you will need to write a proposal to go along with your news release and backgrounder. The proposal can be as simple as a cover letter on top of a news release, suggesting that you are available for an interview. Or the proposal may suggest a complete program special on your company that you believe would be interesting and suitable for a particular show. If you have previously had programs aired about your products or company, you should mention these in your proposal. And by all means, find out the name of the person who makes the programming decisions for the station or the program before you send in your proposal. (This is often the *producer* of the show.) An unsolicited program proposal without a source name will usually go directly into the trash.

## News Conferences

When news is important or timely and you want more attention than a news release can provide, putting on a *news conference* (also called a *press conference*) is one way to get a number of media folks together at one time. News conferences allow you to cover more ground than is possible through new releases alone. News conferences should be scheduled only when you have something important to announce. If the press feels that your news is not important, they will leave you in the embarrassing situation of giving a press conference to an empty room. What is important enough to justify a news conference is determined by the individual situation and your organization's visibility. There are no hard and fast rules—just use common sense.

To schedule a news conference you simply invite the press to the conference, over the telephone if the news is immediate or with invitations several weeks in advance if the announcement is planned. Sometimes advance news releases are mailed out with the invitations. It is advisable to call the press to verify attendance within 48 hours of the news conference.

If you do schedule a news conference, make sure it is well organized. The operative word for a successful news conference is *preparation.* In addition to making your formal announcements to the press in a prepared speech, you should have printed news releases available and

**News Conference Objectives:**

☐ **Responsibilities Assigned:**

Invitations: _____        Facility Coordination: _____

Follow-Up After Event: _____        Key Speaker: _____

Media Kits: _____        Speaker Introductions: _____

Other Company Representatives to Attend: _____

☐ **Media List Prepared and Verified**

☐ **Invitation Mailing Prepared**
    ☐ Background statement      ☐ Location map for the conference
    ☐ Notice of date and time      ☐ Identification of key speakers and attendees
    ☐ Postage paid response card to verify attendance      ☐ Name/telephone number for more information

☐ **Mailing Two Weeks Before the Conference**

☐ **Follow-up 48 Hours Before the Conference**

☐ **All Speakers Prepared and Briefed**
    ☐ Questions and answers list provided to all company attendees
    ☐ All speakers trained to work with reporters

☐ **Facilities Ready**
    ☐ Location convenient and without distracting noises      ☐ Refreshments
    ☐ Adequate heating or air conditioning      ☐ Seating adequate and comfortable
    ☐ Stage or podium prepared      ☐ Electrical outlets adequate for equipment
    ☐ Lighting adequate and tested      ☐ Audiovisual equipment ordered in advance
    ☐ Audiovisual equipment tested before conference      ☐ Acoustics and microphones tested
    ☐ Security adequate and available (if appropriate)

☐ **Presentation Materials Ready**
    ☐ Speech prepared and rehearsed      ☐ Visual aids completed and reviewed
    ☐ Handouts duplicated for press

☐ **Media Kits Complete**
    ☐ Photos related to the news event      ☐ Speaker photos
    ☐ Complete news release      ☐ Backgrounder
    ☐ General corporate information      ☐ Contact names and numbers for information

☐ **News Room Prepared for Media Representatives**
    ☐ Telephones      ☐ FAX machine
    ☐ Typewriters or personal computers with modems      ☐ Copy machine with paper and supplies

Figure 4.3. News conference checklist.

backgrounders for the press. If the event includes multimedia materials such as videotape or slides, copies of these should be available so the press can better remember what you said. The person who makes the presentation should be well prepared and well informed. There should be ample time for questions and answers after the announcement (and the person presenting the news should prepared for tough questions from the press). It is also traditional to have some kind of refreshment for the press such as coffee, juice, and snacks at the very least.

The physical facilities are very important to the success of a news conference. The room should be large enough to comfortably seat everyone and the lighting should be adjustable, if possible. If television representatives will be in attendance, the room should have adequate power outlets and be convenient for TV crews with heavy equipment. Ventilation and air conditioning should also be a consideration in choosing a location. A large number of people, hot lights, and electrical equipment can raise the temperature to uncomfortable levels in just minutes. Excessive heat will make your presenter sweat, which looks unprofessional.

Make sure there are no distracting noises in the vicinity of the news conference such as planes going overhead or noisy machinery running in adjacent areas. Microphones are sometimes more sensitive to picking up irritating background noise than the human voice.

During the presentation, the use of visual aids including colorful slides, flip charts, or videotape to augment the news announcement is often advisable, especially if the news involves multiple announcements or topics. Make sure the microphones and visual aids equipment are all in working order before the presentation. There is nothing that will turn the press off more than disorganization by the company making the announcement because it wastes their limited time. If you want positive treatment by the media, you and your company must look professional at all times.

## Press Tours and Special Press Events

Another tool for handling complex and important news events, such as new product announcements or corporate restructuring, is to take a *traveling news conference* around the country, otherwise known as the *press tour*. Press tours can be one-on-one meetings with individual press people around the country or multiple news conferences held simultaneously in different cities. As always, when trying to get publicity make sure you have printed press materials and backgrounders available for all your contacts and verify all your appointments in advance. All the considerations for news conferences apply to press tours. If your press tour

---

# THE MISSING PRESS MATERIALS

One of our advertising accounts took care of its own publicity and press tours, and they usually did a great job. But one time, things didn't go as planned on an expensive but very necessary press tour to Europe.

After months of arrangements, the company's CEO and the Vice President of Marketing Communications departed for London with several pieces of luggage and a suitcase full of press materials and personal effects. Arriving early morning London time with a meeting scheduled in the early afternoon with an important editor, the two executives realized that their baggage containing their clean clothes and PR materials was a no-show.

In panic, because of the tight schedule of many meetings across the continent, the two execs hurriedly called home and received faxes of the PR materials for photocopying. The supporting literature could not be photocopied or faxed, so they had to do without it. After the rushed purchase of new clothes and toiletries, they were near exhaustion but ready for their first editor. Vowing to carry a change of clothes and press materials onto the plane as carry-on luggage next time, the two learned a valuable lesson.

On arriving home nearly a month later after an exhausting press tour, they received a phone call from the airline that the missing luggage turned up in Hawaii and would be returned to them the next day. So much for planning.

---

involves taking your contacts to lunch, make sure you make reservations, check out the menu, and verify the facilities in advance.


## Press Photos

Pictures, illustrations, videos, charts, and photos can help get your news releases read and published—so they are an important part of your publicity toolbox. Include photos relating to your news story whenever possible. Editors are always on the lookout for visuals to jazz up a story, so good ones are of immediate interest to them. Newspapers and trade magazines are always looking for interesting photos to liven up their pages. When including photos in your news releases or media kits follow these guidelines:

1. Use a professional to take the pictures, unless you have someone on your staff with equivalent skills and equipment. Refer to the chapter on hiring vendors if you haven't done this before.
2. Make sure your people look natural. Announcement photos and head shots can be posed, but make sure the character of the person comes through. If possible, show people in their work environments for interest. If you take pictures of people during

an event, ensure they don't look posed or uncomfortable, even if they are.

3. Use action shots if possible. Action in a photo always gets reader attention. For example, in a simple product shot of an expensive pen, you might show a handsome hand writing a letter using beautiful, flourished calligraphy. Or if you are selling a new line of frozen yogurt, show the product being eaten by happy children, with the package clearly displayed. Readers favor attractive product photos with real people in them, even if the photos are of everyday products or mechanical equipment. However, if the people look posed or contrived, it is better to leave them out. Be as imaginative as possible and you will have a better chance of getting the photos published.

4. Use interesting backgrounds and props. However, don't use the "Sears Fall Scene" in the portrait studio or anything like it. These artificial backdrops look like cheap sets and should be avoided. If you can't think of something interesting, use something simple.

5. Use 8 × 10 inch black and white photo reproductions for newspapers. For magazines that carry color pages, submit 35-mm transparencies (slides) in addition to the black and white photos. If you are unsure, include both black and white and color photos. Make sure the photos and transparencies are clearly captioned with the subject, company name, and telephone number. Date them on the back or on the slide frame. Photos and the news release materials often become separated and you don't want another company's photo going into your news story. There are photo houses that specialize in duplicating public relations photos that will add the captions to the photos for you. If you can't find one in your area, call a public relations agency for a recommendation.

## BUILDING YOUR MEDIA LISTS AND FILES

In publicity, understanding the tools is not enough; you must also develop press and media contacts. The development of positive relationships with key editors, industry writers, journalists, analysts, and other VIPs (politicians, authors, etc.) who have influence in your market is part of any effective publicity program. Your media lists and media files should include all the contacts and people to whom you will be sending news releases and making contact to get publicity.

Developing your press contacts and media lists is the most important part of getting your publicity tools to work for you. You should include the following information for each contact in your media file:

- Name and title of the contact.
- Publication, station name, or other affiliation.
- Address (including zip code).
- Information on this contact's news interests and specialties.
- Readership profile and circulation information if you have it available.
- Deadline dates for publication, if any.
- General notes. Include the dates and details of previous discussions and meetings with this person. Include any personal information you may discover about the person, so you can personalize your conversations with this contact over time.

Keeping the media files and mailing lists up to date is an important and on-going process. Press people move around and some change positions frequently. Magazines and newsletters come and go. If you use a publicity professional or agency, they should keep the lists current for you, but you may want to periodically verify that they are kept complete and up to date. And you may have names of your own that you want added to the lists.

---

## ✎ TIP: GET THE NAMES OF EDITORS FROM THE MASTHEAD

All publications include a masthead in the first several pages to show who publishes it. Most mastheads show not only the publisher, but also the senior editors and contributing editors. The masthead also includes the publication's mailing address and phone numbers. Voilà! An instant mailing list!

Note that managing editors and advertising people may also show up in the masthead. Neither directly concern you; the managing editor is usually a financial business-oriented person and the advertising people sell advertising and don't write articles.

---

The mailing lists and contact files are easy to keep up to date using a simple computerized database program. The database program makes sorting mailing lists for specific releases very easy and most programs let you print *personalized* letters automatically. If you don't use a computer, keep the file information on alphabetized index cards. The mailing lists themselves can be typed on preformatted forms, ready for duplication on mailing labels designed for the copy machine. There are forms for creating photocopy-ready mailing lists at any local stationery store. If your mailing lists are long, however, use a computer or a local mailing list service for tracking the names and printing the labels.

## Customizing Media and Contact Lists for Your Business

Your media lists should be targeted specifically for your company and industry. Most companies, even small ones, use a number of media lists, each one targeted to a specific kind of news and interests. For example, a large electronics company may have a national news list, an industry-specific publications list, a local list for each city in which the company has offices, other geographically targeted lists, an industry analysts list, a key customers list, a political and government officials list, an international list (targeted by country or continent), and a news services/wire services list.

News releases are sent to those on the list or lists that are most appropriate for the specific announcements or stories. A news release of general importance may go to everyone, whereas a specific announcement may be sent to only those on one list. A small company, such as a local restaurant, may also have segmented lists for targeting news releases for maximum exposure, including restaurant reviewers, newspaper contacts, trade press, community associations and clubs, a VIP list, a television list, and a radio list.

There are a number of standard list sources available at almost all libraries. In these references you can find detailed information on local, national, and industry-specific media for creating the media lists and files. The most commonly used references include the following:

*Broadcasting/Cablecasting Yearbook* provides information on TV and radio stations and cable systems. This reference also supplies phone numbers, call letters, and other information on the format of the stations.

*Editor & Publisher Yearbook,* published by the newspaper trade publication *Editor & Publisher,* provides the names of the editors and top reporters for almost every newspaper in the United States. In addition, it provides listings on the wire services and the names and specialties of the syndicated news services.

*Gale Directory of Publications and Broadcast Media: An Annual Guide to Newspapers, Magazines, Journals, and Related Publications* provides information on U.S. and Canadian publications and stations.

Standard Rate and Data Services produces reports on publications that carry advertising; these are especially useful because they list circulation figures as well as advertising data.

In addition, there are other sources for lists of VIPs and industry contacts, including state government directories ("blue books"), research reports by major industry and financial research firms (Dataquest, Infocorp, Dun & Bradstreet, and Reuters, for example), the *Congressional Directory,* Chamber of Commerce directories, professional association and club membership directories, and, of course, the local telephone book.

# THE SOURCES FOR PUBLICITY AND HOW TO WORK WITH THEM

There are a wide range of media sources available for publicity programs. Your publicity efforts should include as many media sources as possible. The major media sources for publicity and how to contact them effectively are described below.

## Newspapers—Daily and Weekly

Though newspapers have lost some of their dominance in the news arena to television in recent years, most media lists and publicity programs still start with the papers. New York City has more than 40 regularly published newspapers. Even in small communities there are usually more than one: a daily newspaper, weekly community papers, and perhaps an entertainment tabloid or two. As your company, market, and news interest expand, you can add newspapers across the country to your media files.

Newspapers have a number of editors who cover news for specific topics and there is one or more who covers your subject area. It is always best to get the correct editor's name if you can by calling the newspaper. If this isn't possible, send your release to the topical editor or news desk most likely to be interested in your news, such as the business editor, food editor, city desk editor, or national desk editor. If the newspaper is very small, you will probably send your news releases to the Editor-in-Chief of the paper, who is responsible for the entire publication—but never do this with larger papers. The Editor-in-Chief in larger papers has topical editors to handle the news and doesn't review the individual press releases.

You will want to include the following in your media list, depending on the size and interest appeal of your news:

- National newspapers (i.e., *Wall Street Journal, USA Today, Investor's Daily, Christian Science Monitor, New York Times*).
- Local newspapers—including general interest and business papers.
- International newspapers.
- Local news and entertainment tabloids.

## Magazines and Trade Journals

As already covered in the advertising chapter, there are thousands of magazines published in the United States and thousands more internationally. Magazines can have a tremendous impact on a target market and therefore on the success of your company if you receive positive coverage in them.

Many magazines publish general news so you should include as many relevant magazine editors in your media list as possible. *Relevance* is the key word in getting magazine coverage. As you did with your advertising, match the magazine demographics to your target market and your news messages.

When sending news releases to magazines, use specific editors' names. If you haven't updated your mailing list lately, verify that the editor is still with the magazine with a telephone call before you send out a news release. Sometimes it is useful to include more than one editor from a publication on your lists, as they may not necessarily share information with each other. In addition, some magazines use freelance editors and writers for their articles, so you will want to put these people on your mailing lists.

When you contact a magazine editor over the telephone, ask what the magazine prefers for submission of news materials and releases. Editors for the key magazines in your industry should be sent updated backgrounders and media kits on your company regularly.

The list of specific magazines and related publications to use in a publicity campaign is too vast to include in this book, but here are some general publication types you should consider when developing your media lists:

- National news magazines—weekly and monthly.
- International news magazines.
- Industry-specific magazines and trade journals.
- Popular and special interest magazines.
- Local interest magazines.
- Industry newsletters.

## Special Interest Newsletters and Company Publications

Because of easy-to-use, affordable desktop publishing technology, newsletters are cropping up from almost every company and organization. These include Chamber of Commerce newsletters, insurance company newsletters, power company newsletters in with your monthly bill, software company newsletters, and others. Large, local homeowners' associations even have newsletters. Since many of these publications are consistently short of article ideas they are a good possibility for local businesses to get products and services mentioned. Many of these new publications need fresh news, more so than other media, so make sure to search them out and include them in your publicity campaigns.

## Television Sources

Based on many recent studies, both the general public and frequent readers prefer television over newspapers as their primary source of news. With the growth in cable television and public access channels, there are more opportunities for small companies to be interviewed or featured on television if they have something of potential interest to present.

Before you send off news releases to television stations, however, become very familiar with television programming—the program schedules, program contents, and focus of the programming. Once you know the shows that are potentials for your news, call the station to find out the contact person who reviews news releases and program proposals. Mail your news release and program proposals to this person and, as always, follow up to get their reaction to the news. If your news is of national or regional scope, the wire services (covered later) will send news releases to all the pertinent television stations.

If the contact person is interested in making more than a brief announcement on the air, they will usually set up an information interview to discuss your program proposal. Sample programming ideas include a feature presentation of a new technology on a science program such as Australia's widely syndicated *Beyond 2000*. If you sell Chinese Woks, you might suggest a Chinese cooking segment using your products on a specialty TV show on gardening or cooking. If you have just started a new training program for your employees, you might suggest a feature on the positive benefits of the program in stabilizing local employment to a news show.

General program sources for your media list for television include:

- News programs—local and national
- Talk shows—local and national
- Public access stations
- Public television stations
- Cable channels with specific business and news orientation, such as *CNN* or *Financial News Network*

At the very least, volunteer for the fund-raising campaigns on public television channels. It is a good form of secondary publicity and the channel often mentions your support on the air and displays your company's logo in the background.

## Radio Sources

Creating radio contacts is much like working with television. Again, start by becoming familiar with the programming. In general, radio stations

# TELEVISION AND RADIO SHOWS: HOW TO SOUND AND LOOK CALM AND COLLECTED, EVEN WHEN YOU'RE NOT

Television and radio exposure is excellent publicity. If you are lucky enough to get an interview on these important media, you need to be prepared for a session in front of hot lights and the eye of a camera or, in the case of radio, a microphone so big that it looks as if it can hear your inner thoughts as well as your voice.

Interviews for both radio and TV are divided into two categories—controversial and public relations (PR) oriented. A PR-oriented interview is a simple question and answer session requiring a moderate tone of voice, a smile in the case of TV, and little thinking on your part. Most of these are taped days or weeks before airtime and a friendly interviewer will arrange to edit or retape a flubbed response or comment on your part. The host will ask you prewritten questions that you have already reviewed or discuss simple topics with which you are familiar and comfortable.

A controversial interview is sweaty-palms time—with broadsides hurled by the host that you must tactfully counter and turn to your advantage whenever possible. What makes it rough is that what looks like a simple PR interview can be a disguise for something more like a cross-examination for the unwary. Prepare for the worst, because that way you will always come out looking the best.

To get ready, spend time preparing for the interview. Look into the background of your host. Does he or she have a reputation for asking embarrassing questions with no warning? Is there a reason why he or she doesn't like you or what you stand for? If so, be prepared for hostile questions and trouble.

Have a co-worker, friend, or spouse ask you the most difficult questions you can think of that are related to the topic. Practice giving clean crisp responses, even if it takes hours to *coach* you adequately. Have your trainer ask questions on personal matters or ones that are potentially inflammatory so that you can practice waiting and thinking up a response before blurting out something embarrassing that you will regret later.

If you're going on radio, take along something small and discreet that you can play with in your hands to focus nervous energy. On radio you can bring notes to review. On television, you can't—so you need to be sure of your material.

If you're discussing a heated or difficult topic and sweat forms on your forehead, the audience will assume you are nervous because you have something to hide—even if it is only because the lights are hot. So make sure your makeup will take care of it. This is usually done by using perspiration-absorbing powder with the regular makeup. (Yes, men should wear makeup too.) The station will usually have a makeup artist to help you. If you're prone to sweating, let this person know.

For TV and personal appearances, always wear conservative, simple clothing. If you're not sure what to wear, hire an image consultant or ask for help in a quality clothing store.

Remember that the better you look and sound, the better you will come off in the audience's eye, ear, and mind. Remember also that it is better to be short on words than to provide a blusterous response that can cause you grief if it is quoted and requoted down the years. Remember Richard Nixon and the *Checker's Speech?*

make general announcements of local events and news more readily than television. There are also opportunities for interviews and general publicity. For these, you will again need to produce a program proposal in addition to a news release and send it to the appropriate program coordinator responsible for selecting the people to be interviewed. The major wire services also send news releases to radio stations. General program sources for publicity on radio include

- News programs—local and national, including both AM and FM channels
- Talk shows—local and national
- College radio stations—community colleges, four-year colleges, and universities

## Wire Services and News Syndicates

Wire services and news syndicates (companies that specialize in gathering and distributing news for use by the media) can be used to send news releases to a wide number of publications and stations at one time. They are best for news that has national, international, or broad industry appeal. Wire services are especially important for small newspapers and television stations as a source of national news.

Wire services generally have the reputation of being objective news-gathering sources. The wire service reporters and editors will modify and summarize your release as they see fit in an attempt to balance the news they send over the service. It is worth the effort to develop good relationships with the wire services and their reporters, but remember that they are usually interested only in *major* news or stories that are particularly odd or humorous. The positive impact of having your product or company mentioned over the wires is immeasurable.

The largest wire services include the Associated Press (AP), United Press International (UPI), and Reuters (business news). There are both general news services and industry-specific services available. There are also local wire-service bureaus. Wire-service bureaus can help you identify the correct services for your news release, if you have not sent one to a wire service before. You can locate these in the *Yellow Pages* of your telephone directory. In addition to wire services, there are also special news and feature syndicates and services for specific industries and topics that supply information to the media.

If you have news of national or international interest that you intend to send "over the wires," make sure to send the release to *both* AP and UPI. These agencies are very competitive and one hates to see someone *break* news that the other one doesn't have. As a policy, it is not good to alienate one of the major services, as you usually need them much more than they need you.

## Articles and Books as Publicity Options

Having a major article published about your company or product in an important magazine, or even better a complete book published by a major publisher, can often do more for sales than an expensive advertising campaign. One of the added benefits of articles and books used for publicity is that the magazines and publishers often pay you for writing them, although you won't make much unless the article is for a major national publication. The bigger personal reward is usually getting your name in print as the author.

The process of getting an article published about your product or company is very similar to getting publicity about your product—the difference is that you develop a contract with one specific magazine rather than sending news releases to everyone on your list. You then develop the article within a specified schedule and actually write the article for the magazine (or get a professional to write one for you under contract).

Articles can be written about a new technology, a major business success, an innovative approach to doing business, customer applications of your product, and the lives and personalities of important people in your company. Pick up the magazines you use in your publicity activities and look at the articles—they frequently focus on specific companies, key executives, and new products. If you can suggest stories such as these (or even better ones) on your own company to the editors—you may be able to get similar articles published for your company.

Like a news story, a feature article must have a specific angle, it must be relevant, and it must be well written. Most articles should be accompanied by illustrations and photographs with descriptive captions.

Occasionally, editors will be so intrigued by a simple news release that they will come to you for additional information so they can write a feature article on your product or company. When your company is really in the big time, the media will come to you regularly looking for articles and feature stories—just as they come looking for news. Until then, the process of getting a full-length, feature article published usually involves the following steps:

1.  Know your media options for articles. Be familiar with the editorial coverage (articles) in the specific magazines and papers that are of interest to your business.
2.  Know the editors. The way to do this is through the same process used for gaining publicity talked about earlier.

3.  Know the magazines' publication schedules. Be aware that articles are written two to three months (or more) in advance of the publication of a magazine.

4.  Tailor the article idea for a specific magazine. Make sure the article fits into the format and focus of the magazine. Make sure it is written to the magazine's primary market. The central idea or topic should be relevant and informative. An article should be more than just a glorified press release—it should inform and fascinate the readers.

5.  Before you write the article, send in a query letter for your article idea to the appropriate editor. Send the letter to one magazine at a time, unless you tell the editors that you are making multiple submissions of the idea. A query letter is a special letter to an editor that describes the article you would like to sell to the magazine. It should explain why your idea will be of interest to the readers and why you are the right person or company to write the article. Include a title, specify a proposed delivery date, and specify the length of the finished article.

Most trade industry articles are about 1,000 to 1,500 words, though some are longer. Use past issues of the magazine as your guide when you propose a length for the article. It is not necessary to submit the finished article. If an editor is interested, he will ask to see part of the article or will offer alternate approaches for covering the topic.

Having a book written on your product or company is a process similar to getting articles published, but it takes longer. Most of the time books are proposed to publishers before they are completely written. If you don't have the expertise or time to complete a book, it is possible to hire professional authors to co-author or ghost-write a book on a contract basis, just as it is possible to hire people to write articles for you.

If you want your book published and distributed by a major publisher, only books about well-known companies, interesting corporate histories, or products with a large customer base (usually technical products) will normally have a chance of finding a publisher. An alternative is to publish a book yourself through a publisher that specializes in self-published projects. To be effective, you will need to promote and distribute the self-published book.

Before you decide on using a book to promote your company or product, pick up one of the many reference books available on writing and selling books available in any bookstore or library. The good ones will explain how to write a book proposal and how to find an agent to sell your book idea to a publisher. The books will also explain the ins and outs of self-publishing.

## Miscellaneous Sources for Publicity

In addition to the standard media, you should make contact with and be aware of the following potential sources for publicity if they are applicable to your industry and business:

- **Consulting Firms, Data Research Firms, and Industry Analysts.** These are crucially important in some industries because many of the influential firms produce newsletters and industry reports that are widely read by investors and customers. The analysts working for these companies can also provide the names of other contacts and financial resources you should know in your business or industry.

- **Professional and Political Organizations and Associations.** There are hundreds of these, and some of them can be helpful to your organization. For local organizations, watch the activities columns in the local newspaper. For names of national organizations, read the announcements in the major industry publications.

- **Special Interest Clubs, Sports Groups, and Fraternal Organizations.** Sending a news release about a special offer or a new product to a local club or organization can often result in immediate business. For small and large companies, it is a good idea to know which clubs and organizations are most active and influential in your community and to be a part of them if possible.

With all the sources available, who you include in your publicity efforts depends largely on the news you have to tell. If your company is small and local, then you will probably stick to local sources. As the size and influence of your company increase, you will branch out. And if you are part of an industry with specific journals and newsletters, include these regardless of the size of your company. Some industries have columnists and other VIPs who frequently write about companies and their products, and these people should also be among your contacts.

We have provided a general list of many possible sources for publicity for companies of various sizes. If you search, you may find more. There are always new magazines, newsletters, and television programs. Many of these need your news as much as you need their publicity. So always watch for new sources. Even if you have a public relations agency that keeps your press lists for you, provide them with a copy of any names or new media you discover. You may find a new magazine or editor even before the agency does.

# MAKING ALL THE NEWS THAT'S FIT TO PRINT:
# HOW TO PRODUCE A QUALITY NEWS RELEASE

A good news release is the bread and butter of positive publicity. If you are a small company, it is okay to prepare your own news release as long as your writing skills are up to snuff. If, however, you aren't confident in your writing abilities, hire a freelance writer or a public relations agency to help out. If you work in a large company, you will probably have easy access to publicity professionals—use them.

Editors expect news releases to be in a standard format; even the story of the century, if not in proper format, will not get read. The diagram provided annotates the generally accepted format for a professional news release.

The first step toward getting your news release printed is to get the release read. In a large newspaper, editors may get hundreds of releases every day. To get the editors' interest, your news release must be interesting and easy to understand. If you use a handsome format, quickly indicate the importance of what is contained in the release, and specify all vital information, including your name and the name of the company, dates, and contact telephone numbers, your release will have a much better chance of being read.

The steps for preparing a news release include the following:

**Step 1. Know what you want to tell the world and be able to explain why it's news.** If you can't explain why your news is important, it may not be. Remember that news should be timely, significant, and straightforward to clearly communicate a message.

**Step 2. Determine to whom you should send the release for maximum news exposure.** Using your targeted media files and lists, determine the best contacts for each release. Do this before you write the release, because you will want to tailor the news for the intended audience.

**Step 3. Draft a one- to two-page (three-page maximum) news release.** A news release that is longer will probably not be read. (The exception to this rule is a scientific or technical release, which may be lengthy in order to explain a complex premise or theory.) If you need to provide more information than a news release to the press, provide a backgrounder as supplementary material.

Releases for radio and television require a special style for reading over the air that doesn't apply to news releases intended for publication. Sentences should be simple and varied in length and the writing should

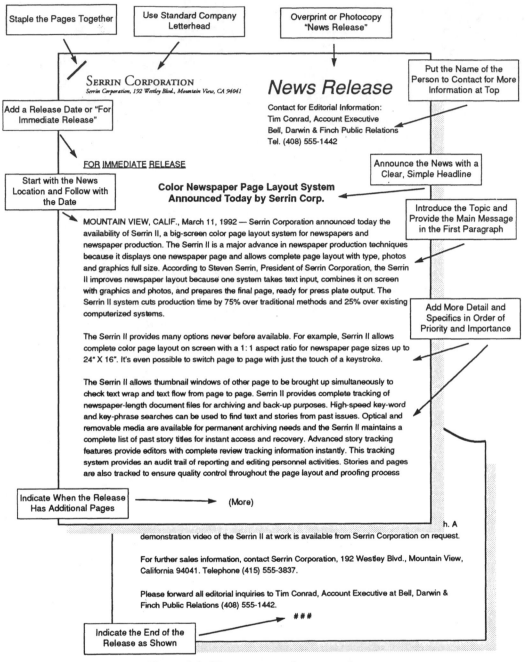

Figure 4.4. The anatomy of a news release.

use a strong, active voice. Attribution should proceed, never follow, the quotations in the release. If you don't have experience with writing for broadcast news, hire a professional to help.

When you are ready to draft the final news release it should include the following:

- **The date and location of the news release.** This is obvious, but sometimes forgotten.

- **A concise, impactful headline.** The headline should explain exactly what the news is and intrigue the person to read on.

- **A strong lead paragraph.** The first paragraph, called the *lead*, should provide the salient information about the release. This first paragraph should be the paragraph you want printed if only one paragraph from the release gets *picked up* (publicity talk for *published* or *aired*) by the media. It should arouse the curiosity of the reader or listener.

- **Answers to the who, what, why, when, and where of the news story in the body of the release.** Who is responsible or involved? What happened? Why is it important and why did it happen? When did things happen? Where did things happen? These are the supporting details and if the release does not answer all five questions clearly, it is unlikely that an editor will pursue the story. Make sure that the body of the release supports and substantiates the lead paragraph.

- **Quotes from key people if appropriate.** Quotes from a company executive or industry VIP add interest and weight to a news release. Use but don't overuse them.

- **Clear, concise writing.** Avoid vague, meaningless, or excessively superlative language. Every word counts, so use them wisely. Be honest, complete, and simple in your explanations.

- **Name, phone number, and address of the person who should be contacted if there are any questions about the story.** You'd be surprised how many news releases cross an editor's desk without a contact name or phone number.

**Step 4. Decide if a photograph, diagram, or illustration would be appropriate to support the release.** Even a basic photograph of a key person or product from the company never hurts. As mentioned, news releases that include a photo are more interesting and more likely to get "picked up." Make sure you allow enough time to shoot and reproduce the picture for inclusion with the release mailing.

**Step 5. Have the release reviewed by an objective outsider.** It is always a good idea to have someone else read the release to make sure the message is clear and that no typographical errors have been incorporated.

If you work inside a large company, have the release approved by the appropriate managers. News releases can have sales, legal, and personal ramifications, so it is important that everyone affected by the announcement approves of (or at least knows about) what is being released to the media. The corporate lawyer or legal department, in companies big enough to have one, should be a part of the routine sign off on all communications including news releases.

**Step 6. Duplicate the news release with quality photocopying or printing.** Use original letterhead for each release. Do not photocopy the letterhead. Copied letterhead looks unprofessional and lacks impact. You can photocopy onto the original letterhead if you have a quality photocopier available. If not, and your mailing is quite large, consider using a competent quick printer or copy center to duplicate the release on your blank letterhead.

**Step 7. Mail the release with first class or priority mail postage.** Splurge on the postage! Press materials sent bulk rate have a poorer chance of arriving on time. If you include photos or other fragile materials, make sure they are appropriately protected against bending, crushing, and other postal system mishaps.

## THE BASIC PUBLICITY RULES

Beyond the ability to write a good news release, there are some unwritten rules in publicity that everyone should know. To help as you begin to work with the press, media, and industry representatives, here are some time-proven principles that will result in more and better publicity.

**1. Always treat the press people and analysts with respect and deference.** Be aware of their heavy schedules and demanding deadlines. Be cognizant of the fact that you are not the only person to whom they need to talk. And most important, even if you disagree with a press person's opinion, be professional about it. Yelling at a key editor in an influential magazine never helps—even if you are right.

**2. Don't demand anything from the press.** It is true that you are entitled to consideration by the press when you have news, but the press doesn't owe you anything unless you convince them that you really have a story. It is their prerogative to choose how they cover your news and where they place it. That includes cutting the contents of your release, changing positive information into negative, including your news in a larger article that also covers your competitors, or giving you a write-up on page 417. This is one of the downsides of publicity—but if you treat the press with understanding, they will usually treat you the same way.

**3. Be as influential, knowledgeable, and charming as possible.** If you aren't particularly articulate, have someone do the leg work for you or get coaching on the answers. Professionalism is a must in all relationships with the press. Most PR agencies or publicists will help draft answers and provide basic media training for inexperienced managers. Everyone on staff that has any contact with the press can benefit from this training—and expect that many people in your organization will come into contact with the media over time if your publicity efforts are successful.

**4. Have everyone on the staff prepared for dealing with the press and VIPs.** People who may possibly come into contact with the media contacts should know the names of the key people on your lists and, if not their names, they should at least be able to identify the magazine or newspaper. This means receptionists, secretaries, and any other people who may answer the phone when someone from the press calls should know how to respond and what to say. They should know where the media kits are and how they should be distributed, just in case no one else is available to handle them. Even in small companies you should let the staff know that you are expecting calls from media representatives or VIPs and they should know how to answer the questions and take messages. The staff should also know to whom to refer the caller and when not to make comments.

**5. Anticipate questions and have answers prepared in advance.** Have someone readily available to answer questions the press may ask. If you or your representative to the press don't know the answers, check and then get back to them quickly. Prepare answers, in writing, to the obvious questions in advance. That way you won't stumble when an editor from *Business Week* calls to talk to you.

**6. Follow up with the press—but do not bug them.** After sending out a news release, follow up to see if the editors or writers have any questions about your release. With magazines make the follow-up within a couple of weeks. For daily media, follow up in a couple of days. You may want to ask the contacts' opinions about improving your release.

Invite them out to lunch or breakfast just to chat. But don't call every day to see if they have seen and read your release. Keep in mind that they get hundreds, if not thousands, of releases every month. Yours is just one of them. Be persistent and consistent in working with the press and media representatives, but don't waste their time.

**7. Never send out a press release or let the news leak out until you and your organization are absolutely ready.** Advance publicity can be the undoing of a company or product line (not to mention your job). If you let people know about your new products too soon, the competition can beat you to market. If you don't deliver when promised, you can lose credibility and customers in the process. Sometimes it seems compelling to let the press in on a "secret" in advance, but in most cases this will deflate interest when the announcement is finally ready for the press. News has a way of leaking into the wrong hands, no matter how careful your contacts are. So, if you are not sure the timing is right, don't let the cat out of the bag.

**8. Always know what the competition is doing.** This is as true for publicity as it is for advertising. You should know which stories are being published about your competitors. You should always be ready to talk to the media about how your products differ (positively) from the competition. When you talk with media representatives you should never be derogatory about your competition, but you should be knowledgeable. Be honest, truthful, and put your own products in the best light. As you become known for your knowledge, ethics, and trustworthiness, the media will come to you more often for your opinions.

---

## THE EXCLUSIVE

A powerful PR tool is the *exclusive*. You've probably heard it called a *scoop*, where one media source gets an important story before anyone else. Of course if the scoop is important, it will help a publication sell more copies than a competitor, or, in the case of TV or radio, viewer ratings will be up and that means increased advertising revenue.

So, if you have a particularly newsworthy event and agree to let one media source have an exclusive on it, you should get special treatment in the form of a cover story or a special feature. A little negotiation with a friendly editor may turn your news into a major event! But be careful, you don't want to alienate all your other media friends who you may need later. Let them in on the news as soon as the story is about to break.

# YOUR PUBLICITY PLAN AND WHAT GOES INTO IT

As with all marketing communications, positive publicity programs start with planning. As already emphasized, publicity is best when treated as an on-going process rather than a one-shot event to be brought out of the closet when deemed necessary. The primary goal is to get mentioned in the press in a positive manner as frequently as possible. But publicity also needs to be coordinated with advertising and other marketing communications to be most effective. Thus, a long-term publicity plan is required that dovetails with the rest of your marketing communications efforts.

Publicity efforts should begin before you start a new advertising campaign, for example, so the press and the advertising will support the messages and announcements you want to make. Since publicity may take longer to show up than ads, begin the publicity program days, weeks, or months in advance so it will catch up with and support the ad program. If the overall plan is executed with consistency and professionalism, your company will get positive publicity.

Of course, in addition to planned publicity, you need to be ready for unplanned events and notices, which is why you produce backgrounders and media kits and have them available at all times.

Usually a one-year publicity plan is adequate, although some companies have five-year goals for their publicity efforts. A publicity plan, which is a subset of a complete public relations and marketing communications plan, should include the following:

• **A clear statement of your company's mission, corporate objectives, and product sales objectives.** Every marketing communications plan, including the publicity component, starts here. We mention it again because it is so important.

• **Measurable publicity goals as they relate to the company mission and objectives.** This should include a prioritized list of people you want to reach and the image you want to project to these people. You should also specify goals for frequency of mention and ways to measure your publicity success.

• **A calendar of media events and news releases for each news event.** Limit your *big* stories to one or two a year and have lots of *little* stories to fill in the gaps. If you know you have specific events during the year, such as new product announcements or holiday events, mark these down first, and do your planning around them.

• **A clearly defined primary audience for each news event or announcement.** This is done so you can target the mailing of your news releases for maximum exposure. The audience should be defined by geographic and lifestyle or industrial interests. Answer the questions: Who would want to know about this and where would they most likely read or otherwise find out about the news? This is much like determining the target market and demographics for an advertising campaign.

• **A list of all the potential story angles for each news event or announcement.** The stories will ultimately become your news releases. Most events have potential for more than one release. Specific releases may be tailored for each of the target audiences and media sources you intend to use to gain publicity for the event.

• **Assignments of contact people for each story and publicity event.** The people who will be involved with a publicity program should know well in advance that they will be called on to work with the media. Give them ample time to prepare. Get the most senior, knowledgeable people in the organization involved. The more important the person speaking to the press, the more important the media will regard the news.

The central idea behind the publicity plan is to ensure you have strategy and tactics determined in advance for an on-going program with the media. At the very least, a small company should send out one news release or initiate one public relations event a month. Two is better. Large companies should have a publicity plan that involves weekly activities and someone should be doing something involving public relations and publicity every working day—whether it is taking an editor out to lunch, speaking at a seminar, phoning editors to touch base, writing an editorial thank you response to a magazine, or sending out news releases.

The publicity plan should be reviewed for completeness and impact at least quarterly and revised as necessary. If you aren't getting enough publicity, as measured by the clippings and announcements in your clipping file, do two things: Increase your efforts and review your past efforts to make sure the material was properly presented and newsworthy.

Between reviews, there may be ideas that just occur to you that you don't include in your plan, and that is to be expected. Just make sure that all spontaneous publicity activities complement the rest of your communications strategy.

## PUBLICITY FOR GOOD NEWS: DAMAGE CONTROL FOR BAD NEWS

Even the best planned publicity campaign can go wrong for a number of reasons and you end up receiving negative publicity, the kind you do not want. In all your dealings with the media, you should be aware that publicity has two sides—the positive and the negative. On the one hand, public relations and its tools can be used as an important component of your overall marketing communications program. Publicity gained from public relations activities can have significant promotional, image development, and general communication value. However, publicity also serves companies when they need to handle negative announcements—for example, the fraudulent activity of one of the board of directors, a poor quarter of profitability, or the recall of a new product because of manufacturing defects.

The media thrive on conflict and controversy and they're always looking for a new angle. The press may claim to be objective, but how many stories have you read or heard lately that don't have an obvious bias? This implicit viewpoint in the news, whether positive or negative, is partially established by how you execute your publicity efforts.

If in your attempt to gain publicity you alienate the press or if they feel that your products lack value or features, you can do serious damage to an otherwise well-executed marketing communications program. This generally will not happen if you follow the steps and rules presented in this chapter, but be aware that every company has bad news at some time and learning to handle bad as well as good news with the press can make all the difference in the future of a company. If the relationship you have developed with the press and media over time has been generally good, the treatment you get in the media will be generally better when dealing with negative announcements than if this is the first time they have heard of you.

---

### ✎ TIP: PREPARE A DAMAGE CONTROL PLAN *BEFORE* YOU NEED ONE

Damage control in difficult situations is an important aspect of publicity, especially for large companies. In many negative situations, the goal of the publicity program is to get no publicity at all. By having people prepared in advance to deal with potentially damaging media situations, negative publicity can be minimized. Many companies have damage control or crisis containment plans ready to execute at any time, even if there is no negative media situation anticipated. These plans include having media kits available at all times, identifying and training specific people to talk to the media, and scheduling regular rehearsals for answering hypothetical questions on negative, unplanned scenarios that could develop.

---

When the media are out to get you, for whatever reason, there are a few simple rules to follow to keep your dignity and your skin intact:

1. Be honest and straightforward. If you don't know the answer or can't comment, state this—but don't sound evasive.
2. Prepare a written, formal statement as quickly as possible to distribute to the appropriate media representatives.
3. Don't go into more detail than necessary when asked questions, especially if all the facts are not yet available. You might end up with your foot in your mouth.
4. If it is possible to do so without looking insensitive or dishonest, develop an angle on the story that emphasizes as many positive aspects of the news as possible to offset the negative ones.
5. A backgrounder on the history of the situation should be provided if there is time, emphasizing positive company accomplishments and putting the problems in the "proper" perspective.

If you are adept at handling a potentially damaging situation, you may even be able to turn the press around to your side. Consider the electronics company, Solid State Circuits, that had a disastrous toxic chlorine leak only six months after moving to Springfield, Missouri. According to the article in *Small Business Reports,* the town was never too happy about the circuit board plant being located near residential areas in the first place, but after the chemical leak, the local citizens were up in arms. In fact, the citizens had to be evacuated while emergency repairs to the leaking valve were initiated.

The leak was covered on all three local TV networks, emphasizing the negative reaction of the community. But Solid State Circuits handled the situation with professionalism and honesty. The president of Solid State, Thomas Kawaski, quickly mobilized a company-wide public relations/publicity program. The company opened their doors to the community and began to address the community's concern for safety. The company took immediate corrective procedures involving removing faulty chlorine tanks, voluntary contact with the Department of Labor to review the facilities, and completion of a comprehensive safety survey. The positive actions were well promoted in local television feature programs and in the newspaper. The company also met with community leaders and invited the public in to see the plant. In a week the headlines in the local newspaper read "Solid State, Community Get Friendly."

Solid State remains active with the community. The company offers its facilities for local fund-raising events and charities and supports local recreation and cultural activities. Solid State and the community are now on good terms, as a result of positive, planned publicity and public relations programs.

This example illustrates the whole secret to gaining positive reactions from the media and your customers—planning, honesty, and preparation, on-going relationships with the media and the community are always your best tools in any publicity situation.

# 5 | Special Events: Producing Seminars, Conferences, and Community Activities for More Recognition

Though publicity is great if you have news to tell, sometimes it doesn't have the direct contact you need to reach your audience with impact. In this case, to make your public relations efforts work you need to produce your own special events for recognition. This chapter provides ideas and implementation advice for a number of special events and activities your company can use to promote its products and enhance its image—without using advertising or other paid media. Special public relations events and tools include seminars, conferences, community activities, company picnics, presentations and speeches by VIPs, stockholders meetings, and other occasions you can use to your advantage.

Special events are best for making the public aware of you and enhancing your image and standing in the community. Sometimes an event and a special promotion are combined for maximum effect. For example, you may offer a training seminar for free—and give a coupon for a reduced price on your product to people who attend the seminar.

Simple events can be handled by almost any organized, detail-oriented person in the company. Complex events with large audiences or events held in multiple cities will involve many people and considerable coordination. Sometimes your public relations agency or an agency that specializes in coordinating events will get involved and other times someone in your organization will be assigned as the project manager for a special event. Like the other marketing communications tools, special events should become part of your overall marketing communications plan and goals and should be well coordinated with your other marketing communications activities. And, as always, careful budgeting and clear objectives are central to their success.

## SPECIAL EVENTS POSSIBILITIES

Though every company should try to generate publicity through news releases and press contacts, not every company will use special events. Many small companies, including restaurants, retail stores, and small manufacturers, can use special events as a primary tool for promoting their products. Some companies use events to complement advertising and other promotional efforts. Other companies won't need to use them at all, concentrating instead on other communications to generate awareness. The decision to use special events depends on two primary factors:

1.  If you need direct contact with your market to help sell products more efficiently, then use special events as much as possible. For example, if your potential customers need education or training on your product before they are likely to buy, special events will play an increasing role in your marketing communications strategy. Products that are likely candidates for the strategic use of special events include technology products, products that replace traditional products or are designed to save time, and many kinds of services and educational programs.

2.  Even if your customers don't need a demonstration or education on your product, special events will play a role if long-term image and community relationships are important to your company's strategy. Large companies almost always have public image goals that can best be supported with special events and community activities. For smaller companies this is not usually as imperative, although many small companies support events because they are community minded and like to get involved in improving the community.

Based on these factors, special public relations events are most often used to build awareness, improve corporate image, establish standing in the community, or educate a marketplace about a new product or technology. In addition, there are some benefits that are unique to using special events to make the public aware of your company and products:

1.  Many events can be produced at a relatively low cost compared to commercial trade shows and advertising. Of course, they can also be very expensive—depending on the type of event you want to produce.

2.  People remember a positive event longer than ads or other marketing communications tools. Thus, events can have long-term impact on a target market or community.

3.  Because you are in contact with the audience and potential customers, special events provide an opportunity for gathering direct feedback on product ideas and programs that other promotions do not provide.

| Kind of Event | What They're Best For |
|---|---|
| Educational Seminars | Persuading a Market Why It Needs to Buy an Expensive Product and What Makes It Worth the Price<br><br>Explaining Very Complex or Technology-Based Products |
| Community Events | Keeping Your Name and Products in Front of Your Local Community Members—Particularly Useful for Retailers of All Sizes |
| Conferences/Company Sponsored Tradeshows | Increasing and Maintaining Awareness in Markets Comprised of Industrial or Technology Products |
| VIP and Celebrity Presentations and Speeches | Useful for a Variety of Purposes—Most Effective When a Prominent Celebrity is Used or One that is Important to the Market Like Henry Ford Speaking at a Large Ford Dealership |
| Holiday Events | Useful for Maintaining Community Awareness or Developing Ongoing Rapport with Current Customers |
| Public Product Demonstrations | Similar to Mini Educational Seminars—Useful for Showing "Wonder" Products and Products with More Capability than is Physically Obvious such as Cooking Tools |

Figure 5.1. Choosing a special event to meet your objectives.

4. Events can be used to develop positive relationships with the community at large. This positive relationship with the community can have many benefits, including the enhanced image and positive attitudes of potential customers and employees developed through these activities.

5. If your company doesn't have much other news, special events can be used to generate publicity in the media, which has a broad impact on public awareness. Thus, putting on an event has a double benefit: generating publicity for the event and providing direct customer exposure accomplished by the event itself.

The downside of using events is primarily one of risk. There is no guarantee the right people will attend or see your event. Of course this is true of advertising and other marketing communications in general. There are also a number of things that can go wrong when coordinating events, and simple problems such as equipment failure or a speaker with laryngitis can destroy the impact of an otherwise well-planned activity.

If the steps presented here are followed, however, the commercial ben efits of a well-executed event far outweigh the risks.

## PLANNING AND IMPLEMENTING SUCCESSFUL SPECIAL EVENTS

There are some basic steps that are common to managing any successful special event. These include the following:

**1. Define the objectives for the event.**　Do you want to build general awareness or announce a specific product? Do you need to support your advertising messages? Do you need to reach a wider audience? Do you need to educate a new target market? Events without clear objectives are events that probably don't need to happen.

**2. Define the target audience for the event.**　Selecting the appropriate target market applies to events, just as it does to producing other marketing communications, like advertising and publicity. Before you decide on an event, be clear on who you are trying to reach and where they are.

**3. Determine a realistic budget for your special events.**　Based on your overall marketing communications budget, determine the importance of the events relative to your other marketing communications. If events have a high priority in reaching your customers, this should be reflected in the budget allocation for events. The scale of your event will largely determine the budget. All the small details that go into planning events have costs, so do not underestimate the budget you will require to pull things off professionally. Here are the standard expense categories for most events:

- Facilities rental.
- Equipment rental, including audiovisual equipment, lighting, and furniture.
- Honoraria and fees for speakers, special guests, and performers.
- Decorations and flowers.
- Promotion.
- Entertainment.
- Travel and lodging for guests and employees.
- Food.
- Hospitality costs for guests or presenters, including meals, limousines, and special gifts.
- Presentation media, such as slides, videos, or background music.

To avoid surprises and panic when managing your event, always put together a small contingency budget for the last minute details that are inevitably overlooked in even the best-planned affairs. The costs for putting on events are often hidden. Costs that people often forget when planning an event include the following:

- Producing and printing the invitations and press releases. If professionals have to design and write these, don't forget to include their fees.
- Speeches and presentation materials. Again, if someone is going to write the presentation speech for you, include the costs of the writer and the cost of the slides or video-production.
- Postage charges. It is surprising how many people plan the mailings but forget the costs of postage, which can be considerable.
- Telephone calls and travel expenses for arranging facilities and food, following up with invited guests, and working with the press and media who will cover your event.
- Special construction costs for stages, signs, special lighting, or booths.
- Fees for the facilities staff for special services, including food servers, bartenders, and even carpenters if you will be building a stage or speaker's platform.

The most frequently underestimated expense is the personnel cost in time and money for the executives, managers, and staff who will be working on the event. The people from your own company need to be scheduled and because they have other work to do, their time needs to be appropriately allocated. While people are working on the event, other work they normally do will not be getting done. If this is not considered, the people will not have enough time to prepare and support the event appropriately. If people resent working on an event or feel overburdened, it will be reflected in the quality of the event. If the event will negatively impact other aspects of your business, or there aren't enough resources (people and money) to pull it off effectively, consider another form of promotion.

**4. Select the appropriate type of event for the objectives, the target audience, and budget.**   Your objective and target audience will determine to a great extent the scope and nature of the event that will have the desired results. If you want to educate a new target market, then a seminar, conference, or product demonstration is a possibility. If you just want to make your local community generally aware of your existence, a holiday party might meet your needs. If your funds are limited, you may want your events to consist of limited presentations and demonstrations. And, by all means, be creative if you have it in you.

**5. Identify the best timing for the event.** After you decide on the kind of event that best meets your needs, be careful to select the appropriate timing. The times for some events, such as holiday parties or anniversaries, are pretty much predetermined. However, the scheduling of other events can and should be controlled. Availability of facilities, weather, and competing events should be considered before selecting a date.

Don't schedule events too close to major conferences or tradeshows if your customers are likely to attend these. Avoid overlapping your events with those of the competition. Avoid times of the year when the weather in your area is undesirable (unless you hold the event in another location). Although you can't forecast the weather in advance, at least be prepared for the worst case scenario—no matter where you end up locating the event. And make sure there is enough time to prepare the event before you finalize the date. It won't matter how good the date is if you are unprepared when it arrives.

In addition to choosing the date, you will also need to consider the time of day for some events. If it is an all day affair, then choose a day when the most people will be able to attend. Don't schedule a family event on Sunday morning during church hours. Don't schedule a business event on a Saturday. If you plan an after-work event, allow for commute times and give the people a few minutes to relax with a drink or refreshments after work before getting started.

**6. Identify the best location for the event.** The location of the event is critical to its success. If you do not have appropriate rooms or facilities in your own company, rent them. The location should always be accessible, easy to find, and comfortable. Hotels, conference centers, club facilities, and even some well-appointed restaurants are all possible locations if your own company facilities aren't appropriate.

If you are putting on a large-scale event, locate it somewhere close to a major airport if possible. Make sure adequate hotel and transportation facilities are available. The rooms for the event should be a major consideration in your choice of a facility. They should be able to accommodate your best case attendance estimate. Make sure the seating is comfortable. Avoid gaudy, brightly colored, or cluttered rooms. Neutral environments that you can dress up with your own decorations and signs are best—unless you are giving a formal dinner in a gala ballroom. Look at many possibilities before choosing the location. Consider things such as electrical facilities, air conditioning and heating, close proximity of the rest rooms, and the general services and equipment provided by the facility.

**7. Establish a team or event committee for coordinating large events.**   For a small event, a competent, organized person can probably handle most of the planning and coordination. But for a large event, no single person has enough time to plan, organize, and implement a special event. In this case, many companies form event committees, in which one person acts as the project manager for the event and other people are assigned specific aspects of the events, such as publicity, decorations, presentations, and logistics. The key to using a committee effectively is the skill of the project manager in coordinating and managing the team.

**8. Publicize the event well in advance using standard publicity techniques.**   You should treat your special event as news and should follow all the guidelines for gaining publicity for the event that were covered in the last chapter, including sending out press releases in advance and following up with your media and press contacts. Timing the press releases is crucial; you want coverage before the event, but not so much in advance that it is forgotten. There are also community calendars in most newspapers that you should use for events that are open to the public. Listings in these are usually free, so it is worth the time to send the editor in charge of the calendar a notice, even if you do not send out formal press releases. For large-scale events you may want to do some advertising in newspapers or trade journals.

**9. Invite people in advance and follow up whenever appropriate.**   In addition to publicity, you will probably want to invite people from your mailing lists, including customers, press and media representatives, prospects, or community leaders as appropriate. These invitations should be mailed about three weeks before the event and if there are people you really want to attend, follow up a week or two in advance with a personal reminder call.

**10. Make sure all the company participants are trained and clear about their responsibilities.**   If multiple people will be involved in an event, keep them informed about the progress on the event and the activities. All participants should have agendas in advance. All speeches and presentations should be practiced in advance in the actual room if possible with the lights, audiovisual equipment, and microphones. For large events, it is advisable to have a meeting the day before the event where all people are briefed on protocol and responsibilities. The responsibilities for problems, food, VIP coordination, and facilities should all be clearly specified in a list that is provided to each person on the event team.

**11. Follow up after the event to get reactions from the participants.**   To improve your events, call selected attendees or send out questionnaires

**Special Event Objectives:**

☐ **Responsibilities Assigned:**

Invitations/Publicity:_____ Food and Beverage Coordination:_____

Decoration/Facility Coordinator: _____ Entertainment: _____

Event Planning:_____ Event Manager: _____

☐ **Event Advertising Placed (If Appropriate)**

☐ **Mailing/Phone List of Invitee's Identified and/or Acquired (If Appropriate)**

☐ **Mailing/Phone Invitations Two Weeks Before the Event (If Appropriate)**

☐ **Follow-up 48 Hours Before the Event (If Appropriate)**

**Schedule of Activities:**

| Time | Name of Event | Description of Event |
|------|---------------|----------------------|
|      |               |                      |
|      |               |                      |
|      |               |                      |
|      |               |                      |
|      |               |                      |

☐ **Music Ready (If Used)**

☐ **Facilities Ready**
    ☐ Adequate heating or air conditioning        ☐ Seating/standing room adequate
    ☐ Music/sound equipment ready                 ☐ Decorations complete

☐ **VIP Facilities and Arrangements (If Required)**
    ☐ Hotel/transportation arranged               ☐ VIP briefed on speech/activities
    ☐ Podium/microphones set up and checked       ☐ Person to meet and transport VIP to event

☐ **Presentation Materials Ready (If Used)**
    ☐ Visual aids completed and reviewed          ☐ AV equipment ready and tested

☐ **Food**
    ☐ Menu prepared              ☐ Refreshments ready
    ☐ Caterer or preparer selected   ☐ Over 21 servers for alcohol (most states)
    ☐ Tables/chairs ready        ☐ Condiments and place settings ready

☐ **Give-Aways and/or Contests Ready**

Figure 5.2. Special events checklist.

to determine what they liked and disliked. What topics should have been added to the conference or presentation? Which activities were too long? Which activities were too short? What did they think of the food? Were the location and facility appropriate? The more you learn from your events, the more success you will have putting them on in the future.

## USING VIPS IN YOUR EVENTS

The use of very important persons (VIPs) can be a powerful force in the success of an event. The primary idea behind having VIPs at your event is to profit in some way from their appearance—more attendance, positive associations between your product and the VIP, and more press coverage because the VIP is there.

If you decide to use VIPs in your event, you will need to care for these people. Some VIPs are more VIP-ish than others. Surprisingly, some small-time VIPs, including local radio disc-jockeys or vice presidents of companies, actually expect more VIP attention than famous names and established public figures. The big names often have an agent or private secretary to contact to determine specific preferences and procedures. For less than national figures, you will have to use your common sense to keep them happy. Here are some tips on the things that most VIPs expect if they are invited:

• The financial arrangements with VIPs should be specified clearly in the early planning stages. Fees, honoraria, or other remuneration should be agreed to before publicizing the event. Some VIPs command large fees or honoraria for even brief appearances. If they are both notable and talented, it is usually worth it. For national figures, the financial agreement is usually handled by the VIP's agent. For others, it is handled personally. Responsibility for expense accounts, travel, lodging, and even meals should all be agreed on in advance, in writing.

• Publicity and media coverage of the event are expected by most VIPs. If the VIP is especially notable, a pre- or postevent news conference may be in order. At the very least, most notables expect their picture to be taken with an appropriately high-ranking person from your company. Contact the VIPs in advance to establish their preferred way of dealing with the media.

• Allow the VIPs some time to think, breathe, eat, and look around. Don't schedule every minute of your VIPs' time. If you run the people ragged, they won't perform or look as good either. Remember, they may be famous, but they're still just people.

• Always make sure that the VIP receives a complete agenda for the visit in advance so changes and adjustments can be made if appropriate. In addition, provide an outline of the event itself and some background on your company. Your media kit is usually adequate for this purpose. Also, make sure the VIP is informed about the dress requirement for each event—casual, black tie, business, or whatever. Military VIPs are very particular about the dress requirements, so be specific. VIPs have to pack too, just like other people, so don't surprise them with a white tie dinner at the last minute.

• If the VIP will be giving a speech prepared by your company or PR agency, make sure the person has enough time to review it, change it, and approve it before the event. Any speeches that others will be giving should be provided as background information.

• If you will be responsible for the travel arrangements, you will need to establish the VIP's preferred method of travel and preferred carriers. Verify the arrangements just before the travel dates. Allow enough time for airport transfers and commuting. And make sure the VIP is met by someone from the company who is knowledgeable about the event and the facilities available in the city.

• Some VIPs prefer to make their own hotel arrangements, but others do not. Book the best room possible within your budget. If the person is very notable, hotels will often provide suites for free or for reduced rates. (This doesn't seem fair does it? The more successful you are the more you get for free.) Find out if the VIP will be bringing a spouse or other guests and determine bed preferences and sleeping arrangements—twin, king, or whatever. One room or two? If possible, have flowers delivered to the room and a fruit basket, a (good) bottle of wine, or favorite liqueur or other appropriate welcome gift. The stature of the offering will depend on the stature of the VIP.

• Find out if the VIP has friends or relatives in the area, and if so, allow time for the VIP to visit with these people if desired. You may want to make arrangements for these people to meet the VIP during a dinner or formal luncheon, if this is an option.

• Ask the VIP in advance if there are any special requirements. These include special diet preferences, presentation equipment preferences such as a favorite type of microphone, or medical considerations such as allergies to flowers that might be used in the meeting room.

• As a last point, always, always make sure someone is assigned and available to the VIP at all times for special requests or as a resource when the VIP has questions.

## THE SUCCESS SECRETS BEHIND SPECIAL EVENTS

Why is it that some events go so well and others flop? So that you don't find yourself in a room without an audience or on stage listening to boos and hisses, here are some simple secrets to making special events work for you instead of against you:

• **Welcome the attendees at the beginning.** Use people's names whenever possible. The power of calling someone by name is immeasurable. Provide name tags for the attendees to avoid the stress of trying to remember everyone's name.

• **Prepare contingency plans for every possible problem.** Try to anticipate everything that could possibly go wrong—bad weather, speaker gets sick, equipment doesn't work, or whatever you can think of. Without contingency plans for late speakers or other predictable mishaps, an event can quickly fall apart. The more problems you can imagine and plan for, the more likely the event will go without a hitch. Of course there is always the problem that no one anticipates, like the time a TV celebrity with a reputation for being a friendly easy-going type of guy, turned out to be a completely uncooperative jerk and ruined an expensive event put on by a major corporation. But, if you are otherwise prepared, havoc can be kept to a minimum.

• **Remember the details.** It is the details that make events special. Things such as boutonnieres and corsages for the speakers add a touch of class. Printed agendas with the names of key speakers are a must. Tasteful decorations and flowers on the dinner table or on the stage can turn an ordinary event into a gala affair. Quality signs that make rooms and activities easy to find are not only considerate, but help reinforce the importance of the event. Pencils and note pads on the tables are a thoughtful and appreciated addition.

• **Make the event entertaining and informative.** If your event includes presentations, use speakers who are lively and entertaining—not dry and monotonic. Limit formal speeches to 15 minutes or less. Use a variety of media in your presentations whenever possible. In large-scale events, such as conferences or company sponsored tradeshows, have multiple activities scheduled simultaneously.

• **Remember that the way to a customer's mind is through his stomach.** Almost every special event should have some kind of refreshment. It doesn't have to be haute cuisine or even expensive, but there should be something of quality. Snacks are fine for seminars, but inappropriate for conferences. The more elaborate the event—the more elaborate the food. If you are having a large event catered, have the hotel provide samples of the food before you make your selections—the catering departments will do this at no charge for large affairs. And make sure you choose food that the majority of people will find pleasing. Sushi may be fine at a trendy party for a new retail store in Beverly Hills, but as the main offering at a tradeshow for truck drivers in Cleveland, it's not a great choice. Many times people remember the event by the quality of the refreshments—and the quality of the food reflects on the quality of your company and your product—so be picky. The food budget may turn out to be the single largest expense in putting on an event—and worth it if the food is memorable for the right reasons.

• **Give the people something to remember after the event is completed.**   Little gifts such as a small box of candy at the end of a dinner, an embossed notebook at a seminar, or a carryall bag at a conference provide positive reinforcement of time well spent. The remembrance doesn't have to be expensive; imagination and utility often count more than cost.

• **Time the activities and presentations for maximum impact.**   The key to keeping people interested in your event is timing. In a conference, make sure there are a variety of activities. A highlight event should be scheduled every hour to keep people interested. Make sure the capstone speeches occur when people are most receptive—between 10 a.m. and noon for daytime events, and before 8 p.m. for evening events. Late evenings and early mornings are best for social interactions and introductions.

• **Always know what the competition is doing.**   If your competition is giving a one-week training seminar in the Bahamas, all expenses paid, then you know what you have to compete with. You should not necessarily mimic the competition, but you must take them into consideration when you develop your event strategy. Sometimes it is appropriate to be a copycat—but it is usually better to do something of equal or better quality with a much different theme and approach. People will judge your company and your products based on the organization and impact of the event, so if your event is poorly prepared when compared to your competition, people will assume that your product is also of lower quality. If you can't afford to put on an event that competes in content, creativity, and organization, it might be better not to put on an event at all. Or, as an alternative, put on a number of smaller, more personal events of high quality as opposed to one colossal event that drains your budget and your resources.

• **Always thank the guests for attending.**   For most events the "thank yous" should be done twice—at the event and in a note sent after the event with a personal signature. (The note may be printed, but the signature should be personal. A printed thank you signature is tacky.) In large events with hard-to-identify audiences, make sure you personally thank as many people for coming as possible. The more people feel special at your event, the more they will appreciate you and your company. And that's the whole point of special events, isn't it?

# 6 | Collateral Materials and Direct Mail: Choosing What Works and Making It Happen

Your prospective customers may need more information before they can decide on your product, so you hand them a colorful brochure. Or you need to get the word out to your market quickly—and don't have the time or budget to use advertising—so instead, you mail your promotion to a carefully selected list of likely prospects. These examples illustrate two important and very powerful marketing communications tools—collateral and direct mail. Both of these tools allow you to say just about anything you want, any time you want and are limited only by imagination and available budget. When you use collateral materials and direct mail promotions, you are entirely in control of the message, the production, and the distribution of the materials—so these tools can have significant advantages over advertising and publicity in controlling a message and targeting a specific marketplace.

Collateral materials include brochures, catalogs, annual reports, datasheets, price lists, newsletters, and other printed materials that work with other tools to enhance and complete the sales process. Collateral materials are used to provide customers with details and information not possible in an ad or news release. Most collateral is distributed in person or through the mail in response to direct inquiries by a potential customer.

Direct mail is specialized collateral that is mailed to prospective customers instead of being given out by a salesperson. Direct mail in its simplest form consists of a letter or postcard mailed to prospects. More complex direct mail projects use a mailer designed expressly for this purpose or consist of a product brochure sent along with a personalized letter to customers. Because direct mail programs often use materials created in a manner identical to collateral materials, the use and production of both of these marketing communications tools are covered together in this chapter.

## COLLATERAL FILLS THE GAPS LEFT BY ADVERTISING AND PUBLICITY

Advertising and publicity are potent tools for getting the word out by creating both awareness and need for a product. But since ads and press coverage can't always present the complete information required by customers making a buying decision, a "follow-up" tool—collateral—is needed to add detail and better explain the product and its benefits. Collateral is used to build and enhance the awareness initiated through media-based tools and direct mail. It can also be used as a powerful image-building tool to enhance a company's credibility or technological prowess.

Collateral is always used to support the sales process, although this support may take a number of forms. In the case of products sold by an outside salesforce, the collateral may include presales brochures and price lists. In the case of a mail order company, their catalog is usually the major force in moving products. A charity may support a door-to-door soliciting program with a small brochure that adds weight and credence to the solicitor's verbal assault.

Collateral can also be used to support future sales. Many consumer goods manufacturers stuff literature into product packages to support the buyer's belief that he or she has purchased a "quality product." This postsales literature is provided in the hope that it will motivate customers to buy more of the company's merchandise in the future.

## Brochures Specify Benefits and Enhance the Company Image

The most familiar collateral format is the brochure. A brochure is a multipage booklet, ranging from 4 to 24 pages in length. (More than 24 pages and you usually have a catalog.) The size of the brochure depends on how it will be distributed and the whims of the designer. We've seen brochures as small as 4 × 4 inches and as large as two-feet square.

Brochures are best for delivering strong benefits and sales messages. They are also a good choice for enhancing overall corporate image. Product specifications and technical details are best covered in another kind of collateral called a datasheet or white paper—or these details may be relegated to a back page of the brochure. There are several categories of brochures, including the following:

- **Corporate capabilities brochures.** These typically expensive brochures are designed to convince customers and investors of the stability and integrity of the featured company. Corporate brochures expound the company's advanced technology, financial resources, and customer base. These brochures cover the company's full spectrum of services and resources and the value the company offers its customers. They are typically used as "leave behind" pieces by a salesforce along with specific product brochures or included as one component of a complete media or literature kit distributed to VIPs and the press.

- **Product sales brochures.** Product sales brochures are benefits-oriented promotional pieces for a product or product line. Usually, but not always less expensive than corporate brochures, product brochures are used directly in the sales process. They are used at tradeshows or as a leave behind piece used by the salesforce working in the field. These brochures may also be displayed in retail environments. Costs permitting, these brochures can be mailed as part of a direct promotional campaign.

- **Educational brochures.** These are designed to support other collateral by providing customers with an education on competitive product issues or an explanation of a new technology employed by the company. The purpose of a well-crafted education piece is to show customers what to look for when evaluating competitive products or reviewing similar technology. Of course this "education" is inevitably self-serving and portrays exclusive aspects of the company's product as more important than those of a competitor's. Sometimes educational brochures can be simple "white papers" produced to look like a scientific report. Other times they are just as elaborate as a product or corporate brochure. Again, it is the audience and the budget that help you decide how much to spend on producing any piece of collateral material.

- **Internal promotional brochures.** Large companies often have a need to promote themselves or their programs to employees. They do this by creating brochures for use inside the company. Examples of internal promotional pieces are elaborate human resources brochures used to attract new employees and company benefits brochures.

## Price Lists and Datasheets Provide Detailed Information in Inexpensive Formats

Price lists and parts lists are some of the simplest collateral pieces. Taking a variety of formats, they may consist of tiny stand-alone booklets or quick-printed black and white pages to be inserted into a three-ring binder.

Datasheets are also simple collateral pieces, typically one to four pages in length. Unlike a brochure, which focuses on delivering a product sales message, datasheets generally focus more on product features and specifications. Datasheets are usually less expensive to produce than product brochures. They typically employ one- or two-color printing and simple photos and illustrations. The inexpensive format allows for frequent updating at minimal cost as a product changes and evolves. Product brochures should work together with datasheets. The brochure creates the image and expounds the overall benefits message and the datasheets summarize the brochure's message and add the indepth technical specifications and operational details.

## Catalogs Perform "Show and Sell" Functions

Catalogs are used to display a wide range of products for immediate and direct sale to customers. Catalogs typically make copious use of photos and illustrations to display the goods and come in various sizes, though standard 8 1/2 × 11 and 9 × 12 inch formats are most common. Catalogs that are familiar to almost everyone include those produced by Sears and Best Products. These are as big as a phone book and sell everything—clothes, furniture, cameras, and more in one volume. Manufacturing companies also produce catalogs of products, parts, and equipment.

Recently catalogs have again become a popular direct marketing tool for a wide range of products. Catalog-based companies have sprung up for all kinds of unique and not-so-unique product lines, including clothes, specialty foods, business products, exercise equipment, and leisure time products. Recently we received a catalog of portable wine cellars with prices starting at $3500. We still wonder which mailing list targeted us for that one.

## Annual Reports Turn Required Disclosures into Positive Promotion

Annual reports are required of all corporations by law. In some ways similar to a book-length brochure, they include the following components: corporate background information, a letter from the president, financial reports, and a list of company officers. Annual reports may be as simple and inexpensive as photocopied typewriter output bound with a staple for a small privately held firm. But rather than just produce the required financial disclosures, most publicly held corporations use the annual report as both a promotional tool and a financial report. A major corporation may produce an elaborate eight-color annual report with embossing and special papers costing $250,000 or more. The original purpose of an annual report was to keep investors and prospective investors apprised of a company's financial status. Now they are often used to build image through the corporate information section and the obviously expensive design, photography, paper, and printing. Some companies use their annual reports in the same way a corporate capabilities brochure would be used.

# PRODUCING COLLATERAL MATERIALS: STEP-BY-STEP

## All Collateral Follows the Same Path to Completion

Although collateral includes a long list of diverse materials and encompasses a wide range of sales and marketing objectives, the basic steps for creating all collateral tools are (fortunately) nearly the same:

- Establish objectives for the piece.
- Define a format for the piece.
- Determine a budget for the piece.
- Hire the right vendors to produce the piece.
- Develop the concept and write the copy.
- Design the piece for visual impact.
- Complete the preprint production.
- Print the piece.
- Distribute the finished collateral piece.

These steps will now be covered in depth and tips and hints for making the process go smoothly will be provided, so your collateral materials will have maximum effectiveness in getting the word out about your products and company.

**Step 1. Establish objectives for the piece.**   The process of creating cost-effective and persuasive collateral material begins in the planning stages. More so than other tools in the marketing communications toolbox, collateral materials must be carefully orchestrated to work with other promotional programs and the sales process to be fully effective. Many collateral pieces must wear several different hats to meet an organization's needs. Of course some companies create individual pieces for each need and you can too, but this uses money that could be better spent elsewhere.

Selecting the right format for a collateral piece and setting and sticking to a budget for the project are central to the success of collateral projects. Since outside vendors are often required to write, design, produce, and print them, the development of clear objectives and guidelines is crucial. Like most other communications efforts, the process of creating effective collateral material requires careful balancing of the need and function for the piece against the price tag and physical requirements of the format. Although a full-color brochure with 24 pages of expensive photos and expressive text is useful for almost every kind of product, it may be cost prohibitive. Instead, a simple two-color, four-page piece may cost substantially less, work just as well, and take far less time to execute.

Be very clear on what uses and functions the collateral material will serve. You should be able to explain in two sentences why each piece in a collateral strategy is needed and how the pieces will work together in the sales process. Unless you have a lot of money, avoid the "grand scheme" of several levels of collateral recommended by income-seeking design firms and agencies. Consider tiered literature schemes only if each piece is justifiable and useful on its own without the rest of the scheme.

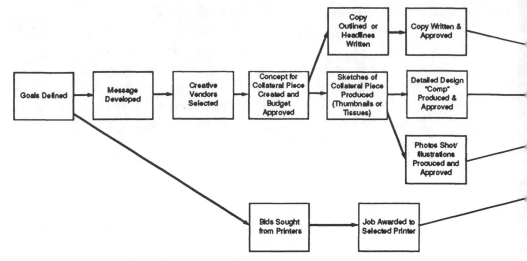

Figure 6.1. The process of producing collateral materials.

Remember, the only people who will bother to understand your literature strategy are you and your agency.

You can establish specific objectives for your collateral materials by answering questions such as the following:

- Who is the audience for the piece? As always, this is the first question you need to ask.
- How will the piece be distributed?
- What is the expected life span of the piece?
- Who in your organization will be distributing or using the piece? Salespeople? Public relations department? Executives? Personnel department?
- What functions will the collateral piece serve that are not served by other marketing communications?
- At what point in the sales cycle will the piece be distributed to the potential customer or other audience?
- What messages will the piece communicate? (Refer to Chapter 2 again for a list of possibilities.) Be careful to keep the messages focused. One common mistake in collateral materials is the attempt to say everything about a product or company in one piece.

Be open minded as you define your collateral requirements. The project that you originally defined as one brochure may turn out to be more cost-effective in the form of several less expensive product brochures—or the reverse may be true.

**Step 2. Define a format for the piece.** After careful review of your objectives, you must determine roughly what kind of piece you need in

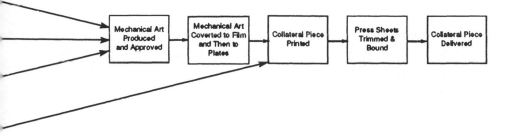

terms of format. Format includes specifications for size, number of colors, and paper quality. What makes this a bit tricky is that the format dictates your budget, but at the same time your budget dictates the format.

Here are some things that can help you determine a rough format for your next collateral piece:

- Collect copies of your competitor's materials to see what format they use (number of colors, size, complexity of design, number and quality of photos and illustrations, quality of paper, and printing).
- Assemble the collateral projects used by your company in the past and review them for effectiveness. Pile the ones that worked best in front of you and put the others aside.
- Make a list of major topics to get some idea of the page count. If the number of topics becomes excessive, eliminate less important ones or combine them if it makes sense to do so. Effective collateral contains one major focus per page. This focus might be to showcase a single product or product line or describe what makes your company better than the competition.
- Choose a physical size format for the piece based on the number of uses for the piece. 8 1/2 × 11 inches is standard for most brochures, catalogs, and datasheets because it fits conveniently into file folders and provides lots of room on each page. A slightly larger size sometimes works for a corporate brochure because it sets the piece apart from smaller product brochures and gives it more presence. For consumer products, a smaller size may work

depending on how the brochure will be used. For example, a brochure promoting an expensive line of cosmetics might be sized 4 × 4 inches to fit easily into a woman's handbag. A brochure used in a retail store might measure 8 1/2 × 3 inches to fit in a mounted literature holder. If a brochure will be mailed in addition to being distributed by hand, then it must fit into standard envelopes and floor displays, if used.

- Select the approximate number of colors for the piece. Study your competitor's materials and your pile of "effective" literature to see how many colors were used. If the budget is tight, use as few colors as possible to keep costs down. Use more if your company has relied on a colorful look in the past or if your competitors use them. Why? Because your one-color piece will look uninteresting to a customer reviewing your literature alongside a competitor's when making a buying decision. Note, however, that in the case of a charity or not-for-profit, the opposite may be true. In that case your competitor's four-color piece will look like an imprudent use of donations against your simple one- or two-color piece.

- Select any special "extras" required by the project. Examples of extras include *business reply cards* (BRCs), or special print treatments such as foil stamping, varnishes, embossing, or coil binding.

- Select a paper type appropriate for your project. This is a subject to be discussed with prospective designers and printers if you are new to marketing communications. We have also put some basic information on papers in Chapter 8 to get you started.

- What quantity will be printed? Normally, allow enough collateral to last at least six months and up to two years, depending on how the piece will be used and distributed. The more you print the first time, the less each individual piece will cost.

These specifications will help you set limits on the budget for the project and will provide guidelines for the vendors you hire. The vendors might ultimately make a few changes and recommendations to improve your rough specifications after the concept and design are proposed, but your initial format specification will establish your expectations so the vendors don't blow the budget on a design that you can't afford to execute.

**Step 3. Determine a budget for the piece.** With the plethora of format decisions made but not cast in concrete (yet), you can now solicit estimates for writing, design, production, and printing. Based on your format decisions, complete a Collateral Specifications Worksheet such as

Collateral Project Name: _____ Date: _____

Kind of Collateral Piece: _____ Desired Completion Date: _____

Physical Size after Trimming: _____ Number of Panels: _____

Number of Spot Colors: _____ Process Color? Yes    No

Spot Colors to Be Used: _____ .

Number of Halftones: _____ Number of Process Color Images: _____

Are There Large Areas of Solid Color? Yes ☐    No ☐

Are There Screen Tint Colors? Yes ☐ No ☐    How Many? _____

Paper:   Coated Stock ☐ Uncoated Stock ☐

Paper Brand Name_____ Paper Weight _____

Proofs:   Blueline ☐ Chromalin ☐ Match Print ☐ Color Key ☐ Dummy ☐

Special Treatments:  Foil Stamping ☐    Embossing ☐

Varnishes? Yes ☐ No ☐    How many? _____

Printer Bids (Get bids from three printers and have them quote on three different quantities):

Printer#1: Name: _____ Phone Number: _____

Quantity _____ Price _____ Quantity _____ Price _____ Quantity _____ Price _____

Printer#2: Name: _____ Phone Number: _____

Quantity _____ Price _____ Quantity _____ Price _____ Quantity _____ Price _____

Printer#3: Name: _____ Phone Number: _____

Quantity _____ Price _____ Quantity _____ Price _____ Quantity _____ Price _____

Figure 6.2. Collateral specification worksheet.

the one illustrated and send a copy to prospective vendors for each of the primary services that will be used to produce your collateral project. As a control factor, look up last year's projects to see how much was spent for a similar piece.

**Step 4. Hire the right vendors to produce the piece.**  After getting the bids from the vendors, you will need to decide who to use to bring the project to fruition. You can hire a full-service agency or design firm that specializes in collateral materials or use freelancers to write, design, produce, and print your collateral projects. In addition, you will need to choose a printer with the appropriate level of skill and equipment to print your piece.

Be aware that vendors who specialize in the development of print collateral materials have skills and portfolios different from advertising specialists. Selection of talent for the project is critical to producing an effective piece on time and within budget. For example, a writer capable of creating a lengthy brochure is often different from an advertising copywriter. A few writers can do both well, but usually someone who is good at producing a one-page ad will become bored with writing a 24-page brochure and taking the copy through several drafts until completion. The steps and pitfalls for choosing vendors are detailed in Chapter 9. After making your vendor choices, you will need to establish a schedule for the project on which everyone can agree. As explained in Chapter 10, a detailed schedule is an important part of controlling project delivery.

**Step 5. Develop the concept and write the copy.** All but the simplest pieces require a writer to produce ideas and copy for the project. The process of writing a collateral piece starts with a concept (idea) along with headlines for each page or spread. The concept for a collateral piece includes a theme, style, and suggested visual imagery. The person who writes the collateral piece or a creative director at an agency is responsible for coming up with the overall concept. This person uses the messages and background materials described in Chapter 2 as source material. Writers will have meetings with you or other people from the company to ask questions and verify details to be used in the copy.

After specifying an overall concept and organization for the piece, the concept should be reviewed and approved. Then the writer creates a first draft of the copy for review, while coordinating ideas with the designer to make sure the design and the copy fit. The writer should also describe and caption all the visuals to be used to reinforce the messages in the copy.

---

✎   **TIP: THE ENDLESS "TOO MUCH COPY" CONFLICT**

Many collateral projects suffer from the *Too Much Copy Conflict.* It is a problem that often begins with you. If you have too much to say on a page of a brochure or datasheet, the designer must either clutter up the design with too much type or resort to setting it in tiny seven- or eight-point type—extremely hard to read. Your writer may be guilty of the same problem. He or she may become unusually prolific on a given topic and force in a lot of secondary detail, obliterating the key messages. Your designer may advise cutting the copy; however, if your designer has his or her way, no copy would be used because it clutters up the design. Ultimately, it is your job to make sure the message gets across with the right number of words.

Depending on you, the writer, and your organization, the copy may be accepted nearly verbatim at the first draft or it may continue through as many as 10 rewrites before acceptance. Strong, concise writing and clear, unambiguous organization are the keys to making a piece enjoyable and easy to read and that is what you should look for when you read the draft. If the draft goes through more than three revisions, then either the writer is wrong for the project, your review process is not productive, or there are internal political problems in your organization that need to be resolved before work on the piece continues.

After the final draft of the copy is approved, the writer's final contribution to a project will be to proofread the ready-to-print mechanical assembled by the designer.

## WE CAN'T LEAVE OUT ONE WORD!

On a rush project we completed, a client needed to assemble a six-page catalog of their wares in a hurry for use at a tradeshow that was only one week away. A visit to the client for an input session disclosed that they had already "written" the piece. They presented 24 pages of dense copy, typed single space from margin to margin on each page in tiny type produced by a computer printer. When walking out the door, the company's owner told the us that "not one word of the writing could be left out because it really catches the gist of the product."

After frantically designing the piece and chopping the copy down (with a machete), we presented the comp, copy in place, to the client. An informal review with all partners in the business left us sitting in the waiting room. The original copy had been chopped to less than 5% of its original size and completely rewritten. An hour later, a beaming company president emerged from the review meeting with the statement, "I'm so glad you managed to get it all in. We've only got a couple of word changes for you to make." Astonished, we made the changes and sent the project off to print before anyone could compare the final copy to the original and change their minds.

**Step 6. Design the piece for visual impact.**   After the concept is approved, the designer's work begins, though sometimes the designer and writer will work together on a concept for a piece. Designers are used to creating the look and feel for most collateral projects. Many designers and design firms specialize in collateral only, taking on other communications projects such as advertising only if times are tight. The designer or design firm is usually responsible for taking the project from tissues all the way through print.

Well-designed collateral is a pleasure to look at and read. Captivating photos catch and keep the eye and their captions provide just enough detail to get the reader to read the copy. Charts explain concepts difficult to illuminate in words alone. Color makes the piece vibrant. The choice of type, visuals, and space on the page results in overall cohesiveness.

---

## ✎   TIP: AVOID TRITE THEMES AND PHOTOS

There are a number of cliches to be avoided when planning collateral materials. The more obvious ones to avoid include the following:

• Unless your headquarters is a landmark such as the Eiffel Tower or the Transamerica pyramid or your building is significant for some other reason, leave the photo of it out of the brochure. Use the space for something important to your readers.
• Avoid shots that say nothing. For example, almost every computer software brochure has a picture of an anonymous person sitting in front of a computer doing nothing in particular. Photos likes these convey no message.
• Skip themes using puzzle pieces, children's building blocks, and board games. Thousands of others have already beat you to these tired themes. Not only that, but in the case of board games, the manufacturer may sue for copyright infringement if you show the game in a photo without permission.
• Don't use *your* baby or child in photos. You may think he or she is completely adorable, but your readers may not share your view. If you must show a child or young person in a photo let the designer select one from a modeling agency.
• Choose something other than shots of underclothed models to sell your products unless you sell bathing suits or lingerie. If you do, you will potentially alienate one or both sexes of your market.

---

The design process for collateral is similar to that followed for print advertising. First, the designer creates tissue drawings of the piece. A tissue may be a miniature *thumbnail* sketch or full size. Most designers draw these sketches using pencil or colored pencils in the case of a multicolored piece. With your approval of these sketches, the designer will prepare a *comprehensive* (or *comp* for short). This is a full-size color mock-up of the piece showing *greeked* copy, headlines, and sketches of all photos and illustrations. Before a final comp is produced, it is important that the designer and the writer communicate on a regular basis to ensure that they are clear on the concepts and that the space allowed for the copy is adequate.

After the comp is approved, the designer sets type, has photos taken with a professional photographer, and has illustrations produced to create the components necessary to produce a printer-ready *mechanical*. At this point, the job is ready for the production step.

### Step 7. Complete the preprint production.

Production is the term used for getting a project ready for printing. This starts with assembling the type, photos, and illustrations into a mechanical. The mechanical is then sent to the printer for stripping (the process of converting the mechanical into film that will be used to create plates used for printing). The printer completes halftones and color separations of the illustrations and photographs and strips them into the film. Then the plates are "burned" for printing the piece. We have included more information on prepress production in Chapter 8.

Most designers oversee these production steps or do it themselves. Designers use two methods, depending on the nature of the job and the designer's preferences, to complete production steps—traditional drafting board methods or desktop publishing systems.

*Traditional production:* The designer (often using a paste-up artist to do the dull work) assembles the components of the job into a mechanical. The mechanical consists of sheets of illustration board with pasted down type, overlays for each color, and placed photocopies of images so the printer can see where to put them. The finished mechanical is then ready for the printer, who will complete the stripping, halftones, and color separations.

*Desktop publishing production:* With the advent of desktop publishing designers can now produce ready-to-print film with the aide of their own computers and desktop publishing software. The designers use an outside service bureau to output the film or resin-coated paper used to produce printing plates. One piece of film is used for each page, and in the case of multicolored pages, one additional sheet of film is required for each page. This output usually includes all elements of the page including images, type, and color information.

### Step 8. Print the piece.

The final step in producing collateral materials is for a print shop to lock the finished press plates onto a press and print the job. After printing, many jobs go to a bindery for trimming, folding, stapling, and special effects such as foil stamping or embossing. Usually your designer will attend a "press check" at the print shop to verify that everything is correct before the entire job is printed. If the designer will not go to the press check, you should.

**Step 9. Distribute the finished collateral piece.**   Finally, after delivery from the printer, the project is complete and ready for distribution. Most collateral material is stored and distributed as needed or sent to a distribution center. Distribution centers may be part of a department within large corporations or they may be completely independent businesses that handle materials from a number of different companies. The key to distribution, whether it is done from within the company or by an independent organization, is making the collateral tools easily accessible to those who need to use them.

Some collateral materials are sent in response to a phone inquiry, a bingo response from a magazine ad, or a business reply card. In these cases the requestor's name and address along with a special code number identifying the request should be quickly forwarded to the literature distribution center. A well-equipped center uses this code to produce the appropriate form letter on your stationery; it then picks out the right brochure and envelope from its inventory, and after stuffing, addressing, and adding postage, it drops the package into the mail. These centers may also be used to distribute packages of literature to sales offices and retail locations.

## GETTING THE MOST FROM COLLATERAL PROJECTS

To be effective collateral must get noticed and read. Here are several guidelines that will help.

- If you provide collateral to your dealers or distributors, make it free or inexpensive to use. After reviewing last year's budget, many companies decide to charge their retailers or distributors for all the brochures they are "wasting." It is not uncommon for these companies to charge inflated prices for the collateral too. The rationale is that dealers will hand out literature only to serious customers. The reality is that in many cases the dealer will resort to handing out muddy photocopies of the literature to avoid paying the bill. In extreme cases, a dealer or distributor will forgo using your materials and essentially stop selling your products. If you can't afford to distribute a piece of collateral for free, don't produce it.
- Make the literature ordering process easy. Many companies suffer from bureaucratic inertia. If the process to order literature is clumsy and slow, your salesforce and customers will quit requesting it. A busy distributor who is forced to spend an hour on the phone with a manufacturer to get literature will probably

not bother to repeat the process next time materials run low. He may also drop your product as sales fall off. Other companies make the mistake of locking all of the literature in a closet and rationing it piece by piece to the salespeople because it costs so much to produce. Like the distributors, your sales team will resort to ugly photocopies and leave the literature locked in the "vault."

- Some companies use a combination of collateral materials together in a folder called a *literature kit* (known as a *lit kit* in the trade) as a sales tool. Lit kits can include a capabilities brochure, product brochures, and perhaps a white paper or clippings of significant press materials. If you use a lit kit, make sure it contains all the information required to educate customers and nothing more. One company we are familiar with has a lit kit that contains 16 different items! Busy customers receiving this package can't tell the important from the superfluous and may miss the important material as a result. Keep your lit kit organized and hone the items down to five or six important ones—no more.

- Make copies of your basic literature available at tables in your lobby and anywhere else your customers or company visitors congregate. For example, if you run a car dealership, put stacks of literature in the service waiting area. Who knows, someone might come in for an oil change and leave with a new car!

- Make sure that all your collateral looks as if it came from the same company. Cosmetically different collateral confuses customers and reduces the overall effectiveness of your image-building efforts. This is sometimes difficult to control because each time you work with a new designer or design group, they will attempt to create their own look for you after tactfully criticizing the work done by others. Insist on keeping the look you already use. If you must change it, do it slowly and progressively unless you are entering a completely new market where few customers will have seen your existing materials.

- Avoid creating expensive collateral for a product that may change quickly or for a market that is new or unknown. Producing an expensive piece in these cases may tie you to ineffective materials that you can't afford to redo. Consider using a less expensive temporary piece instead until the elements stabilize.

## DIRECT MAIL: A POWERFUL SELLING TOOL FOR ALMOST ANY MARKET

For products with an audience identifiable by name and address, direct mail is a powerful yet economical tool for getting the word out. In fact, direct mail is frequently referred to as the world's largest promotional channel. Because a mailer can contain considerably more information than an ad, you can generate product awareness, and in most cases you can provide all of the information necessary for completing the sale in one promotion. Direct mail is a powerful tool for getting action from recipients and you should plan your mailers with that in mind by asking for a response and providing a means for making it.

Use direct mail to announce a sale or to introduce a hot new product. Make your mailers timely so people want to respond *right now*, because once they shelve your mailer, it is unlikely they will get back to it and respond. With the volume of direct mail many recipients receive, it is likely that without a means for immediate response, your offer is destined for a nonstop flight to the waste disposal facility.

As potentially persuasive as direct mail is, it has some serious disadvantages to consider. It will not work for products with target customers who are impossible to identify by address. For low-cost, mass-market products, such as shampoo, an extensive direct mail program may be too expensive to be cost-effective—although sending out samples in recent years has proved effective for some consumer goods manufacturers. Expensive consumer goods such as cars and furniture are difficult to sell directly with mail promotions, although you can use direct mail effectively to announce a sale or special promotion for these products.

One of the biggest difficulties with using direct mail is that it is increasingly abused as companies attempt to keep advertising expenses down. Most people receive piles of mailings both at work and at home. Some of these mailings offer nothing of interest and have no compelling appeal to respond. People get tired of the junk offers, so they quit opening or responding to any direct mail. As a result, direct mail marketing efforts must be especially well executed to stand apart from the trash.

## Direct Mail Formats Meet Different Objectives

There are two important components to direct mail promotions: the mailer itself and the mailing. The mailer consists of the physical piece of collateral to be sent to prospects. The mailing consists of selecting a mailing list and then sending the mailers to prospects on the list using the most expedient mailing method within the project's budget. Direct mailers can use a number of formats. The most common of these include the following:

**Letters and Postcards.**   The simplest form of direct mail is a letter on company stationery making a pitch for a new product or special offer. Letters and postcards are the rock-bottom direct mail option, but they can be effective if the letter is well written or the postcard is unusually compelling. For some markets such as fund-raising, this inexpensive tactic works well with hand-written addresses and signatures because it makes the effort appear more personal.

Use a letter approach if your budget is extremely tight and if the personal appeal of a letter is appropriate for your market. Don't use the letter approach unless you can make it look personal. Note that printing your signature in blue ink as is often done will not fool anyone. Use the postcard approach only if you can afford to print the card with at least a second color and preferably use an oversized card for better impact. Postcards work well for advertising hotels, property, new model cars, and grand openings of retail outlets. Put a four-color picture of your product on one side and then details on the back in two colors. Don't use this format if all you can afford is a small black and white postcard—you may alienate more customers than you gain and you certainly won't get their interest.

**Brochure and Letter Combination.** The brochure/letter combination is a very effective mailing technique that uses an existing brochure accompanied by a letter to personalize and introduce the product. The letter calls the customers to action by making a special offer or by asking them to respond in some way. This is a straightforward technique that works well for almost any product, particularly if you overprint the envelope and have an especially well-designed brochure that is ready to mail.

Use this approach if you have a very sales-oriented brochure already printed and you can afford to mail the quantity of the piece required for your market. If you are selling very upscale products such as luxury cars or palatial homes in the country, this is a tasteful approach, although it may take a while to get a noticeable response because of the long sales cycle associated with such products.

There are three weaknesses to consider if you choose this format:

1. If your brochure is expensive to print and your mailing list long, it may not be economical.
2. Unless your brochure is very "buy me now" oriented, you may not get the response you intended even with a strong letter. (Many recipients don't read the letters.)
3. Lengthy, full-sized brochures can be heavy to mail and the postage charges may swallow your budget.

**Custom Mailers.** For maximum impact a custom mailer is usually best. A custom mailer can be designed in any shape or size that can be easily mailed. It may be a dazzling six-color piece that stands out among the contents of the mailbox or it may be a minibrochure produced exactly as detailed in the collateral section. The total package may consist of an envelope packed with information, a catalog, coupons, or all three. Because a custom piece is planned as a mailer you can include plenty of "buy now" information and also provide as little or as much product detail as appropriate.

Use a custom direct mail piece whenever possible because you can impart a timely message to your customers and create just the right look to get noticed. Brightly (but tastefully) colored pieces work best, but if your budget is tight consider doing a one-color piece with a striking color such as bright turquoise. Surprisingly, grays sometimes work well for this kind of piece because they offend no one and they look different from all the brightly colored designs. To get maximum impact choose a designer with a real eye for design and an understanding of color and don't skimp on paper quality.

**Hop-Along Mailers.**   *Hop-alongs,* also called *hook* mailers and other less attractive names, are promotions sent with other mailings. These include advertisements stuffed in the same envelopes as credit card bills and stacks of postcards mailed as a block by magazines in technical industries. These can be effective promotions, but since they are usually going along for the ride, you will have little control over who receives your mailer. More importantly, the format may be extremely limited—usually a tiny insert produced on a lightweight paper to keep mailing costs down. In addition, your insert may get buried in a pile of similar promotions for other products.

Since many of these mailers are stuffed in monthly billings, recipients may not be in any rush to open the envelope. They also may have a negative mindset when they finally do get around to opening the bill. Hop-alongs are best used if you need to reach a large group of prospective customers and you aren't too choosy about timing or readership. This tool works well for selling perfume through department stores and magazine subscriptions through established channels such as Publisher's Clearing House. *Postcard packs* assembled by magazines targeted to niche technical markets often draw strong responses as well.

Don't use hop-alongs if your target market is comparatively small and focused because it won't be cost-effective. Don't rely on this tool for making short-term offers such as a two-day sale or a limited-time price reduction because you will have little control of the timing.

You can find out about hop-along possibilities by contacting an advertising agency that specializes in direct mail. Look in the telephone book under *Advertising—Direct Mail.* An alternative is to contact specific companies directly and talk to their advertising departments.

**Newsletters.**   Because of the ease-of-use and low cost of desktop publishing technology, a growing number of organizations are mailing regular newsletters to customers and prospects. Although a newsletter may appear to have more in common with a newspaper, its real purpose is to keep the company's name and products under the recipient's nose. The most effective newsletters offer special promotions and/or provide useful advice.

Newsletters are a different kind of direct mail tool because the best ones advertise products and services under the guise of education. They are effective for generating repeat business with existing customers but generally are not good for soliciting new customers. A well-assembled newsletter sent to the right person will not only get read, it may get saved for future reference, which gives it a longer life span than other kinds of mailers.

If you sell products that require substantial customer education such as computer software or expensive kitchen equipment such as food processors, newsletters are a good tool for maintaining customer loyalty. Use this tool only if you can dedicate the resources (people and money) to produce the newsletter on a regular basis and that means a minimum of four quarterly issues to be effective.

Keep in mind that newsletters require an established mailing list of customers compiled by salespeople or compiled by entering information from invoices or product registration cards. If you are contemplating such a project, check that such a list is available or initiate a program to build one.

On the down side, newsletters require a lot of work on a regular basis and once you have begun a newsletter program, your customers may object if you suddenly cancel it, mail it on an irregular basis, or let the editorial quality slip. It takes only one or two poor-quality issues for your customers to stop reading your newsletter, so you must be able to guarantee quality stories and writing as a part of this long-term commitment.

Don't use newsletters for inexpensive products sold to mass markets. No one wants to read a monthly newsletter on toothpaste or light bulbs and you will spend a lot of money on postage and printing to service such a large user base. By the same token, some products are simply not very interesting, even though customers could benefit from customer education. It is likely that a quarterly newsletter on maintaining stain-resistant carpet or on getting the most from a washing machine will hit the trashcan unread by the majority of recipients.

## Integrating Direct Mail with Other Promotions

Some companies thrive solely on direct mail promotions, including catalog houses and specialty product manufacturers. Other companies are spending a larger portion of their promotional budgets on direct mail promotions because of the controlled, targeted distribution and the relatively low cost. For most companies, however, direct mail is most effective when integrated into a balanced marketing communications mix. For example, focused advertising and publicity can be used to generate awareness and then direct mail can be used to close deals by building on the media-generated interest. Direct mail is also good for special offers and announcements that are not appropriate or effective when promoted through advertising media.

For companies that sell expensive or technologically sophisticated products, direct mail is usually not sufficient to promote products. Although your mailer may be persuasive, many customers will want to see a little more industry or market presence before taking a risk on your product. This presence is best built through advertising and public relations. As your reputation and credibility are enhanced with the other marketing communications, your direct mail efforts will be easier.

## THE DIRECT MAIL PROCESS: STEP-BY-STEP

Direct mail promotions follow a logical set of steps starting with objectives and concepts and ending with the customer response—the desired end result of all mailing programs.

**Step 1. Establish objectives for your direct mail campaigns.**   Like all forms of marketing communications, direct mail works best when goals for a program are set and the mailing program is designed to fulfill these objectives. Setting an objective for the direct mail campaign provides a yardstick with which to measure its success and helps keep the project focused throughout its implementation.

Targeting a direct mail Program is in many ways similar to targeting media advertising, to get the right message to the right people. This is accomplished by creating a mailer that appeals to and educates your market and then mailing to the list that contains the largest percentage of recipients from your target audience.

As in advertising, frequency in direct mail is also important. If you run a shop that sells tires and you send out a bimonthly mailing to residents in the area, your message may fall on deaf ears most of the year, but will get read and responded to when one of these people decides that the car needs new tires. That is why, depending on the nature of your business, you need to put together a complete direct mail program with multiple mailings and a schedule for the year. Some businesses mail as frequently as weekly, switching mailing lists to keep their message fresh and to reach a broad range of prospects. Other companies mail rarely but regularly—every time a special sale or offer is planned or when a new product is introduced. Most direct mail programs are planned on an annual basis with a mid-year review to accommodate market changes, surprises, and new promotional ideas.

**Step 2. Establish the mailing list sources.**   After establishing your objectives, which includes the target audiences you want to reach, you should choose a mailing list or lists that meet your audience requirements. The mailing list is central to the success of any direct mail program. You must choose the lists now because you can't assemble a budget without knowing how much postage will be required and how many mailer units must be printed or otherwise created. Rental lists vary considerably in price depending on degree of accuracy, size, and quality; this cost should go into your budget. There is a section with detailed information on selecting and using mailing lists later in this chapter.

**Step 3. Budget your direct mail program.**   After you know the objectives and mailing list options, you have to establish a budget for individual mailers and the entire direct mail program. The budget will include the costs for producing the mailers, the rental costs of commercial mailing lists, and the fees charged by the fulfillment house, if you use one, for handling your direct mail responses. Use the steps from the collateral section and Chapter 10 for determining your direct mail budget. And don't forget the charges for the postage. If you use a business reply card, remember that you have to budget for the return postage as well.

For a large mailing, a successful response is typically 2–5% of the people on the list. If you are selling expensive products the success rate may be less. There are some programs that generate a response as high as 25% or more, but these are rare. Before you finalize the budget and decide on the number of mailers to send out, consider the return on investment in your program. If you get a 2–5% response in the form of new sales, will this generate enough revenue to justify the cost of the promotion? If you are not sure of the response rate, conduct a pilot mailing to a well-targeted but small list to determine what you can expect.

**Step 4. Define the selling propositions for your direct mail piece.**   The propositions will be the focus or *hook* for the promotion, so the product and company messages you incorporate in the mailer will have a chance of being read and acted on. Effective direct mail promotions relay a sense of urgency and require immediate response from customers. To get customers to respond you must establish a proposition that will motivate them to take action. Some common propositions that work well in direct mail marketing include the following:

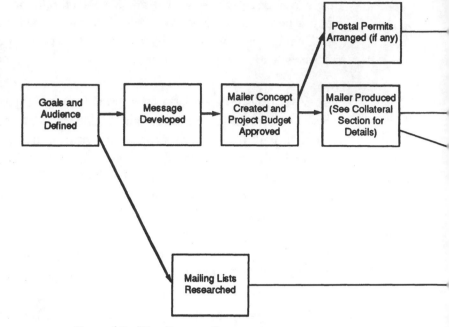

Figure 6.3. The direct mail process.

- Special pricing—including discounts, rebates, and introductory pricing.
- Combination offers—buy one product, get one free, or buy this product and get another kind of product for free.
- Contests or sweepstakes.
- Free gifts for trying a product out.
- Product trials and trial subscriptions.

In most direct mail propositions it is also important to emphasize guaranteed satisfaction, risk-free offers that encourage prospects to buy with confidence. In addition, the offer should be easy to implement. Whenever possible, take all forms of legitimate payment, including checks and credit cards.

In addition to the proposition, you must always plan the desired response before you create any direct mail promotion. Unlike advertising, which can be used to establish awareness or to build image and credibility over the long term, mailings that don't call customers to action have little impact and are usually forgotten. The only exception to this rule is the use of newsletters, which often include useful product information and may be kept longer than other mailings.

Means of response vary from product to product and company to company. If you run a retail store and you promote a big two-day sale (preferably starting the day after the mailer arrives), you have provided

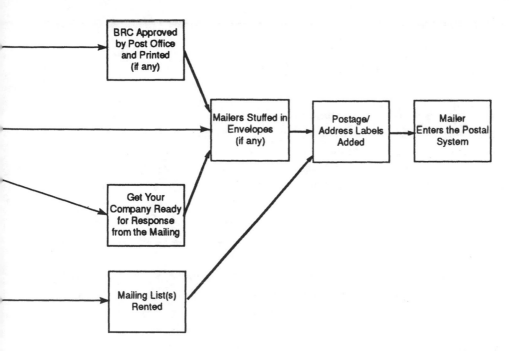

an intriguing special offer and an immediate means for customers to respond. If you are introducing a new product include a business reply card (BRC) in your mailer and a prominent toll-free phone number for customers to call for more information. Your salesforce can then follow up on these leads directly.

Couponing is also a viable tool for direct response. The mailer may not last more than seconds, but if the product is of interest, the coupons will get saved and used—even if they get passed to Aunt Hattie down the street. For some products offering a trade-in on a competitor's product is a powerful response generator. After taking (and most likely junking) the trade-in, you sell your product with a discount based on the "trade-in" value of the product. Another workable tactic is to provide a key or magic code that can be used to open a trunk of prizes or claim a numbered gift. This is a good way to get customers to visit a store to test their luck.

**Step 5. Establish a format for the mailer.** The format you choose for your direct mail campaign must match the objectives, audience, and your budget. Consider the standard options discussed earlier and see how they relate to your market and product image. If you decide that a custom mailer is right for you, follow the steps for establishing a format and design covered earlier in the collateral section of this chapter.

---

✎ TIP: GETTING NOTICED AMONG THE PEAS AND
CARROTS IN THE MAILBOX

Because there is such a high volume of direct mail activity, your first job is to stand out from the crowd in a prospect's mailbox whether at home or at the office. Bright colors, unusual shapes, intriguing statements, or the use of hand addressed envelopes are all excellent tools for getting your mailer noticed. If you are packaging a mailer in an envelope, get it overprinted with bright colors or captivating statements. At the very least stamp it with a large red rubber stamp that says something along the lines of "IMPORTANT INFORMATION ENCLOSED!" To get a better idea of what your competition is doing and how to look different, just open your mailbox.

---

As part of making a format decision, collect your competitor's materials to see what approaches they use. Consider imitating the format and improving on it. If your competition sends out a cheap black-and-white mailer with minimal design, hire a competent designer and print yours two-color! It is also helpful to find out which mailing lists your competitors use, but short of sheer luck if your name happens to be on the list and you can trace it to the list source, this is difficult.

**Step 6. Produce your mailer and any peripheral components such as giveaways, coupons, mailing envelopes, and dots to seal self-mailers.** If you are creating a custom mailer, follow the design, writing, and print steps presented for collateral materials. If your project includes a give away item such as a pen or other gee-gaw (see Chapter 6), these products typically take five to eight weeks to produce, so make sure they will be ready in quantity by your mailing date.

**Step 7. Arrange postage for your mailer and the business reply card if used.** If you are using bulk rate or a postage-paid BRC, allow several days for this process. You will need to get a permit and bar code for BRCs, which need to be printed on your card. You will also need to make an advance deposit with the post office for the return postage. And always review the final mechanical art for BRCs with the Postal Service—there are myriad specifications and requirements for BRCs and one "expert's" advice may differ from another's. It is a good idea to write down the name of the person who approves your reply card in case there is a problem later.

**Step 8. Get ready for responses in advance of the mailing.** If your direct mail program is worth doing, assume it will be successful. This means you will get more orders, phone calls, or customers in the door.

You must plan for handling these responses and inquiries well in advance of the mailing. Define an organized response system within your company or hire an outside fulfillment house (again, look under *Advertising—Direct Mail* in the *Yellow Pages*) to handle inquiries, purchases, or phone calls based on the mailing. If you are simply providing literature, make sure it goes out no more than 48 hours after the request is received. These requests must be serviced quickly so respondents don't forget what they requested.

---

### ✎ TIP: PUT YOURSELF ON THE LIST

It's a good practice to put yourself on all mailing lists your company compiles or uses. If you are renting a magazine list, become a subscriber. If you are using a list based on responses to a certain catalog, buy something from the company. At the very least have a mailer sent to you with every mailing. Getting yourself on the list is useful for several reasons. First, by slightly misspelling your name, say by adding or changing a middle initial, you can track where the list goes. If you find yourself receiving mail from a competitor who used that spelling on the mailing label, check into it. Second, you can check to see how long it takes to receive your mailing. Third, you can see the condition in which your mailer arrives after traveling a circuitous route through the Postal Service. And fourth, if you are using a mailing house, you can monitor how long it takes them to handle the mailing and whether your instructions are being followed to the letter.

---

If the response involves customers coming into the store for a sale, make sure your sales crew has seen the mailer and is ready for questions and increased traffic. Also ensure that adequate product inventory is on hand to meet the increase in demand.

For mailings that generate sales leads for an outside salesforce, have all salespeople return calls quickly and efficiently and document the customer's status after the phone call. There are inexpensive sales-tracking programs for many personal computers to handle this work. These programs will automatically schedule a sales call next week, document long-term interest, or put the lead in a "dead" file along with other unqualified prospects. In the case of return BRCs, don't be so eager that respondents get called the minute the cards cross your door. This implies that you are either desperate for business or use high-pressure salespeople—something experienced buyers have learned to avoid. Be responsive, but not overly zealous.

If yours is a large organization, ensure that the telephone receptionists know where to direct callers from your mailing. Some of these callers may be shy, confused about your company and its organization, or poor speakers of the language. Your receptionists should know to ask any hesitant caller if they are "phoning in response to the XYZ program they recently received in the mail," and then efficiently guide the caller to the right person.

If the mailing included BRCs, ask the person or persons responsible for sorting the mail to handle the BRCs as a priority, putting them on so and so's desk within an hour of receipt. All incoming BRCs should be logged to help you build your own mailing lists for future use and to make sure that leads are followed up, not just forgotten.

**Step 9. Mail the materials.**   Get ready for mailing by adding address labels and postage to each mailer. This may be done by you, a temporary employee(s), or an outside mailing house (most of these companies can also help with fulfillment after the mailing). Consider using a charity organization or group of handicapped people for this chore—every city has several organizations that will handle mailings efficiently and at the right price—and it helps them raise money for their worthwhile programs.

If your requirements demand presorted mailing labels by ZIP code, most mailing list providers will provide labels or lists arranged in this order. Just be careful to keep them and the resulting mailers in the proper order.

For high-volume mailings done in house, an automated postage machine speeds the process, but it takes some of the personal quality out of the mailing. If you are attempting to target your mailer to arrive on a certain day of the week, consider staggering a national mailing to give farther-traveling units more time to arrive.

The timing of your mailing is also important. Time the mailing so your promotion arrives on a good day—that is a day when your prospective audience will be the most receptive to your message and there is less competing mail. For business to business mailers, Monday is usually a tough day at the office. Tuesday through Thursday are good days to get to businesspeople in their most receptive mood. Friday is usually a poor choice because although your audience may be in an upbeat mood, they may forestall action until Monday and subsequently forget your offer. Remember that if you are mailing to large companies, your mailing may spend a full day in the mail room and internal delivery system before it arrives at its destination. That means that your Thursday arrival may turn into a Friday delivery.

---

### ✎ TIP: GETTING STUFFED AND MAILED THE EASY WAY

If you are managing a large mailing project with a big list, consider using a mailing house to handle the entire process. There are local, national, and international companies that specialize in handling all phases of direct mail promotions. A big mailing house is capable of providing you with a well-qualified mailing list (from a large catalog of possibilities), can help you develop the mailer, and will take the individual components of your package, *stuff* them in the mailing envelope by machine or using a team of people, and apply the address labels and postage. Best of all they will even drive the mound of mailers to the post office in a tractor trailer if necessary, ready for immediate departure to points south. And when the leads start coming in, they can enter the information in computer databases and even ship your products or literature. It costs more to have them do all this, but it is easier and more efficient.

Timing for mailing to a residence is different than to a business. If your product sells to homemakers, any weekday is a good possibility because people who don't work outside their home have lots of time to read their mail and act on it. If your product is a consumable likely to be purchased by working spouses, a Friday delivery is a good date because many of these consumers do their shopping on Saturday or Sunday. Weekends are also "home improvement" and "fix the car" days, so Friday or Saturday is a good arrival time for promotions that appeal to these activities.

**Step 10. Manage the responses expediently.**   The response mechanisms covered in Step 8 should already be in place, so it is now time to aggressively deal with all the leads and sales you will receive. If you've done it right, you shouldn't have long to wait! But you can't rest yet—if your mailing schedule is aggressive, it's time to start work on the next mailer!

## GETTING THE MOST FROM DIRECT MAIL PROMOTIONS

Here are some ways to make your direct mail promotions reap more positive responses:

- Keep your copy short, tight, and easy to read. If your customers need a lot of information before purchasing the product, consider providing this information as a follow-up to phone calls and returned BRCs. Or include the information in a separate document sent in the same envelope, but make sure that the first thing recipients notice is your primary proposition, not the details.
- Display your address and phone number in more than one place on the mailer, so people can't miss them. If your mailing is being sent to non-English-speaking countries, include a FAX number so people can place orders or get information quickly without having to cross the language barrier.

- Never mail the same mailer or letter to the same people twice. Don't print a three-year supply of a mailer expecting it to be relevant that long. The same mailer the second time around has almost no impact.

- Avoid the "deluge approach." This is when an organization mails to the same list as frequently as once a week. Although becoming more common for highly competitive local promotions offering specials for pizza delivery and a variety of tacky supermarket coupons, there are far too many of these circulating to be effective. Recipients may enjoy the attention initially, but quickly become annoyed with the constant clutter in their mailbox. This is particularly true of mailers that look basically the same from week to week and repetitive mailings from companies in which recipients have no interest.

- Avoid adding gift items to your package unless they are properly packaged. For example, if part of your mailing includes a free pen, the machinery at the Postal Service will usually not harm the pen, but the printed surface of your mailer will be damaged if you don't protect it.

---

### ✎   TIP: SELF-MAILING OR PUT IT IN AN ENVELOPE?

Depending on the nature of your piece, you can choose to mail it in an envelope or to use a self-mailing format with the customer's address stamped directly on the piece. The advantage of a self-mailer is that an exciting piece can get immediate attention and there is no cost for envelopes. The disadvantage is that the piece may become soiled and wrinkled in the mail.

If you use a self-mailing format, take precautions in the design stage to give your piece the best chance of survival. First, make it smaller than 8 1/2 × 11 inches when folded closed. A compact mailer has a better chance of arriving unscathed than a larger piece. Second, use a stiff paper stock for the job. Stiff paper holds up better through the mail. Third, use a paper that doesn't take marks easily. If you print on a fibrous uncoated stock, it gets smudged instantly by dirty fingers and machinery. And fourth, if the piece folds, close it securely so it can't "spread its wings" on the postal conveyor and get damaged. Round adhesive dots work well for this. Avoid staples because the postal machines reject them and recipients break fingernails and cut themselves on them.

---

- Try to avoid mailing during the Christmas season, from Thanksgiving to after New Year's Day. Mail volume is horrendous at this time of year, so your mailer will have even more competition. Also if your mailing requires timely delivery for an upcoming event, with the mass of Christmas cards and gifts taxing the Postal Service resources, you will have no guarantee of arrival dates. Business-to-business mailing during this period suffers too. While most companies don't see the volume of Christmas cards and packages that residences do, many people don't really get their mind back to work until mid-January. This means that recipients may be interested in your offer but shelve it for response "next week" and then forget about it.

- Be aware of international mail regulations! If mailing from the United States to Canada or vice versa, postage rates are different and bulk rate and BRC permits are not valid across borders. Make sure that your mailer plainly displays *Printed in {country}* or postal inspectors can refuse to accept it. If mailing to Mexico send it airmail if you want the piece to arrive on time. Mark the mailer with a large red *AIRMAIL* stamp. And always put the name of the country prominently on all mail that crosses borders. One of our letters to a relative spent a month in Ontario, California before being forwarded to Toronto, Ontario, because we forgot to add the magic word, *Canada!*

- If you are doing your own addressing and the list is sorted alphabetically, look for duplicate addressees and weed them out. Recipients who receive twelve of your "limited special offers" will not take your offer seriously. Quality rented lists rarely have this problem, but if you are using several related lists this is a common occurrence. To avoid this problem when renting multiple lists from the same mailing list provider, ask them to do a *merge-purge* on the lists to identify and eliminate duplicate names. This means that with the help of a computer, they will merge all the lists rented into one master list to find and erase the duplicates. If there is substantial duplication, you should not have to pay for the names that were removed.

- If you are mailing a "price-reduced" mailer to prospects, try not to send it to your existing customers. Few things irritate purchasers more than receiving notification that the product they paid $350 for two weeks ago can now be bought for just $99. If your company has a return policy, you may see more merchandise returned and then repurchased at the lower price than you see new sales.

## CHOOSING A MAILING LIST

There are four broad categories of mailing lists to consider for your direct mail needs: *compiled lists,* based on compilations of names from telephone books, product registrations, memberships in associations, or many other sources; *response lists,* based on customers who have responded to mailings in the past; *business lists,* based on business-to-business marketing and including names, titles, and company locations; and *house lists,* compiled by individual companies for their own needs.

The best lists for your direct mail project are the ones that reach the maximum number of recipients potentially interested in your product for the least cost. For example, if you are looking for money for your not-for-profit community action group, you would do better mailing to a list of people who have contributed money to similar causes in the past than to mail to a list simply culled from the telephone book. The latter list will cost you less to rent but your "hit rate" will be substantially lower and a larger percentage of your mailers will fall on deaf ears. Response lists, whether you rent these or create your own, are generally more effective (and more expensive) than arbitrary compilations because the people have a qualified history of buying products similar to yours through the mail.

If you choose to rent a list, it may be available in a number of *sort* formats. For an additional charge, the recipient's phone number may also be available. So you might rent a list of male homeowners living within three specific ZIP code areas making more than $35,000 per year. You then pay the small extra charge for the phone numbers so that your salespeople can follow up on the mailing with a timely phone call.

---

## ✎    TIP: COMPILE YOUR OWN RESPONSE LISTS FOR CUSTOM TARGETING

Many companies fail to track inquiries or responses to their mailings and lose the repeat business possible from these names and addresses. With the help of a computer database program or an index card system you can easily maintain information on all customers and prospects who have done business or inquired about your products. In addition to their names, addresses, and phone numbers, include information on what they bought, how much they paid, and when they purchased. In companies that sell high-ticket items that rely heavily on personal contacts for sales, add a level of depth to the database that includes background on spouses, children, personal preferences, and interests.

---

### Where to Rent Mailing Lists

Mailing lists are available from a number of commercial sources. You can go to a mailing list broker to find mailing lists or have lists created for you by compilation companies. Look for both of these services in the *Yellow Pages* under *Mailing Lists* or *Advertising—Direct Mail*. The most common source for locating mailing lists is the reference section of a well-stocked public library. There you'll find the standard *Direct Mail Lists and Data* and *Guide to Consumer Mailing Lists* produced by the Standard Rate and Data Service (SRDS).

The directories published by SRDS include descriptions of the lists, rental rates, and restrictions. The listings for each source provide detailed information on the demographics of the list, market segmentation criteria, and prices quoted in dollars per thousand names. Companies and sources that compile and sell their mailing lists through SRDS publications and list brokers include:

- Magazines.
- Mailing list companies that develop mailing lists based on a wide variety of sources.
- Credit card companies and banks.
- Direct mail advertisers or companies that sell their own list to make a few extra dollars.
- Clubs, not-for-profit groups, and professional organizations.
- Tradeshow companies that track participants.
- Catalog companies.
- Phone company listings. Yes, an increasing number of regional and national phone companies and long distance suppliers will rent mailing lists of telephone service subscribers. It is faster than copying the phone book.

When you consider a list in a SRDS reference or through a broker, look at the buying history of the list being offered for rental. There are three things to consider: recency, frequency, and unit sale. The *recency* of the list is based on the time between the date the list is rented and the date the people sent in their last order or inquiry. More recent is better. The *frequency* is the number of times a prospect has purchased from the company renting the list, the length of membership, or the amount of time someone has been a subscriber. The more frequent, the better. *Unit sale* is the highest dollar amount of purchases the customer has made through the mail. If your product is expensive and the amount is low, consider a list with a higher unit sale.

Most list providers guarantee list accuracy by setting a maximum percentage of *dead labels*—recipients who have moved, changed jobs, or fled the country. A validity of 95% is a common figure for most commercially available lists. The list provider will reimburse you for excessive returned mailings. Read the fine print in the rental agreement to see how this works and what the percentage of guarantee is for a given list before renting it.

If you plan to use the same list more than once, buy it for all of your mailings at the same time to receive the multiple-use discount. This can save you a substantial sum of money when renting a large, high-quality list for several mailings spread throughout a year or more.

---

### ✎  TIP: REMEMBER THAT MAILING LISTS ARE RENTED, NOT PURCHASED

Renting mailing lists can be expensive, especially if you want to do repeated mailings to the same people with a quality list. You may find yourself tempted to copy the names for future use without paying the rental fee. If so, be forewarned that mailing list providers protect their interests by imbedding "test names" in each list. These test names, usually impossible to separate out, are actually conduits back to the list provider as a check to see if list renters are reusing the list without paying. So, if you reuse a list without authorization and the company gets tipped off, you may receive a bill, or worse, a deputy may appear in your office with a subpoena. A safer, legal alternative is to negotiate in advance a fair price for multiple uses of the list.

---

### Where to Get Names for Free to Make Your Own Lists

There is a wide variety of free sources for creating mailing lists, but with many of these sources no zip codes are included. Get around this with a copy of the inexpensive zip code directory from the Postal Service or use one of the computerized zip code search programs available for personal computers. Although looking up names in a directory is tedious, particularly if you are attempting to assemble a long list, the price is low and you own this list rather than having to pay a rental fee every time you use it! Common sources for compiling your own mailing lists include

- New business listings and vital statistics columns in newspapers.
- Chamber of Commerce listings.
- Industry guides.
- Names collected from a contest or drawing.
- Telephone books.
- Product registration and warranty cards.
- Tradeshow attendees.
- Salespeople's leads.

### Mailing List Problems

Mailing lists suffer from five major problems that can negatively affect the results of your direct mail promotions.

**1. The list may be stale.**   Mailing lists get dated quickly as people move, change jobs, get married, are born and die, and as companies open and close their doors. The stalest lists are usually the cheapest. Avoid this problem by using criteria other than price to choose your list. Demand a list that enjoys regular updating, testing, and verification. Magazine subscriber lists are particularly fresh because people are paying to get the magazine and will transfer the subscription as they move around on the home or job front. Don't confuse these lists with ones from throw-away magazines sent free or unsolicited. These lists may be years out of date or contain names of people who regularly trash the publication unopened.

**2. The list may be inappropriate.**   Mailing lists must closely match the profile of your intended market. Sometimes only a small portion of a list may really qualify as prospective customers, although you may be led to believe otherwise. Avoid this problem by carefully reviewing the credibility of the list provider and the demographic data on the list, and by choosing well-targeted segments of the list when you place your order. If you are using a magazine mailing list, look through the magazine to see what kind of companies and products are advertised. If they don't match your market, keep looking. If you are considering some other kind of list, ask for references to call that have used it before to evaluate its success rate. If a list provider will not cooperate in assuaging your concerns, find another list provider—there's no shortage of them.

**3. The list may be inaccurate or sloppy.**   Lists are often compiled by bored data entry clerks who make numerous mistakes. Misspelling people's name or sex is offensive even when not deliberate. *Ms. Sunny Baker* for years received irritatingly misaddressed mailings based on a master list that had her down as *Mr. Sony Baher*—three mistakes in one name—who knows what the rest of the list looked like! Avoid this problem by asking to look at the list. Obvious and frequent misspellings of standard names, like common cities for example, point to a serious compilation error rate.

**4. The list may be shallow.**   A single list may not include enough names relevant to your needs, forcing you to buy several other lists to get adequate coverage and penetration. This costs more and may mean mailing to a large number of people with absolutely no interest in your product. Avoid this problem by considering either another list source or forgoing the direct mail route and using advertising to get the word out.

**5. The list may be overused.**   Some lists are used so much that the recipients receive a wheelbarrow full of mail each day. The bulk of this mail never gets opened. Avoid this problem by rotating lists and list sources.

Although you will inevitably encounter an oversubscribed mailing list, through rotation you will avoid encountering this problem on every mailing. Better still, through rotation you may reach people whose names appear on no other lists and subsequently get little competing direct mail.

### Mailing Labels

Unless you address your mailers by hand (always more work than it seems it will be), you will probably resort to mailing labels. The most common format for labels purchased from a mailing list provider are *Cheshire labels.* These are nonperforated, ungummed listings printed four abreast on a sheet by a computer. The labels must be cut apart and glued by a machine designed for this purpose.

Increasingly common, but slightly more expensive, are peel-off labels that can easily be affixed by hand. If you plan to do your own mailing, this is the format for you. If you are working with your own mailing lists, these labels can be purchased by the box and run through a computer-driven dot matrix, daisy wheel, or laser printer to imprint the names and addresses. Make sure the labels you buy are designed for the printer you use because some kinds may leave a label stuck in your printer's mechanism resulting in a potentially expensive repair.

When renting a list, it is important to specify (in writing) what format you want it in. Most lists offer Cheshire labels, gummed labels, and computer tape or disk formats. If you aren't specific, your list may appear as unwieldy Cheshire labels or a useless line listing on a ream of computer paper.

---

 ### TIP: TREAT AMBIGUOUS NAMES AS GENDER NEUTRAL

If you don't know the sex of Terry, Karin, Arny, or Jerry, use Dear Jerry without a title. Although some people may take minor offense at the use of their first name, it is much less objectionable than misidentifying their sex. If you get the gender wrong you will offend your customer. Take it from Kim, the male co-author of this book, who used to receive regular mailings from *Ms. Magazine.* Unfortunately *he* wasn't interested in subscribing. The magazine is no longer published. Could this have anything to do with the magazine's demise?

---

## POSTAL CONSIDERATIONS FOR DIRECT MAIL

The seemingly most obvious approach to postage is to take the cheapest route—bulk rate. But, for many reasons, this is not always the best decision.

First, mail that arrives trumpeting a "special offer reserved for you only" is going to lack credibility if obviously sent bulk rate. Many people look through their stacks of mail and drop all bulk rate material in the trash without opening it. Second, if your promotion is of a timely nature, you cannot be assured of delivery dates with bulk mail. So, you must mail early and risk people forgetting about an event or opportunity, or mail late and risk your proposition showing up after it's over. (It happens occasionally and frustrates interested recipients.) Third, a recent test showed that almost one-fourth of bulk rate mail with deliverable addresses never showed up.

If you have spent $1.50 per mailing for the contents and the mailer doesn't make it to the intended recipients, does it make sense to save a few pennies per mailer? Can you afford to send one-quarter of your mailing to the Twilight Zone? Note that this waste is in addition to the bulk rate mailers with bad addresses, which simply get tossed by the Post Office. Since these don't come back to you, you can't use this information to update your mailing lists.

Instead of bulk rate, consider using presorted mail—it is still cheaper than first class and your mailing will arrive looking fresh and credible. If you have the money and are short on time, use First Class with its speedy and timely delivery. With First Class you don't need to spend time sorting by ZIP code and there are no permits to get or extra trips to the Post Office. You also get undeliverable mailers returned so you can update your mailing lists and First Class mail generally gets the best treatment from the Postal Service.

To get the maximum impact from First Class, don't use a postage meter, because your recipients may not notice the rate. Instead use stamps—handsome commemorative ones work best. Your mailing house (if you use one) may charge a little more to apply stamps but the positive impression is often worth it, especially if your are making an invitation to a customer to attend a special event or special promotion.

Weight is another consideration for your mailing. Assemble a *dummy* made up of all components in the package before you produce the pieces. Weigh it carefully on a properly calibrated scale and estimate the postage. A mailer that is extremely close in weight to the upper limits of a weight category may occasionally go over after labels, stamps, and ink are added or after a faulty postal scale weighs it in. This could result in a substantial increase in postal charges.

Another approach to direct mail that still has impact is to make a "big splash mailing" using overnight delivery by the post office or a private carrier or other similar service. Sound extreme? It is for most markets, but consider a company introducing a new piece of machinery priced at over $200,000 and of use to only 200 companies in the world. By mailing overnight delivery, they can get their message directly to the customer much more effectively than a regular mailing. This approach is still relatively inexpensive compared to purchasing advertising media to reach the same group. And overnight and special delivery mail gets more attention than First Class mail. If you have enough overnight mail volume, you can usually negotiate a reduced rate with the private shipping companies. Considering that salespeople selling to out of town customers regularly make $10 phone calls, hour after hour, the cost of an overnight mailing is easy to justify for some markets.

## Testing List and Mailer Effectiveness

Direct mail programs are measured by the responses they generate. One of the biggest factors in the success of your program will be the quality of the mailing list. If you are unsure about the demographics, integrity, or appropriateness of a mailing lists do a test mailing with the list first. Most companies will let you purchase a small subset of a list, called a pilot list, for this. Using a stale or inappropriate list is like throwing money down the drain. You may get money back on a percentage of returned mailers from the list provider but nothing will be returned by a list with valid addresses but uninterested recipients. In either case you may miss a one-time market window opportunity or have to rerun the program all over again.

If your pilot test doesn't give you the desired response rate, consider, before you dismiss the mailing list, that something may be wrong with the promotion itself. The message may be wrong or the mailer may lack impact. This can be tested in the same ways discussed before for advertising and collateral materials. You may spend money on the tests, but the bulk of your budget remains in the bank while you identify and fix the problems.

Between collateral materials and direct mail, there are a lot of choices and plenty of options. The good news is that you control what you get—the bad news is that you also get what you pay for. Both collateral materials and direct mail play an important role in an overall marketing communications strategy, a role that is often overlooked by your advertising agency if you have one, so it's important to define your own needs in these areas.

One final thought—both elaborate or unusual collateral materials and custom direct mail pieces often get saved. They may get put into a manilla folder on products similar to yours, or they may end up in the hands of someone with an eye for literature that will become collectable in the future. So the piece you produce today could get reread many times. This may mean that today's collateral project may ultimately end up with voice in places you never considered. Before you send something out, make sure it is something you want to be held responsible for in the future.

# 7 | Other Communications Tools: Using Identity, Tradeshows, Packaging, and Special Promotions for Best Results

To this point we have covered the major tools in a marketing communications mix; but there are other important tools in the marketing communications toolbox that you should know how to use. These include company identity programs, tradeshows, product packaging, and special promotional items.

By simply attending the right tradeshow with a credible booth, you can not only generate leads for new business, but can also make a large segment of an entire industry instantly aware of your products and organization. Of course, attending the same show with a couple of wrinkled signs pinned up to the backdrop and a rental table will also make people aware of you, but their perception of you and your products will most likely be negative. The tools described in this chapter are important image builders. Used incorrectly, they can do sizable harm; used correctly, they can go a long way to building or reinforcing a positive image and some of them can be used to generate immediate sales. The chapter provides advice that can help you use the tools effectively to get positive results at the lowest cost.

## TRADESHOWS BUILD AWARENESS AND IMAGE

Tradeshows are organized events attended by large numbers of people sharing similar interests. Shows and conventions come in all sizes and cover almost all products and services. There are industry tradeshows, consumer tradeshows, recreational tradeshows, conventions for professional organizations that incorporate product displays, and even special interest shows, such as the ones for Star Trek fans. Tradeshows may be international, national, regional, or local in appeal. Like advertising media, every tradeshow has a target audience and definable demographics.

Many tradeshow attendees are prospects, considering a purchase of goods or services displayed at the show. Other people who attend include the press, job seekers, consultants, industry analysts, and, at some shows, pickpockets and thieves. Depending on the show, there may be a narrow range of closely related products featured, or a wide range of vaguely related wares as displayed in "home improvement shows."

Attendance at a tradeshow requires three basic things—begetting a booth, be it a folding table or multimillion dollar colossus, renting a display space on a show floor, be it a dusty area in an dirt arena or the precisely measured concrete floor space of a massive city convention center, and staffing the booth with enthusiastic, knowledgeable people to discuss your products with show attendees.

## Tradeshows Give Companies a Physical Presence in the Market

Most companies choose to attend tradeshows to supplement other communications activities because, by themselves, tradeshows are not always effective selling tools. Although some products get sold at shows, few expensive purchase commitments will be made by attendees not already familiar with an exhibitor's products.

Tradeshows are best used for:

- Building company and product awareness among prospective customers.
- Building industry presence.
- Generating sales leads.
- Closing sales on inexpensive "impulse" purchases.
- Keeping an eye on the competition.
- Building press awareness.
- Announcing new products.

Attending a tradeshow is a lot of work, and it can be costly in terms of money and time, but for many businesses the rewards substantially outweigh the effort and expense. Because tradeshows can provide immediate, targeted visibility, a growing number of companies are exhibiting in as many shows as they can afford. This in turn has spurred more and more shows, which have become increasingly specialized along product and interest lines.

Even cities are getting into the act by building bigger convention facilities capable of housing several large shows simultaneously and spending considerable sums attracting shows of all kinds. And what better way for a bored middle manager to take a three-day vacation with the company's money than by attending a show in a favorite city?

On the downside, with the burgeoning number of shows, it is becoming difficult to choose just the right one(s) in which to participate. Exhibiting in all prospectively useful shows is cost prohibitive for all but the largest corporations.

### Finding Out About Tradeshows in Your Industry

How can you find out about tradeshows in your industry? If you read the standard trade journals and publications for your industry, you will find out about them because the important shows and conferences are reviewed and promoted in these sources. The Chamber of Commerce is often a good starting place for finding out about smaller, local shows. A full-service advertising agency will also be able to advise you about the shows in your industry that work and the shows that are duds. Ask them, or ask people who have been in the industry for a while. In addition, industry associations and clubs are good sources of information about tradeshows. In fact, many of them have their own conferences and tradeshows that you may want to attend.

If you want to look at a wide range of tradeshow possibilities across industries, there is an annual guide produced by Meetings Databank out of New York called *Tradeshows and Exhibits Schedule* that lists the locations, dates, and producers, among other information, about shows, conferences, and exhibits around the country.

## THE TRADESHOW PROCESS: GETTING THERE IS HALF THE FUN!

Tradeshows can be bewildering because of the sheer amount of detail required to acquire and outfit, ship, and then effectively staff a booth during the show. Here is a summary of an effective step-by-step process for maximizing your results from tradeshows:

**Step 1. Educate yourself about the shows and then establish your objectives.** Like all marketing communications activities, attending a tradeshow should start with planning. If you do your planning right, you can choose the shows most appropriate for your company. Start by requesting the show kits and reading them. Then, go to some shows to learn about them. Evaluate each show's effectiveness at drawing the right profile of customers for your market. Some shows get much lower attendance than the literature claims. You certainly don't want to go through the expense and work to reach a show with low attendance.

Visiting shows also provides an excellent opportunity to study your competitors' booths and booth traffic. By watching their booths, you will get an idea of how successful they are selling goods, taking orders, or getting leads for future follow up. Your competitor's success (or lack of) demonstrates whether the right kind of customers are at the show. Some shows will be more precisely tuned to your market than others and by watching how the competition fares, you can decide whether your participation is justified.

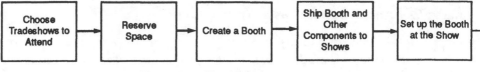

Figure 7.1. The tradeshow process.

Use this review process to get a jump on your competition's booth design. Study their displays to see what works and what doesn't. When studying a competitor's booth, evaluate the following:

- **Booth size.**  Measure booth size by casually counting your steps as you walk by a booth. Booth spaces are sold by square or rectangular spaces in set sizes, 10 × 20, 20 × 20, or 40 × 60 feet, or metric sizes in Canada. In a convention hall, you will quickly become adept at judging booth size because most halls put all similar sized small booths together in rows. The large booths get premium placement in the center of the show and by the entrances.

- **Booth position.**  In all shows, the prime locations sell out first and there may be a surcharge for them. Most tradeshow companies offer the best spaces to last year's attendees. Although you can't compete with companies that have rented space in the same show for 10 years and subsequently bettered their position on the show floor, you may be able to get better placement than your competition by renting a slightly bigger space.

- **Construction of the booth.**  Is it simple or ornate? Does it look old and dirty or fresh and new? Identify the size and kind of graphics used. Are they lit with floodlights or back lit? Does the booth make use of the space above it? If so, how? Some booths take up two stories of vertical space or have banners hanging from the ceiling. Is it an inexpensive prefab model that folds up into a suitcase? Do they have a display area, seating, or a stage? What is unique about the booth? With this information, you can design a booth that will match or improve on the look used by your competition.

Consider taking a camera on your tradeshow outings and snapping shots of booths you particularly like or dislike for future study. Snap pictures of your competitors' booths too. This will be useful in building a booth that outshines theirs because your booth designer can build on your competitors' examples while not repeating their mistakes. (The lighting in tradeshows is often a problem for photographers. Use a camera

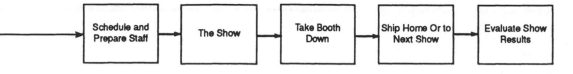

loaded with fast film and a flash with a "long throw" that requires minimal setup before and between each shot.)

After you educate yourself on what shows are available and what your competitors do, you need objectives for the tradeshows you will attend. They can be simple long-term goals such as "continue to build awareness of our company and the new XYZ product line" or short-term goals as specific as "introduce the new ZXY 1000 as a superior solution to the competition's." Having these objectives in mind will allow you to review design drawings or step back from a nearly finished booth and ask yourself, "Does this booth meet this goal?" Your objectives will help you evaluate a booth's overall effectiveness at delivering a strong, but simple message. Yes, even tradeshow booths deliver messages.

After establishing your objectives, you can decide which shows you want to attend, based on the attendance demographics, timing, and location of each show.

**Step 2. Determine the right show and reserve space well in advance.**
Calling the show producer (either a private company that specializes in tradeshows or the club, professional organization, or company that sponsors a particular event) for more information will get you a *show kit*. This kit consists of general information about the tradeshow including time, place, featured speakers, educational events, available space, and rental prices. The kit should also discuss attendance projections and audience demographics.

If you find that the show matches your needs, you will want to see about reserving space. Remember, the earlier you decide to attend, the better the space you will be able to rent. The kit will include a space reservation form and the show's (often extensive) rules and regulations. The kit also provides you with a floor plan for the show with the committed major exhibitor's spaces marked by name. Study this layout carefully to select the best space for your needs. A call to the show's coordinator (his or her name and phone number will accompany the kit) will bring you details of which spaces are available and which are booked. Reserve space verbally and then complete the form and send it along with a check to "seal the deal." Reserve as early as possible because shows sometimes sell out. If you don't book early, you will end up in the show's equivalent of Siberia.

Tradeshow Schedule From (date): ——————————   To: ——————————

Today's Date: ——————————

Shows Selected to Attend:
| Show Name | City | Dates | Booth Size |
|---|---|---|---|
| ———— | ———— | ———— | ———— |
| ———— | ———— | ———— | ———— |
| ———— | ———— | ———— | ———— |
| ———— | ———— | ———— | ———— |
| ———— | ———— | ———— | ———— |

Shipping Company and Phone Number: ——————————————

Other Equipment to Be Sent to Each Show:
| Show Name | Equipment |
|---|---|
| ———— | ———— |
| ———— | ———— |
| ———— | ———— |
| ———— | ———— |
| ———— | ———— |

Booth Arrival/Departure Dates for Each Show (List in Order and Watch for Overlap!):
| Show Name | Arrival Date | Departure Date |
|---|---|---|
| ———— | ———— | ———— |
| ———— | ———— | ———— |
| ———— | ———— | ———— |
| ———— | ———— | ———— |
| ———— | ———— | ———— |

People to Man Booth at Each Show:
| Show Name | People |
|---|---|
| ———— | ———— |
| ———— | ———— |
| ———— | ———— |
| ———— | ———— |
| ———— | ———— |

Figure 7.2. Tradeshow planning worksheet.

**Step 3. Design and construct the booth.**   A basic prefab booth may be bought, rented, or borrowed. Booths may also be custom designed from scratch or purchased used and rebuilt. You will need to have your booth ready to ship at least two weeks before the show. Along with the booth itself, you will need graphics to decorate the booth, display tables, carpet, chairs, and other peripheral items. Many of these can be rented directly from the convention hall itself if you are attending that kind of show, but you must settle for functional and ugly rather than attractive choices.

Even the simplest booth needs the following:

- Attractive, readable sign with the company's name and logo.
- Graphics that explain key features of your product or message.
- Display area for the products.
- Room for literature to be handed out to interested people.
- Room for people to stand and move through the booth.

If you are going to a large industry show, you will also want to create a give-away of some kind—ranging from plastic bags with your logo for holding literature to elaborate gee-gaws, discussed later in the chapter.

When you visit the tradeshows you will see the possibilities and the appropriate kind of design for your space. Booth space is always smaller than it seems in the floor plans—so don't clutter your booth with too many elements. Simple is better in booth design. There are companies that specialize in designing and manufacturing tradeshow booths that will help you review the costs and possibilities.

The least expensive booths are portable, prefab backdrops for small spaces (up to 10 × 10 feet) that attach the graphics with Velcro fasteners. These are best for small local and regional tradeshows. These portables come with shipping cartons with wheels and a handle. They can be assembled by one reasonably tall person. Beyond that, the booth possibilities are endless—again, limited only by budget, audience, and objectives. Companies spend as little as $3500 for an attractive portable booth and graphics and as much as a million dollars or more on booths for major industry extravaganzas. There is more about buying and renting booths later in the chapter.

If you are doing a custom booth, remember that they take lots of time. And always assemble the booth once at a warehouse or at the company to see how it goes together and how it looks in final form. You will almost always want to make changes to the booth once you see it assembled—so allow time for this.

**Step 4. Ship the booth and other materials to the show.**   In the paperwork provided with the show kit, you will find a schedule that details when your booth must arrive at the show and specifies time restrictions for setting it up. Ship all components together and ensure in writing that the shipping company knows and understands the delivery schedule. In addition to your booth and furniture, you need to include the materials

**Booth Hardware**
- ☐ Booth and Fittings
- ☐ Carpet for Booth
- ☐ Chairs for Booth
- ☐ Demonstration Equipment
- ☐ Dolly for Moving Equipment (If You're Doing It Yourself)
- ☐ Extension Cords (Heavy Gauge Preferable)
- ☐ Gloves for Handling Heavy/Sharp -Edged Equipment
- ☐ Graphics
- ☐ Keys for Shipping Cases
- ☐ Lights for Booth
- ☐ Power Bars
- ☐ Tools/Equipment for Set-Up/Take-Down
- ☐ Shipping Cases for Booth and Other Components
- ☐ Tables for Booth

**Booth Supplies**
- ☐ Business Cards (Bring Plenty)
- ☐ Card Imprinter for Imprinting Show-Provided Plastic ID Cards
- ☐ Giveaways Such as Shopping Bags or Gee-Gaws
- ☐ Invoices/Estimating Forms/Proposal Forms
- ☐ Pens (Bring Extras)
- ☐ Press Kits
- ☐ Products and/or Samples
- ☐ Product Literature

**Logistics**
- ☐ Airline Reservations (Bring Itinerary)
- ☐ Booth Assembly Instructions (To Make Assembly Easier)
- ☐ Car Rental Reservations (Bring Confirmation Numbers!)
- ☐ Hotel Reservations (Bring Confirmation Numbers!)
- ☐ Instruction Manuals for Difficult to Assemble Equipment
- ☐ Inventory of All Shipped Boxes and What They Contain

- ☐ Local Telephone Number for Shipping Company
- ☐ Schedules (To Be Given to All Booth Personnel)
- ☐ Shipping Permits and Custom's Documents for Foreign Shows

**Health, Repair & Sanity**
- ☐ Adhesive Bandages for Blistered Feet and Set-Up Scratches
- ☐ Aspirin for Sore Minds and Muscles
- ☐ Booth Locking Tabs (Extras, If Your Booth Uses Them)
- ☐ Contract (Bring a Copy in Case of Disputes with Show People)
- ☐ Degreasing Cleaner (For Removing Stains on Booth and Carpet)
- ☐ Duct Tape (For Mounting Down Cords and Quick Fixes)
- ☐ Light Bulbs (Extras to Replace Broken or Burned Out Ones)
- ☐ Money (Cash) for Tips and Purchasing Refreshments
- ☐ Paperback Book for Airport Entertainment and Evenings Alone
- ☐ Phone Numbers of Friends and Relatives in the Show City
- ☐ Picture from Home If You're On the Road More Than a Week
- ☐ Velcro Strips (For Quick Repairs to Signs and Graphics)
- ☐ Water Bottles (You May Get too Busy to Get a Drink!)
- ☐ WD-40 (For Loosening Stuck Assemblies During Take-Down)

**Dress**
- ☐ Comfortable Dress Shoes for Standing All Day
- ☐ Dress Clothes for Show ( Lightweight—Shows Get too Hot)
- ☐ Old Clothes and Tennis Shoes for Set-Up and Take-Down
- ☐ Sweater or Jacket for Cold or Over-Air Conditioned Shows

**Misc.**
- ☐ Camera and Film to Take Pictures of Booths and Visitors
- ☐ Electrical Converters for Foreign Shows
- ☐ Maps of Show City's Streets and Freeways
- ☐ Travel Guides on What to See and Where to Eat
- ☐ Passports and Travel Documents for Foreign Shows
- ☐ Phone Numbers of Show City's Customers

Figure 7.3. Tradeshow attendance checklist.

to assemble the booth, carpeting for the space (unless you rent this), and bulk shipments of literature and other booth supplies. Ship air freight if you can afford it—your booth and other materials will suffer less handling and the chances of arriving on time are much better than by truck or rail—especially if time is tight. Inspect your arriving shipment for losses and damage and file any claim immediately both verbally and in writing.

---

✎   TIP: GET YOURSELF INSURED BEFORE THE SHOW

Make sure your shipment and your company are properly insured. Your regular business insurance rarely covers tradeshow damage or liabilities. Ask your agent to provide you with the correct policies for tradeshow equipment and liability. Most large tradeshows demand evidence of liability coverage before you can attend the show.

---

**Step 5. Prepare the people who will staff your booth.**   Before you get to the show, make sure the people who will be manning your booth are trained in booth etiquette and procedures. You should develop a printed booth schedule if multiple people will be manning the booth. In addition, a briefing session the night before the show opens is a good idea, perhaps over dinner or drinks. The idea behind the briefing is to create rapport among the booth team members and ensure that everyone has the same answers to the questions the prospects are likely to ask. In addition, you can clarify the schedule and make sure everyone knows their responsibilities. A list of people to contact in case of booth problems should be provided to everyone.

**Step 6. Set up the booth and equipment.**   All shows will provide a setup time for you or the show's staff to put your booth and equipment together. Set up must typically be completed at least 12 hours before the show opens—your paperwork will specify the times. If you are doing it yourself, prepare for the labor involved by wearing light clothing that is suitable for lifting, hammering, and moving heavy objects. Keep in mind that some halls are neither heated nor air conditioned during setup times and massive doors may be open to the outside weather. As an alternative to getting grimy and sweaty, you can hire professional setup crews to assist you in putting the booth together. Each show has different restrictions about bringing in outside labor, so read the show agreement in advance. Even if you do hire others to assemble the booth, be sure you are there to supervise. Their interpretation of a layout and yours may differ significantly.

**Step 7. Man the booth, talk to prospects, and soak your feet at night.** How you and your staff appear at the show can make all the difference to its success. Since you have already trained them you should be ready to start making sales and getting new leads. You should be energetic, smiling, and accommodating—no matter how tired you are or how much your feet ache. Working the booth floor in a busy show is hard work.

Make sure that all staff working in the booth are properly fed and not worked to death. Even in the busiest shows, breaks must be arranged and refreshments kept on hand.

Unfortunately, there are unscrupulous people who attend tradeshows for quick pickings. Keep an eye on all valuables during a show and consider leaving purses back at the hotel or locked in the trunk of a car for safekeeping. Don't put anything of value in the space behind your booth or in a quiet corner, because it may not be there later.

Any prospects who come by your booth should be offered literature and you should query to see if they have any questions. In most tradeshows you will be able to take names and addresses by running show identification badges through a credit card imprinter, which you can usually rent or purchase from the show producer. If these are not available, ask for the prospects' business cards or have forms available for prospects to fill out.

You should also have a clearly defined way for dealing with press people who will inevitably come to your booth. Usually they should be referred to the most senior person in the booth at the time, given a media kit, and generally treated as VIPs. Most large shows also have a press room that you should stock with copies of your media kits and news releases. The show producers may also offer times and rooms for news conferences that can be scheduled in advance of the show for companies with major announcements. The steps for scheduling a press conference at the show are usually spelled out in the show's information kit.

**Step 8. Disassemble the booth and pack for shipping.**   Once the show closes, you must take down your booth and get it ready for shipping as soon as possible. This must usually be done within 12 hours after the close of the show. Be aware that in many shows this is prime time for theft, so keep your eye on all expensive equipment. Have someone from your organization assigned to monitor the take down process. Even empty packing crates may disappear if another participant is one short. Consider carrying out any item of extreme value—particularly if it is small and easily lifted. Many shows will require you to get a property pass to carry anything more than a purse out, but it may be worth the effort. Once boxed and inventoried, your goods will be taken directly to the shipping docks by show personnel. If you didn't make arrangements for return shipping, the show producers will assign their own shipping company for you.

**Step 9. Ship the booth back home or to the next show.**   When your booth and equipment arrive home, count the boxes to ensure they all made it and inspect them for external or concealed damage. File any claim immediately. Use this opportunity to replace anything damaged, burned out, broken, or lost so the booth will be ready to use for the next show.

**Step 10. Follow up after the show.**    All the leads you get from the show should be immediately distributed to the correct sales regions and appropriate follow-up literature should be mailed as soon as possible. A timely "Thank You for Visiting Our Booth" letter sent to each visitor is recommended. In addition, you should have a meeting to evaluate the effectiveness of the show.

In evaluating the overall show results, consider the following:

- The quality and number of leads generated.
- Press activity during the show that will gain publicity for your company.
- Industry contacts made at the show that may be valuable for joint ventures, investments, or future promotions.

After considering these factors, decide whether the show was a success. If you decide it was worth the time and effort, book your space now for next year's show. If not, spend your communications dollars on something else.

## Tradeshow Space Selection Considerations

More than any other decision, your booth space will determine the traffic you get at your booth. More traffic is definitely better, so when reserving space, consider how people may be drawn toward each prospective location. This is important for a tiny 10 × 10 foot booth as well as a 60 × 60 foot giant. Some areas in a show floor are going to get substantially more foot traffic than others no matter what the show people say. Your show rep may convincingly explain that attendees will find you by simply consulting the map on the show-provided program. This is true if someone is deliberately looking for you, but many attendees never open the program, and explore only those aisles that grab their attention.

Booths located near the front door get the most traffic for obvious reasons. Booths located near concessions, restaurants, and the restrooms also get more notice because of the people walking by to reach these frequented places.

If you are looking for space for a small booth keep in mind that a corner booth gets more notice than one in the middle of the aisle. Not only can people approach from four directions instead of two, but a corner booth can have two open sides rather than just one, making the booth seem larger. If you are using a larger, island booth (a booth open on all sides), try to get space near the largest booths in the show because their openness will make your booth easier to see and these locations are usually the best for foot traffic.

If yours is a small company that sells add-on or peripheral products that work with products made by a large company, try to get as close to this other company's booth as you can. When people head for the big booth they will see you and they may be interested in your product since they are interested in the big company's products. For example, if you sell computer software that runs on Apple Macintosh computers, a booth located next to Apple's is a good location.

In shows that are not sold out, one location to avoid is near the unsold space. Convention halls screen off the unrented areas. If you rent near this space, your booth may end up in an empty aisle surrounded by unsightly drapes.

As previously mentioned, you will be able to select from a wider number of spaces the earlier you commit to attend. If you find that there is little space left and the show's sales rep is trying to talk you into a poorly located spot, weigh how important the show really is before giving in. A really lousy spot may put you in a dark corner miles from the front door or you may have to pick a location among booths featuring products completely unrelated to yours. These poor locations may neutralize the impact of your attendance at the show.

## Booth Considerations

After selecting a space with adequate traffic, designing the right booth is the next critical decision. Booth options range from a rented table surrounded with *pipe and drape* (that ugly fabric mounted on pipes that you see dividing smaller booths at most shows) to multimillion dollar affairs employing motorized decorations, big screen TVs, and laser lights, taking up a city block on the floor of a large convention hall.

To acquire a booth of your own, you can buy a prefab model, purchase a used booth, or build your own. You can also rent or borrow a booth, but the limitations of most rental arrangements make this unworkable for most companies, unless you just want to get your feet wet to see if you want to make a major investment in tradeshows.

Most shows rent standard booths in addition to tables, furniture, and carpeting. These standard booths are identical in size and construction and cannot be customized by your company. Usually arranged together in long rows, these rental models are chosen on the basis of long-term durability rather than good looks, so they tend to be cold-looking affairs that attendees steer clear of rather than visit. They do little to establish identity for your company and are often the least visited booths in the show.

## Prefabricated Booths

By far the most popular booth for small companies and small budgets is the prefabricated booth. Prefabs are available in many formats from a variety of vendors. Many of the models are completely portable and can be assembled by one person in less than an hour. If your company is doing well and wants to grow from a 10 × 10 foot to a 10 × 20 foot booth, many prefabs will allow you to hook two 10 × 10 foot units together to create a larger display.

If you decide that this is the route for you, ask the salesperson to pack the entire unit away and then guide you through the steps from unpacking to complete assembly. Look for a model that is easy to assemble and one that is extremely sturdy, stable, and rigid once put together. Make sure your choice can accommodate small shelves and the weight of sales literature without swaying or leaning. (There are few experiences that rival the embarrassment of talking to a tradeshow visitor and having your booth suddenly collapse or fall over behind you.) Pass on models that seem wobbly or use fragile plastic parts for load-bearing locks, struts, and hinges.

---

    ## TIP: WHAT IF I CAN'T AFFORD A BOOTH?

A practice common in many industries where show prices and space availability have become prohibitive is to skip the show altogether and rent a swank hotel room close to the convention location and organize what's called a *hospitality suite*. There attendees can see product demonstrations, meet the salespeople, and enjoy a relaxed party atmosphere with free drinks and food far away from the hustle of the show floor. This usually costs less than attending the show and requires far less logistic management. And, because the atmosphere is informal, prospective customers are potentially more receptive to sales pitches and persuasion. The key to making these suites successful is getting enough invitations out before and at the show—and the better the food, the more "uninvited" guests you will have coming around.

---

Though prefabs are convenient and inexpensive, when you proudly set up your new prefab at a show and stand back to admire it, you may notice that all of the booths around you are similar or identical models. Because of price, weight, and shipping size limitations, most small prefab booths look very much the same. This is fine if yours is a small company

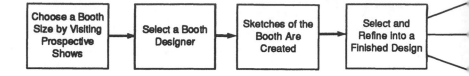

Figure 7.4. Building a booth step-by-step.

or if you attend shows where most of the competing booths consist only of a rented table and a couple of signs. But for larger companies or those in highly competitive markets, the prefab sends a message of "new, small, and not very financially secure" —not the kind of image every company desires.

You can, to some degree, get around the look of a prefab by adding flashy graphics, custom tables, and lighted columns, but using this approach to dress up your booth adds to the cost, shipping weight, and setup time. Before you know it, you might have been better off with a custom design.

## Designing and Building a Custom Booth

Although undoubtedly the most expensive road to travel, by building your own booth you can get exactly what you want and also keep the road open for future expansion needs. Building your own booth usually means hiring a specialist to design it and coordinate the construction effort with several subcontractors. Everything from the booth to peripheral tables, seating, graphics, displays, and even shipping cases must be either bought or built.

As an alternative to "from scratch" construction there are a number of modular booth systems available that offer semicustom construction and may save you substantial time. Since these systems were designed with show use in mind, they are already constructed from lightweight, durable materials and some systems are extremely flexible.

To get started in the custom booth process, you need to locate a suitable specialist for the project. This person is usually a designer who specializes in tradeshow and exhibit booths. Look for one through referrals or in the *Yellow Pages* under *Display Designers and Producers*. These

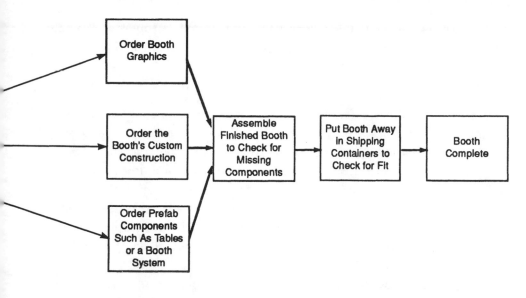

listings will include a variety of freelancers and also large companies that can handle the entire process for you.

When selecting this kind of talent follow the advice in Chapter 9 and keep two additional points in mind.

1.  Many designers will take on a tradeshow booth project at the drop of a hat. Hire only ones with a proven portfolio of trade-show booth design and production. Although many designers can create a beautiful booth design, they may know next to nothing about building one that is lightweight, durable, and easy to ship.
2.  When searching out a booth design firm, look for one with real creative prowess. Many of these firms are simply order takers with little or no creative expertise.

## Controlling and Managing Tradeshow Booth Construction

Tradeshow booths can become political hot potatoes because of their cost, visibility, and complexity. It's best to work with the most senior person possible in your organization to get the approvals; otherwise you may be surprised at how many "experts" your organization has when it comes to booth design. (See the *Everybody's an Expert Problem* in Chapter 11.)

Careful project management is also vital. A large, elaborate booth project can quickly spiral out of control without your careful supervision. Avoid the classic "last month" problem in which companies wait until about a month before the show to begin designing and building a booth. Trying to construct a booth in such a limited timeframe results in a poorly executed project fraught with a fortune in rush charges.

## Booth Graphics

Graphics are often treated as a separate project, especially with prefab booths. The graphics are used to make a booth attractive as well as to deliver a message. Graphics should be treated as an integral part of booth design—whether retrofitting an existing booth or building a new one. For many booths the graphics are the prime attention getters.

Booth graphics come in a variety of formats—from simple poster-like graphics that mount to booth fabric with Velcro to complex back-lit signs and neon lettering. What's right for an individual booth should be up to your designer and you. In general, graphics should be as big as possible. Use a few well-chosen, descriptive words. Use bright colors. Simple, strong designs are best.

To evaluate graphics in a booth layout, answer four basic questions:

1.   Will the attention of a casual tradeshow attendee be grabbed among the competing exhibits?
2.   Is your company's name and basic message apparent?
3.   Does your eye instantly land on an important graphic or does it jump between several elements before finally settling somewhere?
4.   Do the graphics explain in several seconds or less what your company is about and what your products do?

A negative response to any of these questions means adjustments are in order.

---

### ✎  TIP: BEWARE! BOOTH RENDERINGS ARE DECEPTIVE

As a part of the booth design process, you may be shown a *rendering* of the finished booth. A rendering is a detailed drawing of the booth done with colored markers or an airbrush. These renderings are idealized and show the booth in isolation. The perspective used in these drawings is extremely deceptive if you are not experienced at looking at them. Although a 10 × 10 foot booth is too small for more than two people and a small table, a rendering of this same booth will make it look large enough to display a 1959 Cadillac with its doors wide open. Once you see the rendering, you may be tempted to add more elements to the booth or more displays and tables to the foreground. In a word—don't!

To get a real-world conception of your booth's space, tape off the dimensions on a concrete floor or parking lot. After laying out the rented space, mark where the booth will go, keeping in mind that all booths have thickness to them and many designs waste substantial space *behind* the booth. Now add any peripheral elements such as tables and chairs. Block off areas taken up by each element by adding stripes of tape across them. Then assemble the number of people who will man the booth at one time and stand in the remaining area. This will give you a realistic estimate of available space. Don't be surprised if it turns out to be substantially less than you thought.

## Putting It All Together: The Endless Details

Once the booth and schedules are all in place, there are more details to be handled as part of tradeshow participation. First you will need people to staff the booth during all hours that the show is open. This means they must be on hand before the doors open and until after the show closes. In most organizations, getting participants for booth duty is difficult. Prospective booth workers suddenly come up with the most surprising reasons why they can't attend ("I can't go to the San Francisco show because I'm allergic to cable cars.")

The best booth workers are the company founders and executives of small companies and experienced sales and marketing people in larger organizations. Get salespeople to staff the booth by showing how last year's booth duty generated substantial leads and resulted in big sales and increased commissions.

In addition to conscripting booth workers, you must make transportation and accommodation arrangements for these people. You can save money by booking airline tickets and hotels in advance. Most shows offer substantial discounts through local hotels, but the best deals are taken up early, just like the best booth space.

If you are introducing an important new product at the show (tradeshows are an excellent place for such introductions), your PR person may want to arrange a press briefing or lunch with editors to discuss the merits of the new product (see Chapter 4). If this is the case, provide them with plenty of notice because you may be competing with a large number of other announcements.

If you want to make an impact on the industry at a major show, sponsor an after-hours party. They are expensive, but they can make a lasting impression. Most of the large companies will have parties at which key customers and company representatives mingle for the evening. If you want to compete, you should think about a special event—but you will need to plan it and announce it well in advance. By the way, Cheese Whiz on crackers and beer will not draw a big crowd. Do something with some panache and imagination if you want results from a tradeshow affair.

Last, when sending people to a show, treat them well by booking them on transport that gets them there quickly with a minimum of stopovers and hassles. Provide them with comfortable accommodations and make sure the expense account is adequate. If you don't, you may have an expensive booth in an important show staffed with cranky, zombie-eyed staffers who are more interested in sleeping than talking to customers.

## COMPANY AND CORPORATE IDENTITY PROGRAMS FOR STANDING OUT FROM THE CROWD

All organizations have some identity. It may be one that is carefully honed after years of design and refinement or one acquired haphazardly with little active forethought. A carefully designed identity is the key to standing out from the competition and being remembered by customers, the press, and other members of your industry. It also is important in maintaining a positive image or counteracting a negative one.

An identity is the look and feel your company has in the outside world. Several elements are used to create this. First, there are the overt elements such as the choice of logo and the company colors. Second, there is the overall use of color, the style of typography, frequently used design elements, and the way the pieces of the communications program work together. If you have multiple products, you may have subidentities for brands or product lines as well as an overall corporate look.

Identity programs should be consciously designed, tested, and then used consistently on all visually oriented communications from letterhead to television commercials. By establishing an appropriate look and sticking to it, your communications are instantly recognizable to those already familiar with your company and you will easily build an image in the minds of those unfamiliar with your company. A consistent identity also makes the communications process much easier because you have less to accomplish if your audience recognizes you and already has positive knowledge of your organization.

### The Logo

Logos are symbols or marks that are used to identify an organization. Your logo may be as simple as a company name set in a particular typeface and always printed in a specific blue, or as highly refined as a special mark developed by a professional design firm. Large companies may pay several hundred thousand dollars for an appropriate logo.

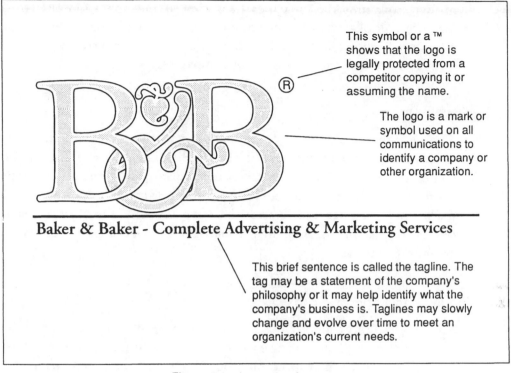

This symbol or a ™ shows that the logo is legally protected from a competitor copying it or assuming the name.

The logo is a mark or symbol used on all communications to identify a company or other organization.

Baker & Baker - Complete Advertising & Marketing Services

This brief sentence is called the tagline. The tag may be a statement of the company's philosophy or it may help identify what the company's business is. Taglines may slowly change and evolve over time to meet an organization's current needs.

Figure 7.5. Anatomy of a logo.

The right symbol consistently rendered in the same color gives an organization a strong identity. It can be legally protected so that other companies can't copy or use a mark that is deceptively similar.

The design of a logo should be handled by an accomplished logo designer if you can afford one. If not, a strong type treatment of your company's name may suffice until more money is available. The logo should not be created in isolation, however. It should be part of an overall look for the company that includes company colors and possibly the selection of a typeface for use in literature that is compatible with the logo.

## The Look

Apart from the logo, companies develop and evolve a look that together with their logo makes them instantly recognizable in a crowd of other companies. The look includes, but is not limited, to the selection of a certain typeface for use on all communications materials, the use of specific colors, and the inclusion of stylistic elements that are readily associated with other materials from the same company.

This look, for maximum effectiveness, is carried through all of the company's communications programs and usually is adaptable to a wide range of implementations. Large companies may put together a style manual explaining the look they have chosen and how to implement it. Since few "looks" remain current and inviting for periods of more than a few years, the style manual should be updated regularly and the look evolved to reflect current taste and company needs.

## The Tagline

Taglines are a brief sentence (no more than six or seven words) that describe a company's business or philosophy. The tagline always accompanies the logo and is considered an intrinsic part of it. Short snappy taglines add identity and can be used to explain your business to the uninitiated. Taglines evolve with the company and it is okay to change one as long as *all* materials that display the old one are replaced within six months to a year.

## Color Is an Important Part of a Look

Probably the most identifying aspect of a company's look are the colors employed in the logo and used consistently in literature design. There are design houses that do nothing but choose colors for companies and spend a considerable amount of time (and your money) researching and testing color combinations. For obvious reasons color is not important in radio, and in the case of TV, anything goes. But for print communications, color can be a major identifier.

Here are a few basic tips when you consider your company colors:

- Avoid browns and greens as dominant colors because they draw a negative reaction from many people. Occasionally they can be used as secondary elements.
- Avoid the obvious use of "business" blue and gray. These colors are certainly the safest route to travel but also the most boring because they are so overused by companies looking for "safe" colors.
- Gray and maroon and maroon on creme were color schemes popular in the 1970s and are now out of date. Using them will make your company appear out of step with the times. Brown on creme is equally passé. However, in 10 years or so, you may find them back in favor again.
- Surprisingly, some *pastel* colors are safe choices and can be very effective when employed by a designer with an eye for color. Because any color can be used as a pastel, this color family offers you a wide range of choices. (Pastels are colors with substantial amounts of white added to lighten them.)
- Signal yellow is a strong attention-getting color. It can be used tastefully to make your literature jump out at readers.

- Gray on gray combinations are attractively conservative and, if handled by the right designer, can make a very appealing color combination.
- Bright colors are strong attention getters and excite people. Dull colors tend to relax (or bore) people. If your company is conservative, use relaxing colors. If your company employs new technology or sells trendy products, use exciting colors.
- Use strong reds and red-oranges to draw attention to a logo or tagline, but do not overuse them. The eye (and mind) is quickly fatigued with too much red stimulation.
- If you make products that compete or work with those sold by a much larger and more recognizable competitor, consider adopting a corporate color scheme similar to theirs but different enough to separate you. (Note that some color schemes are registered trademarks and adopting them is illegal.)
- Colors go in and out of style in cycles. Adopting today's hot, trendy color may quickly date your literature as taste changes. Choose something you will be able to live with over the long haul.
- Consider foil stamping or metallic inks only if you can afford to print them on everything from letterhead to brochures. This gets expensive fast.
- Rules are meant to be broken. A designer with a real eye for color can disprove all of the above suggestions and produce a stunning look using passé colors or ones that are overused. Unfortunately, without a lot of shopping and a budget to match, you are unlikely to find such a person to develop your company's colors. If you are not sure, play it safe and observe these rules.

## PRODUCT PACKAGING FOR GOOD LOOKS AND UTILITY

Most tangible projects require packaging. The obvious exceptions are products such as automobiles and steel girders where the product is the package. Packaging plays several roles depending on the product and its path to sale and consumption. Packaging is used variously to protect products during shipping and handling and to give a product shelf appeal if it's sold retail. Consumer products that depend on this appeal such as shampoos and liquid soaps are usually designed by experts—some with 20 years or more of experience in designing and engineering product packages.

Merchandising, which goes along with packaging, is the display system used to promote products in a retail environment. Examples include cardboard displays to generate awareness for goods and services, neon beer signs, the Goodyear Blimp, and any other awareness generating mechanisms that don't physically contain a product and are neither advertising nor collateral.

## Packaging Primer

If you need to package a product, you must decide what the packaging must do and then choose a format that meets these requirements. If you are currently designing a product that will rely on a potentially expensive package, consider investigating the packaging issues before finalizing the product design. Sometimes minor changes to a product's size or shape can substantially affect the package cost. Ideally product specifications and packaging should be developed in tandem so both items work together for maximum utility and appeal.

Another factor to consider when choosing a package is the manufacturing process. If your product will be stuffed in the package by machine, for example, the capabilities of the equipment must be kept in mind when designing both the product and its package.

The packaging for a single product may include one or more of the following packaging options:

- **Containment packaging.** These packages contain the actual product. Examples are cremes and ointments that come in lead or plastic tubes that require packaging to contain and dispense the product. In the case of more durable packaging such as aerosol containers, the product package is also the shelf package because these containers are more durable than tubes of toothpaste.

- **Utility product packaging.** Many products require packaging that has some shelf appeal but is primarily intended to protect the product during shipping. Consumer electronic products such as VCRs and computers are packaged inside a minimally decorated cardboard box. They are further isolated from damage by the use of carefully designed foam pieces that keep the outside box from making direct contact with the product during rough handling.

- **Shelf packaging.** The objective of shelf packaging is to get the product noticed on a shelf of competing products. The packages must also provide protection during transportation to the purchaser's final destination. For example, in the case of toothpaste, containment packaging is used to contain and dispense the product. Then the tube is stuffed into shelf packaging consisting of a printed cardboard box. This additional level of packaging is used to make stacking easy and protect the tube until it reaches the buyer's bathroom. Most shelf packaging is designed to promote the product, providing enough information for the buyer to make an informed decision before buying.

- **Transport packaging.** Often consisting of corrugated cardboard boxes with little or no printed decoration, this packaging may contain a number of shelf-packaged units. Transport packaging not only protects them from damage, it also makes the product easier to handle. For example, cans of ground coffee are transported in transport packaging boxes to facilitate handling a large number of cans quickly and to protect them from dings and scratches. Occasionally two levels of transport packaging may be required.

- **Image packaging.** Some packaging is actually more important than the product. These are called "image packages." Consider perfumes and expensive cosmetics. Many times the elaborate packages are more expensive than the contents. These packages must incorporate design, shelf appeal, and identity to be effective.

## How Should You Package Your Product?

Product packaging beyond a very basic plain cardboard box or simple shrinkwrap is best left to experts. In addition to being able to design packages that are durable, safe, and appealing, a good packaging designer knows where to buy the most cost-effective materials and fabrication labor. These savings quickly pay for the design services and get you a package that meets your objectives.

Look for a designer or design firm with a broad packaging portfolio using the same kind of materials that you will use. For example, if your product requires elaborate glass bottles, don't hire someone who designs fancy printed cardboard boxes—they won't have the experience you need.

If your packaging needs include custom bottles or plastic containers, you may need to hire both a designer and a package fabrication engineer. Sometimes a designer will render a look for the package and a packaging engineer will implement the final fabrication. The engineer will work with the designer to take the concept from sketches to reality, occasionally rejecting ideas as unworkable or risky.

Here are the basic steps for creating packaging. These hold true whether you are doing it yourself or working with a packaging designer.

**Step 1. Collect samples of your competitor's packaging.** If your product must compete head to head with someone else's either on a store shelf or retail floor, your product must look at least as good if not better than theirs, unless yours costs less. Your designer should study these samples too.

**Step 2. Define how your product will be shipped, displayed, and contained.** You need to consider packaging requirements from factory to end user. Adequate protection during shipping and warehousing is vital to maintaining product integrity and keeping shelf packaging fresh and compelling. Packaging designs must also take into account transportation *after* the sale. For example, a customer purchasing eggs sold in a flimsy container may arrive home to find them scrambled in the carton.

**Step 3. Approve a design.** A competent designer will research your needs and show you several sketches for your approval. If you are designing packaging on a budget, here are several sources for ready-made and semicustom packages:

- You can find standard cardboard packaging through mailing stores or get a catalog from a local box manufacturer. (Found under *Boxes—Corrugated & Fiber* in the *Yellow Pages.*) Some cities have stores that sell only packaging on a retail level. They will have a wide variety of box styles available and the suppliers can special order many that are not displayed. Many of these boxes can be overprinted with your product name, logo, and other text and graphics.
- If you are looking for off-the-shelf packaging ideas other than cardboard, call vendors of special promotional items found under *Advertising Specialties* in the *Yellow Pages.* Many of these companies dabble in packaging and they may have a solution for you that requires only a little custom work. These companies also handle a variety of cardboard and plastic items, although it will cost you more than going directly to the manufacturer.
- Suppliers for bubble packs, foam, and custom plastic packages can be found under the several *Plastics* listings in the *Yellow Pages.*

**Step 4. Assemble a sample to see how the package works.** Once you have approved the design or selected materials yourself, ask for a *dummy* to be assembled from the actual material if possible or get a sample of an off-the-shelf package design if you are using one. A dummy is a proof that closely resembles the finished package. Study it carefully to make sure that everything looks right and, most importantly, that your product fits properly. If your project involves packages within packages, check that they all fit together and that the innermost packages are adequately protected by the outside ones. Test your package dummy for the following:

- **Breakage during shipping.** Drop the boxes onto concrete several times if appropriate to ensure that the product remains intact. In the case of products shipped by truck or the Postal Service,

Product Name: _____ Date: _____

Product Measurements: _____ Product Weight: _____

A. List the Steps in the Shipping Process from Manufacturing to the Customer:

1. _____

2. _____

3. _____

4. _____

5. _____

B. Now, List the Packaging Required for Each Step in the Shipping Process (heavy, box, shelf package, plastic wrap, etc.)

1. _____

2. _____

3. _____

4. _____

5. _____

C. List Out for Each Packaging Type, Who or Where the Package Should Come From (off-the shelf, designer and printer, build it yourself).

Kind of Package from B                                   Where to Get It

1. _____        _____

2. _____        _____

3. _____        _____

4. _____        _____

5. _____        _____

D. Cost per Unit for Each Element

1.$ _____

2.$ _____

3.$ _____

4.$ _____

5.$ _____                = Total Cost per Unit $ _____

Figure 7.6. Product packaging worksheet.

the transport package with the product inside it should be able to stand about a six foot drop onto concrete without major damage.

- **Crushing.** Estimate the maximum weight of packages that could be stored on top of each other by weighing the dummy with the product inside. Then put the dummy on an ordinary bathroom scale and add red bricks until the stacking weight has been reached plus 20% (to make up for packages dropped onto the stack). The product should remain intact and any shelf packaging should remain undamaged.

- **Weatherproofing.** If your product must endure storage outside in the elements, make sure it can withstand sun, rain, cold, and heat.

- **Containment.** If your product is powdered or liquid and is packaged in self-shipping containers, it should not leak after the above tests are performed or when heated or cooled within normal environmental ranges.

- **Gluing.** If your package uses glue, it should be tested for failure under conditions of hot and cold. Keep in mind that a product shipped across the desert by tractor-trailer during the summer will see extreme heat for as much as a week. The area near the ceiling of a sealed truck may reach temperatures of 200°F or more in the sun. A glue that is strong and resilient at room temperature may turn to goo in such conditions. Other glues crack when they get too cold.

- **Hazardous product testing.** If you sell potentially hazardous products, have an accredited lab test and approve the packaging.

**Step 5. Produce and inspect the packaging.** Have the packaging produced and inspect it for defects before accepting the shipments. The steps for producing many of the printed elements of packaging are similar to the collateral production steps covered in Chapter 6.

---

✎ **TIP: THERE MAY BE SPECIAL LEGAL REQUIREMENTS FOR YOUR PACKAGING**

If your package will be used to transport hazardous materials such as pressurized gases and other flammables or foodstuffs such as meat and agricultural products, or if the product contains alcohol or prescription medication, or if it will cross international borders, there are a number of labeling, declaration, processing, permit, and other requirements you must meet. Get expert advice on any such issues before you design and print the package.

## PRODUCT MERCHANDISING FOR MAXIMUM VISIBILITY IN THE STORE

Merchandising is a massive area of communications. All signs and displays that promote a product or company are merchandising. The production steps for most merchandising elements are similar to those already covered for collateral materials. Rather than describe all the merchandising possibilities (that would take a book in itself), here are some effective merchandising ideas that work for a variety of products:

- For physically small consumer products sold retail, colorful cardboard displays work well. They not only grab the eye, but these displays free up valuable shelf space in stores already jammed with merchandise. Cardboard countertop displays also work well in some markets.

- Brightly colored signs generate strong awareness for certain products. Provide your dealers with quality, attention-getting signs. Bright banners, attractive neon signs, and lighted displays all work well. Make sure that any and all printed signs get regular replacement because these fade or become soiled.

- For complex mechanical or electronic products, small signs that explain the operation of each part are a powerful education tool. For example, the technological advantages of a new machine can be explained with small signs attached to each important section. This way, even if no salesperson is available, customers can get a good understanding of the product and what it can do for them. These signs also help salespeople make a more organized sales presentation, acting as cues as they talk.

- For feature-laden products such as consumer electronics, signs that list the features of the product are helpful for consumers attempting to comparison-shop products. If your product has a sign listing features and your competitor's product does not, you have a better chance of getting the sale. This is particularly important in a time when consumer electronics product lines are replaced as frequently as every six months with new models. Few salespeople can keep up with all the new product features.

- For products sold in large quantities to a big chain of stores, providing them with custom display signage is helpful. For example, if your company makes canned soups sold in vast quantities through a chain of grocery stores, providing them with elegant signs that accompany the shelf pricing will give you a visibility advantage over other brands. In this case these signs should be made to fit comfortably alongside the store's pricing signs, usually fitting into a grooved shelf edge.

- Posters are excellent merchandising tools for many markets. They work well in increasing product awareness and building image. The best ones end up permanently attached to dealer's and customer's walls or even framed, giving them a potentially long life span.

The best source of ideas for merchandising your product is to go where your product will be sold and watch customers making buying decisions. This will give you some idea of why one product gets chosen over another. Study your competitor's merchandising schemes as well. You may pick up an idea or see an opening they missed for generating awareness.

# SPECIAL PROMOTIONAL ITEMS FOR LASTING IMPRESSIONS

Special promotional items include a wide variety of items imprinted with your company's name, address, phone number, and often a message. Examples of common items include imprinted coffee mugs, pens, shirt pocket protectors, and notepad holders. Also known in the trade as geegaws or advertising specialties, these items are generally used to complement other promotions or the sales process and help keep the name of your company visible before, during, and after the sale.

Special promotional items are available directly from manufacturers, but a much easier way to buy them is through a dealer that carries a wide variety of promotional items. Although all of these dealers charge a mark-up over factory prices, if you have a problem with a product, they are invaluable in resolving conflicts and getting orders straight.

Specialty advertising dealers can be found in the *Yellow Pages* under *Advertising Specialties.* A few of the companies in this classification imprint only wedding and party items—unless you are planning a wedding or party, stick with the firms that handle business-oriented promotional items. Because there are so many items to choose from, many of these companies print a catalog of their wares, or they will have a showroom of merchandise available for viewing. Some are even equipped with computers that take a word or phrase and search through hundreds of thousands of items to find a match between idea and product.

## What Special Promotional Items Can Do

Special promotional items are used to remind a customer or prospective customer of a company or product. They can also be used to commemorate an event or remind a group of people of a corporate goal or new program. A well-chosen special promotion can have a long life on a recipient's desk or in a home, or it can be used routinely in daily life. This category of communications has the longest potential life span of any tool in the marketing communications tool box. Of course, not all special promotions are that successful. Many end up in the trashcan without receiving any attention whatsoever.

## Selecting Special Promotional Items

When choosing a special promotional item, the goal is to select one that your customers will not only keep, but one they will use or see on a daily basis—that way your name is always on display. What makes this difficult is that many inexpensive gee-gaws are useless to a wide range of people, or they may already have one or more given to them by other companies. Choosing an item of general use is advantageous because more of your customers are likely to keep it. However, if you consider an obvious item such as a coffee mug, many people already have a closet full of mugs given to them by various companies. Choosing an unusual item may give it a better chance of not being redundant, but fewer customers may need it and it will hit the trashcan or be given to the kids.

Good taste is particularly important when choosing these items. Some items are of a sexual nature and destined to be offensive to a wide variety of customers. Some are simply tacky. Many are obviously cheap, and giving someone a piece of junk will not help boost your image in any way. A common mistake when selecting a special promotional item is to look for the cheapest item possible so that a larger number can be handed out. The gift must match the level of importance of the recipient. Giving the president of a major company a cheap plastic notepad holder is a mismatch—he or she may take offense rather than appreciate the gift. Giving a low-level employee in a customer's organization an expensive gift may appear as an opening for a bribe.

Here are some suggestions that you can follow when shopping for the right gee-gaw:

- If your recipients are technically oriented, consider giving them something they might actually use such as a precision ruler, or a fancy mechanical pencil. Neither of these gifts is expensive.
- For management-level recipients, give something that will be useful to adorn their office space. Desk organizers that hold scissors, tape, rulers, and other items are an example of something they might use. A leather day book or notes portfolio is always a good choice. Another appropriate example is a tasteful or unusual clock (not one with an LCD readout). Even if they don't use it at work, they'll probably take it home.

- For recipients in an office environment, consider giving away an inexpensive battery-operated pencil sharpener or electric letter opener. Small computer tool sets are also appreciated by people working with personal computers. Tools to take them apart and hook them up are always in short supply in offices.

- If you must give a coffee mug, choose one that is highly unusual in shape or have a designer put together a brightly colored mug. Although a recipient may already have several mugs, if yours is especially unusual and/or attractive, it will be the one its owner uses. The same thing applies to tee shirts, another standard give-away. Make the design memorable and use quality shirts.

- Avoid giving alcoholic beverages, unless you know the person. Although at one time a bottle of fine wine or imported liqueur was considered a tasteful present, unless you know that the intended recipient enjoys such beverages, this is risky. You might be giving it to a recovering alcoholic or someone who's religion forbids drinking alcohol.

- Pens and pencils have long been standard giveaway items. People actually do use them. Unfortunately, unless you can afford to give away Mont Blancs or at least Cross pens, these items don't have a long life span in customers' hands.

- For retail giveaways, consider selecting a promotional item that goes along with the sale and is useful as a result. If you sell swimming pool equipment, give away an imprinted inflatable beach ball. If you sell expensive jewelry, give away an imprinted ultrasonic jewelry cleaner. Although these may cost you $10 a piece in quantity, if you sell a number of $2500 rings as a result, you can afford it.

- Try to match the gee-gaw to your organization's message or business if possible. For example, one company that makes a product that solves serious computer problems gives out imprinted bottles of aspirin that say, "Without XYZ products this is your only recourse for computer headaches!"

### Ordering and Producing Gee-Gaws

Gee-gaw production is fraught with problems, but you can avoid most of them by following the right steps when ordering and inspecting the merchandise. Because many of these items originate in other countries, quality control often leaves something to be desired. The American and Canadian companies that make custom items and do imprinting are often not very well organized either. Here is how to get the best results when you order your special promotional items:

- If you are ordering an item from a catalog or if you have not actually seen the product, ask the salesperson for a sample. This sample will usually be rushed to you so it will not slow the ordering process much. The actual product may be much poorer in quality than you imagine and you may want to order something else. If the final order is not up to the quality of the sample (a frequent occurrence), you can point to your sample and say "This is what I ordered and this is what I want."

- When ordering anything custom such as an expensive gold lapel pin or something encased in a clear plastic cube, ask that a sketch or rendering be done before the work begins. This sketch may involve an extra charge, but without one you may be very surprised by what you receive when the finished order arrives at your doorstep.

- Put all instructions to the vendor in writing and keep a copy for yourself. Because the information must pass through several hands before reaching the factory floor, there is plenty of opportunity for miscommunication. Written instructions give you a better chance of getting what you order. Additionally, if something does comes out wrong, your written instructions are a free ticket for getting it fixed or replaced.

- When your order arrives, *check all of it carefully*. Without careful inspection, you may not notice a problem until salespeople are already giving the item away. It is not unheard of that part of an order arrives as specified and part has serious flaws (often buried in the bottom of a box and hard to find).

If you are really in doubt about the appropriateness of an item for your market, test it. Get a sample and then ask several of your friendlier customers what they think of it and whether they would like one if you were giving it out. Take anything less than a very enthusiastic "yes" to mean that the item is not appropriate, desirable, or of sufficient quality for your needs.

Taken together, the tools presented in this chapter are used to give your company a physical presence in your marketplace. Tradeshow attendance puts you squarely in front of your market and industry, the company or organizational identity you assemble allows you to put your best "corporate foot" forward, and special promotional items keep your name in front of your customers. Together these tools can give your company a positive, memorable image that helps it stand out from the crowd. These tools help separate you from the "me-too" competitors so common in most industries and businesses.

# 8 | Marketing Communications Mechanics and Techniques: The Basics of Type, Design, and Printing

One of the most intimidating things faced by people new to the field is understanding the technical side of producing marketing communications. Buried in jargon and the subtleties of aesthetics, this is a world of almost imperceptible nuances and never-ending details.

This chapter explains the basics to get you started, but becoming an expert takes years of practice and experience. Exposure to communications projects and your review of competing materials will go a long way toward establishing your credibility. You have been studying advertising and advertising design all your life, so you have a good start. Also, while communications projects vary from small ads to monster tradeshow booths, the basis of taste and aesthetics remain the same—even across cultures and, to some degree, time—though the implementations may change.

When you first begin to work on communications projects, you may feel intimidated by the jargon. Most communications professionals are fond of bantering phrases such as "right-reading negative emulsion down at 133 lines per inch with stripped in screen tints from the amberlith" comfortably. Intimidating? You bet!

Worse, vendors from different companies often engage in one-upmanship with each other (in your presence) by hurling jargon around to test each other's depth of knowledge. They may do this to you to see if they are dealing with a pro who knows the business. Not surprisingly, the less they think you know, the higher the bills.

Your first line of defense is this chapter and the glossary in the back of the book. Covertly study the words to get some idea of their meaning and use. The glossary entries consist of either jargon (words that in communications mean something other than their standard English counterparts) or technical phrases that mean little without a definition. Your second line of defense is to ask the vendors exactly what each phrase means in detail and then further question the explanations until you understand them. A few lengthy question and answer sessions will provide you with a free education and the vendors will cut out the jargon because it extends the meetings. By the way, the entire example above could have been discussed verbally as a "negative," with the fancy details left for the production professionals who care about such things.

## A BRIEF LESSON ON TYPE AND TYPOGRAPHY

Typesetting is the process of converting typed or written words into headlines and body copy for use in print ads and collateral. Type is also set for billboards, packaging, TV commercials, and signs.

Beyond the words themselves, type is important because it conveys an impression to the reader through its shapes and its position on the page. Typefaces convey intrinsic feelings or style. Strong type design gives headlines more impact and makes the copy inviting and easy to read. Poor quality type is difficult to read, forcing the reader to work at getting the message. Most readers will not bother to decipher a cryptic message, so clean, easy to read type is important.

ABCDEFGHIJKLMNOPQRSTUVWXYZabcdefghijklmnopqrstuvwxyz1234567
890,./;'=~!@#$%^&*()_+{}:"?<>¡™£¢∞§¶•ªº–≠""π†®´∑œåß∂ƒ©˙∆˚¬…æ÷≥≤µ˜∫
√ç≈Ω

Figure 8.1. The Times Roman font.

There are probably millions of typefaces available today. The majority of faces support Indo-European languages such as English, French, and German. The remaining percentage supports the world's other languages.

Language is supported by character sets. Each typeface has a set of characters that comprises all the needs of the language it supports. These complete sets of characters are called fonts. A font may contain a complete set of letters, punctuation symbols, and even fractions as part of its character set. One font may have a large enough character set to handle English, German, French, Spanish, and Slavic languages or it may be limited to the support of basic English characters. All fonts have identifying names. Fonts may be named after the designer or after the person or company that commissioned the design. For example, the popular font *Times* was named after the *Times of London,* the publisher that commissioned Stanley Morrison to design it for use in their newspaper during the 1930s.

Typefaces are designed by specialists. These typeface designers are extremely knowledgeable about type and can precisely name a face after only a brief glance. Once carving characters out of wood, today's type designers work entirely on drafting boards or computers to create new fonts.

Much type design is done to further refine the readability or enhance the style of an existing type family. New versions based on older designs also reflect an improvement in printing technology. Today, because of

This is a serif font.    This is a sans serif font.

*This is a script font.*    This is a display font.

Figure 8.2. The four groups of typefaces.

higher resolution printing capability, more subtle changes of shape can be perceived than was possible 50 years ago. Other typeface designers are working to create entirely new families of type for specialized purposes.

Most type can be categorized as belonging to one of four groups and then to families within each group. The four main type categories are as follows:

**1. Serif type.**  *Serif typefaces* are widely used in books, ads, newspapers, and just about anywhere where a high degree of readability is important. The most common kind of typeface, type designers are constantly working to perfect and improve this large group of type families. Most serif fonts have a variety of thick and thin strokes used in each letter. Study the T in "This is a serif font." Note that not all of the lines (strokes) are of the same thickness. The serif shapes originally derived from the way monks completed their hand lettering of religious manuscripts with ink pens.

**2. Sans serif type.**  The word *sans* means without, so these fonts are without serifs. Unlike serif fonts, most *sans serif* characters are drawn with a line of equal thickness. More modern designs, sans serif fonts are strong and effective when used for headlines. Many technical companies use sans serif fonts because of the modern simplicity of the fonts. A well-chosen sans serif font is almost as easy to read as a well-chosen serif font.

**3. Script type.**  Familiar as the form of type used in wedding invitations and official certificates, *script type* is a typeface representation of handwriting shapes. Scripts are usually reserved for very formal documents and, because they are difficult to read, brevity is important. Script faces convey elegance and formalism. Scripts may be either connecting or nonconnecting, meaning that the letters may actually join, or each character, while still looking like handwriting, may not touch its neighbor.

**4. Display type.**   Display type consists of fonts that don't fit into the above three categories. Usually designed with a particular purpose in mind, display type is attention getting and unique. It can vary from letters that look like broken glass to fonts in which all of the letters are made using the shapes of cats. Display type possibilities are limited only by imagination and skill, but never use them for anything but a short headline because, like scripts, they are very difficult to read and ultimately tiresome on the eye. The are best for creating moods, feelings, and style in a communication.

## Type Specification

Basic type specification is a part of every communication that uses type. A designer specs type by marking the raw copy so that a typesetter can see how to set it. It shows how the type should appear on the page, how much space to put between the lines, type sizes, faces, and more. After *specing* the type, the copy is sent to an outside typesetter who then assembles the copy into a finished form. In the case of desktop publishing, this step may be skipped, with the designer/desktop publisher specing and producing the type right on screen as he works.

Advanced typography is a subspecialty of design with a handful of designers handling only artistic typesetting, type specification (or *specs*), and hand-drawn scripts. These type specialists take another designer's type specs and fine tune them to the point of near perfection for maximum impact. This kind of service is used for large billboards and expensive ads where everything has to be just right.

Occasionally a design may demand the use of a hand-drawn headline or logo. Elaborate or crude, this work is highly studied. It typically takes years to fully develop the hand-eye skills necessary to complete competent script designs. Many *script* artists and calligraphers have more in common with illustrators than with designers.

## Type Alignment

Type can be aligned several different ways, depending on the demands of the job. Most frequently, type is left justified (ragged right) or right and left justified. Left justification means that the left edge of the type lines up vertically. The right, however, does not. As the typesetter reaches the right margin, he or she *bumps* the next word onto the next line (computers do this automatically). What happens is that the right edge is *ragged,* with the edges of the lines rarely lining up. For this reason this technique is also called ragged right.

Justified text is text that runs all the way from the left margin to the right and both right and left sides line up with their respective mar-

| Left justification means that the left edge of the type lines up vertically. The right, however, doesn't. As the typesetter reaches the right margin, he or she bumps the next word | Justified text is text that runs all the way from the left margin to the right and both right and left sides line up with their respective margins. Since few lines of copy will be made up of | Right justified text is simply the opposite of left justified. The right edge of the text lines up with the right margin and the left edge is ragged depending on the individual length | Centered text is just that—each line is centered between the margins. Unlike justified text where each line touches the margin, centered text floats in the middle of the page. |
|---|---|---|---|
| **Left Justified** | **Justified** | **Right Justified** | **Centered** |

Figure 8.3. Justified and centered text.

gins. The text in this book is justified. Since few lines of copy will be made up of exactly the same number of letters, the justification is accomplished by adding a small amount of extra space between words and letters to make up the difference. If the type has been properly set, the reader will not notice the extra space.

Right-justified text is simply the opposite of left justified. The right edge of the text lines up with the right margin and the left edge is ragged depending on the individual length of each line. Often called ragged left, this format is used for design impact, but is very difficult to read and follow.

Centered text is just that—each line is centered between the margins. Unlike justified text where each line touches the margin, centered text floats in the middle of the page. Reserved mostly for headlines, poetry, and menus, like right-justified text, centered body copy is also hard to read.

## Leading

Leading refers to the amount of space between each line of text. The expression comes from the old hot type process, where a typesetter would insert a thin layer of lead to separate the metal rows of type from each other. Leading can be used to make type more readable because it adds white space to the printed page. Notice in the example how different the printed lines look using the same typeface and size but with various degrees of leading added.

## How Type Sizes Are Specified

Type is specified by how tall it is, usually measured from the top of an ascender to the bottom of a descender.

The height is measured in points, or in the case of really big type destined for a billboard, inches. A point is 1/72 of an inch. Here are

Leading refers to the amount of space between each line. The expression comes from the old hot type process, where a typesetter would insert a thin layer of lead to separate the lines from each other. Leading can be used to make type more readable by adding white space. Notice how different the lines look using the same typeface and size, but with leading added. Leading refers to the amount of space between each line. The expression comes from the old hot type process, where a typesetter would insert a thin layer of lead to separate the lines from each other. Leading can be

### Inadequate Leading

Leading refers to the amount of space between each line. The expression comes from the old hot type process, where a typesetter would insert a thin layer of lead to separate the lines from each other. Leading can be used to make type more readable by adding white space. Notice how different the lines look using the same typeface and

### Extra Leading for Improved Readability

Figure 8.4. Leading.

examples of several sizes of the Times font. Note as the characters get bigger, they get thicker and more solid looking.

Type is usually specified with two dimensions—the size of the character and the size of the white space between the lines of text. So that means that character size and leading are specified together. Typically this specification takes the form of *12/15* or *12 over 15*. The first number is the size of each character and the second number is the leading (in points) plus the size of the character. So *12 over 15* means 12-point type with three points of leading. The type and the leading together take up a combined 15 points of vertical space.

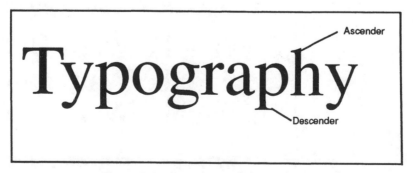

Figure 8.5. Ascenders and descenders.

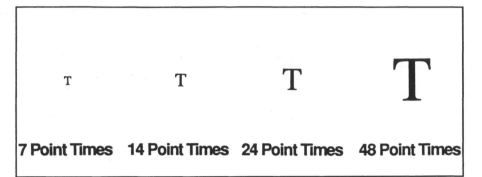

Figure 8.6. Type sizes.

Most book and ad copy is set in 10- to 14-point type because it is the easiest to read while still allowing a lot of information to fit in a limited space.

## Bolds and Italics

In addition to the variety of typefaces available, each face can be rendered as *bold* or *italic* (also known as *itals*). Bolds thicken each letter and on a busy page can catch the eye first. Bold is an effective eye grabber but don't overuse it. Like the exclamation point in writing, a little goes a long way.

Italic is characterized by the slanting of each letter to the right. But there is more to italic that just the slant; each character is a redrawn

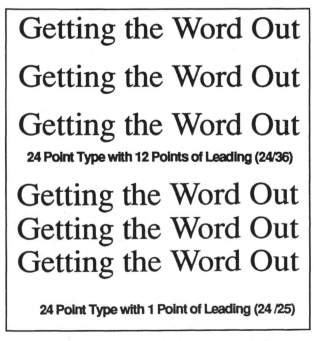

Figure 8.7. Type and leading spec examples.

Regular **Bold** *Italic*
Times **Times** *Times*

Figure 8.8. Bolds and itals.

version with thin diagonal components and other subtle changes. Study the comparison between the standard character and the italic version.

Italics are used to set words off from the rest of a paragraph by looking different. They are used for emphasis, for the titles of books embedded in text, and for secondary headlines. Because italic type is visually lighter because the lines that make up the characters are thinner than normal characters, it appears lighter on the page.

Use italics sparingly because they become tiresome on the eye if used for anything other than a few words here and there.

## Proportional and Fixed Type

Type can be set either proportionally or with fixed spacing. This means that since an "m" takes up more room than an "i," it should be given more space. In the case of fixed spacing, all characters have a fixed amount of horizontal space into which they fit. Most type is set using proportional spacing because it looks better and is easier to read.

## Kerning, Spacing, Compression, and Expansion

In addition to making characters larger or smaller, characters can also be made wider or narrower and the spacing between them can be adjusted. Adding or subtracting space between letters can change readability and make copy fit into smaller or larger spaces in a design. *Kerning* is like spacing, but slightly more complicated. Since many characters don't match up well because of their shape when put side by side, kerning allows a typesetter to improve readability by moving them closer together or farther apart. "T" and "L" are examples of characters that do not mate well.

Times    Courier

Left: Proportional Spacing - Note how the "i" in "Times" wraps under the "T."
Right: Fixed Spacing - Each letter has the same width and takes up the same amount of horizontal space.

Figure 8.9. Fixed versus proportional spacing.

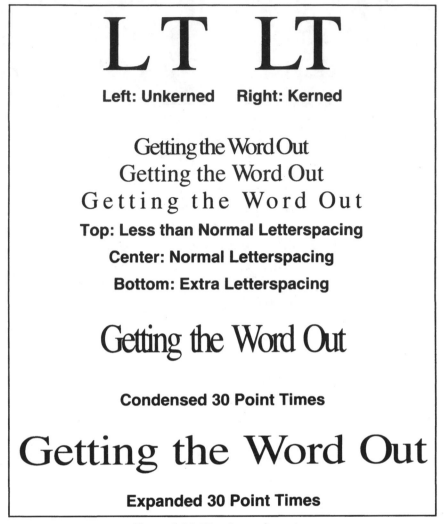

Figure 8.10  Kerning and spacing.

But by kerning, they look just fine (see example). Kerning can also be used to carefully adjust each individual letter in a headline for maximum readability.

The spacing between characters can be adjusted too. Condensing characters makes them thinner so that more characters can fit on a line. Expanding characters makes them appear larger without increasing their vertical size. Supercondensing characters is a useful design practice for creating an unusual look for a company name. Expansion can be used the same way..

### Drop Caps and Raised Caps

Since cloistered monks illuminated their manuscripts by making the first letter in a paragraph or story larger than the others, drop caps and raised

S ince cloistered monks illuminated their manuscripts by making the first letter in a paragraph or story larger than the others, drop caps and raised caps have been employed as a powerful decorative element and attention-getter. Use these tools to enliven long passages of copy where there's little

**Drop Caps**

S ince cloistered monks illuminated their manuscripts by making the first letter in a paragraph or story larger than the others, drop caps and raised caps have been employed as a powerful decorative element and attention-getter. Use these

**Raised Caps**

Figure 8.11 Drop caps and raised caps.

caps have been employed as a decorative element in designs of all sorts. Use these type treatments to enliven long passages of copy where there's little visual relief in the form of pictures or diagrams.

## Pull Quotes

Much like drop caps, *pull quotes* are used to enliven copy-heavy pages. Pull quotes are simply a one- or two-sentence excerpt from the surrounding article. Usually a particularly strong or controversial statement works best because the idea of a pull quote is to get the reader interested in reading the story. That's why they're called pull quotes—they pull in the audience.

One of the most intimidating communications issues faced by people new to the field is understanding the technical side of producing communications. Buried in jargon and the subtleties of aesthetics, this is a world of almost imperceptible nuances that readers must understand to effectively manage communications projects. This chapter presents the basics in simple language with examples to illustrate each topic.

Keep in mind however, that while this chapter will explain the basics, this is a knowledge which takes years of practice to fully build and develop. Exposure to communications projects and your review of competing materials will go along way towards establishing your knowledge. And, you already have been studying advertising and advertising design since you first opened your eyes as a baby. Note also that while communications projects vary from small ads to monster tradeshow booths, the basis of taste and aesthetics remains the same—even across cultures and to some degree, time.

When working on communications projects, you may also feel intimidated by the jargon. Most communications professionals are fond of bantering phrases such as "right-reading negative emulsion down at 133 lines per inch with stripped in screen tints from the amberlith" as comfortably as ordering a tuna salad sandwich from a lunch menu. Intimidating? You bet!

> " Most communications professionals are fond of bantering phrases such as "right-reading negative emulsion down at 133 lines per inch with stripped in screen tints from the amberlith" as comfortably as ordering a tuna salad sandwich from a lunch menu. "

Figure 8.12.  Pull quotes.

## Special Effects

There are a variety of special effects that can be used to enhance type and make it work for special purposes. Although many of these techniques once required expensive handwork or special lenses and equipment, most effects can now be easily and inexpensively rendered with the help of a computer.

## Headlines, Subheads, Eyebrow Heads, Captions, and Body Copy

There are several terms for elements on the printed page that you should be aware of because in the process of writing copy and designing a print project, these phrases will come up. Basically there are three kinds of headlines: *main heads, subheads,* and *eyebrow heads.* The main head should be the central focus on each page or spread and works to reinforce the message of the primary visual. It may convey the one idea you most want readers to remember. Subheads are used to break up copy into readable chunks and should be noticed second to both the headline and the main visual. A good subhead draws readers into the copy and conveys important secondary messages. The third kind of head is an eyebrow head. These are used to *orient* readers to the contents of a page. A brochure that covers the Model 100, the Model 200, and the Model 300

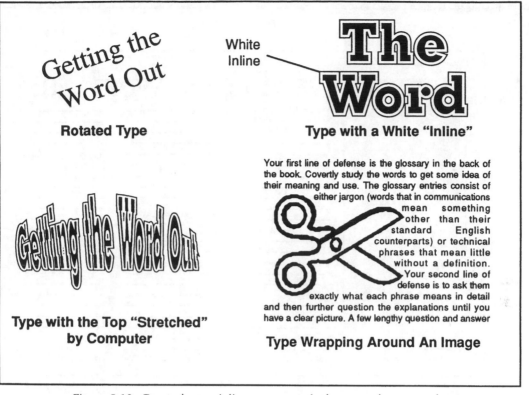

Figure 8.13. Rotated type, inline type, stretched type, and runarounds.

in three spreads, respectively, might have these names used as eyebrow heads on the top of each page to show the reader which topic will be explained on that spread. Eyebrow heads are most often used in brochures and ads and are optional in all print projects.

Captions are used to explain a visual. Often a reader will look at the pictures before reading anything. An interesting visual will attract the eye. The reader will then read the caption.

*Body copy* is simply the text that goes into a print document or ad. Body copy adds detail and explanation to the topics introduced in the headlines and caption. Body copy may be set in one or more columns, depending on the size of the type and the requirements of the document. Avoid very narrow columns because the type may break in undesirable places or become hard to read. Also avoid very wide columns— they are difficult for the eye to track without conscious effort on the part of the reader.

## Avoiding Widows and Orphans

*Widows* and *orphans* are terms for leftover bits of type that appear in undesirable places. A widow consists of a word or less than half a line of text that appears at the bottom of a paragraph. Widows catch the eye,

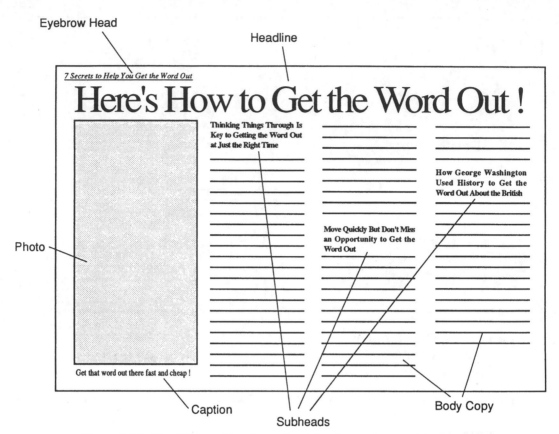

Figure 8.14. Headlines, subheads, eyebrow heads, captions, and body copy.

particularly if they are followed by another paragraph because they expose more white space than the balanced paragraphs do. An orphan is the first line of a new paragraph that falls at the bottom of a column of text or the last line of a paragraph that spills on to the first line of the next column. In practice these terms are often used interchangeably because no one can remember which is which. They also may also be used to describe the last word or sentence of a paragraph spilling over into an otherwise blank column or page.

## A BRIEF LESSON ON DESIGN

Whereas entire books have been written on design, you can pick up some of the basic concepts just by reading this chapter. Design is highly subjective and tastes change by the minute, but the basics of design are easily illuminated.

### Design 101

When evaluating design, your most potent weapon is the first impression. A good first impression of a design usually means that the elements work well enough to at least get a second and more serious glance. A poor first impression probably means that the design suffers from basic problems. Your mission is a seek-and-destroy expedition for design elements that put readers off.

The four basic problems that can happen to any design, whether print ad, tradeshow booth, architectural design, or brochure spread include the following:

1.  The design is too busy. Too many elements compete with each other for the eye.
2.  The design is ugly. Unattractive design stems from a lack of harmony between design elements. This may be a problem with color or poor integration of shapes. It may also be a quality problem where the production is obviously cut rate or inept.
3.  The design is boring. Boring design is usually the opposite of problems 1 and 2. Boring design stems from a lack of elements, or the use of quiet elements that work so well together that the eye could just as easily ignore them as look at them.
4.  The design is unbalanced. In unbalanced design, one insignificant element catches and holds the eye at the expense of other important elements.

Some simple sketches of each problem are provided using a brochure layout as an example. Use your first impression to explore the problems of each. Following each example is a good way to begin to learn about design decisions that you will need to make when you develop your communications.

Start by reviewing the sketch captioned *Too Busy*. In this sketch there are several different elements that grab the eye at the same time. These elements are of similar visual weight and the first impression focuses the eye between the blocks rather than on one of them, or on the headline. The problem is also common when too many competing type styles are used on one page.

When you find that a design is too busy, throw out unimportant elements or merge them. Make the important items bigger or more prominent through the use of color. Make secondary elements secondary. Reduce the total number of typefaces used and consider eliminating all display faces. Too many bright colors can also make a layout busy. Consider reducing the total number of bright colors.

Now, consider the sketch captioned *Ugly*. In this sketch, there are elements overlapping other elements and an obvious lack of visual continuity. The first impression is to reject the layout because there is a total lack of harmony between the elements.

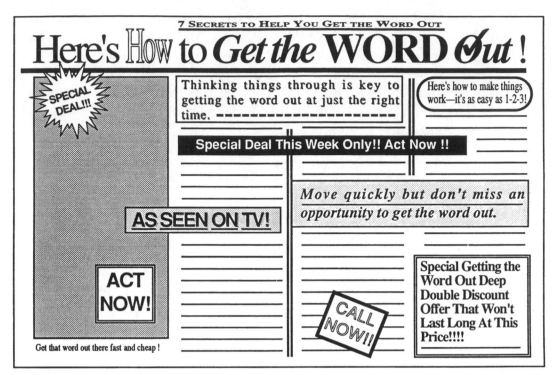

Figure 8.15. Too busy. Layouts with too many competing visual elements are *busy* and fatigue readers' eyes very quickly. A busy layout makes it difficult for the reader to identify the important information and separate it from the mundane. You can identify a layout that is too busy if your eye jumps from element to element instead of being drawn to an important visual or headline.

When you are met with an ugly mess such as this, you may be working with an incompetent or inexperienced designer. If there is time, give the person a chance to fix it or get someone else on the project with an eye for aesthetics.

Next there are two boring sketches to review. In the first sketch *(Boring #1)* there is only one element with nothing to catch the eye. The first impression is one of disinterest. In the second sketch *(Boring #2)*, all of the elements are balanced and fairly equal. The first impression is nonplussed. This second sketch might be acceptable for a page in a book or magazine, but certainly not for an ad or promotional piece.

In dealing with a boring design, simply adding elements helps make your design more interesting. In the case of the second boring sketch, making some elements larger than others will help. And you may want to move them around so the design isn't so painfully balanced.

Finally, review the example of an unbalanced layout. In this design, the important item may be the headline, but it is so dominant that the reader has to make a conscious effort to read the copy or interpret the visuals.

If a design is unbalanced, adjust the size and weight of the elements so all the important elements get attention. Anything that cannot be

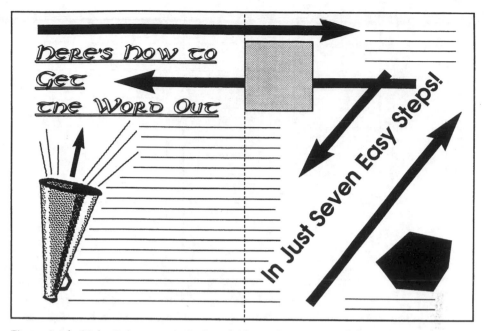

Figure 8.16. Ugly. It is comparatively easy for an inexperienced designer to assemble a number of individually strong elements into a truly unforgivable mess such as this. Unless you have a lot of time to waste, it is probably best to look for a new person to either clean up the mess (if that is possible) or start over from scratch.

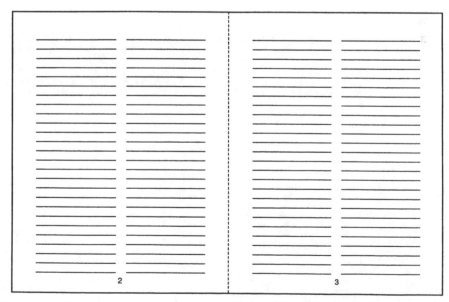

Figure 8.17. Boring #1. In an extremely unimaginative layout such as this, the eye finds nothing to focus on but a lot of copy. The only elements that stand out on these pages are the page numbers! When faced with a two-page spread with no eye-catching visual elements, most readers will be suppressing a yawn rather than excitedly reading the copy.

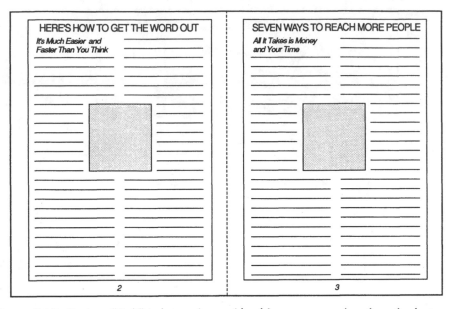

Figure 8.18. Boring #2. This layout is considerably more engaging than the last one, but it still suffers from a lack of interest. The problem with this is that all of the elements are too perfectly balanced. Nothing, not even the visuals or headlines, stand out from the rest of the layout. This format would be acceptable in a low-level design project such as a newsletter.

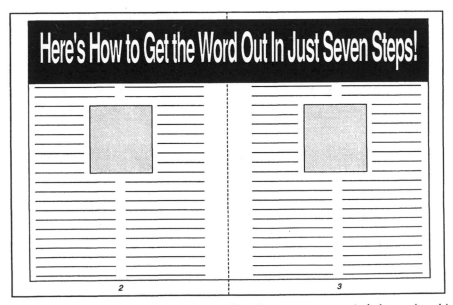

Figure 8.19. Unbalanced. This example suffers from an extreme imbalance, in which one element dominates the rest of the layout. The headline is so dominant that the reader's eyes keep jumping back to it when attempting to read the copy or study the pictures.

brought into visual balance according to its stature in the layout should be eliminated if possible. Occasionally this may be a case of trying to accomplish more than is possible in the available space. Set priorities and make adjustments to the offending items.

# A BRIEF LESSON ON PRINTERS AND PRINTING

There are a number of printing systems in use around the world, but the one used for almost all marketing communications projects is *lithography*. Printing techniques vary in the way they transfer ink to the page. Lithography uses water to resist grease-based inks, so where water is present, no image is printed. Where there's no water, ink is laid down on the paper. This technique is capable of producing highly detailed documents with good control over the amount of ink applied. It also allows long runs at high speed before the press plates need renewal or replacement. In the Western world at least, lithography with its inherent technical advantages is the most popular printing process.

## Three Kinds of Print Shops

There are three kinds of lithographic print shops you may encounter:

**1. Quick printers (also called Instaprinters).**  These are small shops with a single one-color press and only two or three employees—often Mom and Pop. Quick printers are best at fast turnaround of simple documents smaller than 11 × 17 inches with only one or maybe two colors if the job is simple and without large spaces of solid color.

**2. Commercial printers.**  Most commercial printers have large shops, with a number of presses and many employees. There is quite a variation in equipment among these kinds of shops. They may have several two-color presses and possibly larger presses for four-color work. Or, they may have only one press and a *web* for printing newsprint.

**3. Specialty printers.**  The most capable kind of print shops, these printing companies may own several four- or six-color presses. They are appropriate for handling jobs as complex as six-color brochures and elaborate annual reports. However, the quality varies from shop to shop as does their specialty.

## The Color Processes

There are several color processes employed in lithography. Unlike other kinds of printing technology, lithographic presses are capable of only

**Choosing a Printer:**

| Kind of Print Shop | What They're Best At |
|---|---|
| Quick Printers ( Also known as Instaprinters) | Business Cards & Letterhead of One or Two-Colors Where Neither of the Two-Colors Touch (Abut) Each Other |
| | One-Color Brochures Smaller than 11" X 17" Before Folding |
| | Flyers |
| | Price Lists & Part Lists |
| | Simple Datasheets |
| | One-Color Menus |
| | One-Color Newsletters |
| Commercial Print Shops | Most Two-Color Projects Including Newsletters, Brochures, Datasheets |
| | Jobs Printed On Newsprint Such As Local Tabloid Papers |
| | Catalogs That Don't Use Four-Color Images |
| | Direct Mail Pieces That Don't Use Four-Color Images |
| Specialty Printers | Four-Color Jobs Including Brochures, Annual Reports, Direct Mail Pieces and Elaborate Catalogs |
| | Jobs with Multiple *Screen Tints** |
| | Jobs with Areas of *Solid Color** |
| | Jobs that Use *Varnishes** |
| | Jobs with More than Two *Spot Colors** |
| | Jobs that Use Large Paper Sizes Such as Lengthy Brochures and Posters |

* These Terms are Defined Later In This Chapter

Figure 8.20. Which printer to use for what.

printing a dot or not printing a dot. That means that they are incapable of directly printing a continuous tone image such as you see in a photograph. To get around this limitation a number of color processing techniques are used. The techniques may be used together in one job or separately. The most common techniques include the following:

- **Halftones.** A halftone is simply a conversion of a black-and-white photo into a series of dots that can be printed by a lithographic press. The eye perceives these dots as shades of gray ranging from black all the way to white. A solid dot is black. No dot becomes white. Grays in between become partial dots. This system allows one color, black, to be used to produce the complete spectra of grays.

- **Spot color and the Pantone Matching System.** Spot color is simply the placement of solid colors other than black on the printed page. These colors may be used as type, decorative elements, or solid blocks of color. Spot color is usually specified through a (nearly) worldwide standard called the *Pantone Matching System.* This system provides designers and printers with a set of standard inks that can be mixed into a color chosen from the Pantone Color Formula Guide. Using this system, a designer can specify a color in New York that a printer in Los Angeles can match almost exactly.

- **Four-color process.** The most powerful innovation in printing in this century was the invention and subsequent refinement of color printing in which a complex color photo or illustration can be converted into a printed color image. Four-color process begins with the assumption that three colors of inks—cyan, magenta, and yellow— can be mixed in combinations to recreate any other color. Although it doesn't quite provide all ranges of available colors, this system is fully capable of creating convincing color images.

  To print a color image, the original image, usually a photograph or transparency, is color separated. That means simply that a machine is used to scan the photo for each of the standard colors and break them apart. The separation creates a black-and-white halftone for each color, which is used to make plates—one for each color.

  The colors are recombined when a four-color press prints the colors on top of each other. This recreates the look of the original image. But wait! Where's the fourth color? It is black and is used to compensate for the inability of the other three colors to create really dark colors and convincing shadows. A black halftone is also created along with the other separations. So the complete system includes cyan, magenta, yellow, and black.

- **Screen tint color.** In the way that cyan, magenta, yellow, and black can be used to reproduce a photo consisting of thousands of individual colors, these four inks can also be used to create a single solid color. To create a screen tint color, a printer looks up in a book how much of each color to add together to create the desired shade. Not all colors are available through this technique and a solid color printed with Pantone Matching System inks looks more convincing and crisp.

## The Presses You Will Meet

There is a wide variety of press equipment available to meet the needs of various jobs. The small, inexpensive press used by quick printers is usually a machine that can handle only small paper sizes and offers little control of the amount of ink applied to the paper. Usually limited to an image area of less than 11 × 17 inches, these presses cost in the $10,000 to $40,000 range and are relatively simple to operate.

Commercial and specialty printers use one- to four-color presses made by companies such as Heidelberg and Akiyama. Unlike the quick printer's press, these units offer much better control over ink application densities and near perfect control of colors being applied in relationship to each other (this is called *registration*). These presses are sheet-fed. That means that like a photocopier, one sheet of paper is fed at a time. These units are available in sizes that vary from one-color units the size of a big refrigerator to six-color units as long as a truck. A large, high-quality four-color press costs in the region of one to two million dollars depending on the model, the installation requirements, and the shipping charges.

Last, there is the kind of press used to print long runs of magazines, newspapers, and catalogs. It's called a web press because the paper runs through a series of rollers and runners before entering the press. This maze of flying paper vaguely resembles a spider's web. Webs are one or multicolor monsters that feed paper from massive rolls through the press at a very high speed. The paper moves so fast that gas-fired dryers are required to dry the ink so the printed paper doesn't stick together after exiting the press. Webs allow much faster throughput and for a long run are far more cost-effective that sheet-fed presses. On the downside, with their speed, they are not capable of the ink application consistency or registration quality of the best sheet-fed presses.

## The Print Production Process

Before a brochure or other marketing communications can be printed, there are a series of production steps that transform the designer's mechanical into a format used to burn plates that are used to print the piece. Here are the basic steps in the production and printing process that all print communications must go through.

**Step 1. The printer estimates the job.**  He does this by looking at the steps required to get the job ready for press and adding up the hours and materials charges. Next he gets a quote on the paper, sometimes getting a price from several distributors to find the lowest price as well as a delivery window that is suitable for the job. Last he adds the time required for the press run to the estimate. A specialty printer running a complex job on a four-color press may charge $300 to $450 per hour for press time. That time includes the hours that the press will be tied up and the time for a pressperson and one or two helpers.

**Step 2. The job is reviewed.**   When the bid is accepted and the art delivered, the printer reviews the job to make sure it is similar to the job he quoted on and that there are no potential production problems.

**Step 3. The job goes to the stripping room.**   The art is shot and converted into film. During this time, images are converted to halftones and any required color separations are created. Printers may do this in-house or have the work done elsewhere. For really high-quality color separations, most printers send out to houses that specialize in separation and color balance.

**Step 4. The masks are created.**   The finished film of the type, separations, halftones, and any screen tints are composited into a mask. This mask is approximately the same size as the press plates and usually consists of an opaque orange plastic sheet with the film stripped into cut-out windows.

**Step 5. The masks are used to burn the plates.**   One mask is used for each side of paper to be printed and for each color on a multicolor job. A machine called a *plate burner* is used for this process. To use it, the mask with the film mounted into the windows is placed on top of a photo-sensitive plate. Brilliant light then passes through the film windows and etches the image on the plate. Where the orange mask has not been cut away or where the film is black, no exposure takes place. The exposed plate is then developed in a special solution and is then ready for the press.

**Step 6. The printer mounts the plates and adds the requisite inks to the press.**

**Step 7. The printer runs make-readies.**   Junk paper (maybe left over from another job) is run through the press while the pressperson and his assistants adjust ink delivery and blanket pressure. These initial tests are called "make-readies."

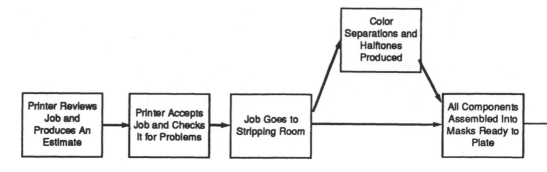

Figure 8.21. The printing process.

**Step 8. A press check is completed by the designer or client.**   After the client approves the run as being accurate and as specified, the printer then runs the job.

**Step 9. The job goes for final assembly or special treatments.**   This may mean going to a bindery for stapling or other assembly, either in-house or to an outside shop. In the case of special processes such as foil stamping or embossing more vendors may be involved.

**Step 10. The job is delivered or picked up.**

## Printing and Proofs

Depending on the nature of your job and the printer's equipment, you may see several kinds of proofs for your review and approval before your job gets printed.

- **Blueline proofs.**   These consist of a paper proof on either a bluish or brownish paper. They allow you to look for missing elements in the design, improperly assembled jobs, or crooked elements and allow you to verify that the mechanical assembly of pages, die cuts, and folds are correct. Some shops do not stabilize these exceptionally fragile proofs. If unstabilized, the proof disappears instantly if brought into the sun or if photocopied.

- **Matchprints and color keys.**   These proofs allow you to check for incorrect color use and colors that don't register properly.

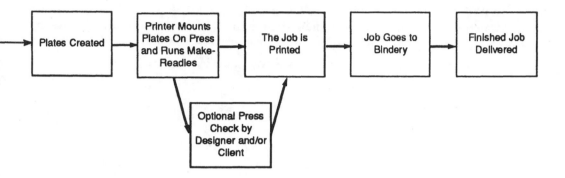

They are also useful for inspecting the overall appearance of a color job.

- **Chromalin proofs.** These are used to check the quality of color separations, the color balance, and the size of the visuals.

- **Dummies.** Dummies are a kind of proof that the printer (or paper supplier) assembles using the actual paper. This sample is blank, but it allows you to get a better idea of how the selected paper looks and feels once assembled into its final form. Use a dummy to evaluate paper weights, opacity, and complex folds and/or die cuts. If your job is an expensive one, you may want to consider several papers and should have a dummy made from each before making a final decision.

## The Ultimate Proof: The Press Check

Along with carefully checking the proofs described above, the ultimate proof of a print job is the press check. Press checks consist of looking at the job on press after the make-ready phase is complete. There you can check color and take one last look for mistakes.

If you plan to press check your job, be sure to let the printer know beforehand. It is best to remind him when you check on the job's progress—quite frequently printers accidently or deliberately forget to call you when the job is on press. If your job is running in a shop that runs 24 hours, the press check may be held at any hour—so be ready to go on a moment's notice.

Once you arrive, you will probably be put in storage until the press-person has completed the make-readies. Large shops with many people visiting for press checks may have entire recreational areas available for the clients as they wait. One printer we used frequently has a complete floor for waiting press checkers. Surrounded by small private rooms for resting and sleeping is a main hall complete with a kitchen, refreshments, and even a pool table.

Once on press, you will need to check for the following:

- Hickies. Small donut-shaped marks caused by debris stuck on the rollers.
- Registration. If it is a color job, use a magnifying *loop* (borrow one from the pressperson) to make sure that all colors line up properly and that four-color images have each color's dots aligned along the edges. If any of the images look slightly out of focus or *soft,* check the dot structure and alignment carefully.
- Scratches. Occasionally a press plate will get scratched on its way from the stripping department to the press.
- Color balance. You may want to bring some colors up or down to make them more lively or less intense. Sometimes in the case of a four-color image, one color such as black may print normally but will make the image appear too dark. With the pressperson's help, you can adjust color. Look also to make sure that the color is even across the sheet. Sometimes a color may be normal in most areas but too light or dark in one band.
- Check that the right paper is being used. Mix-ups or deliberate substitutions occur.
- If a Pantone Matching System ink is being used, verify that the right color has been loaded into the press. Check the printed color against the Pantone chart.

After you make any adjustments and have problems corrected, you will be asked to initial and date the sheet that you approved. This means that you approve the job to run as is. Take a sheet from the job with you. If the shop speeds up the press after you leave (rare) and delivers a job with washed out color, this sample is your proof that the delivered job was not run as you approved it.

## Color Is Subjective

Though a rose is a rose, red is not always red. To give you some idea of how subjective color is, think of the color of Charlie Chaplin's hat when you watch him on TV. Black? Well not really. What you perceive as solid black during the movie is really the dull green of the tube that you see when the TV is turned off. Color appears to change with the environment around it. For example, grass looks greener on cloudy days and just after sunset because the eye becomes more sensitive to green than other colors in lower light levels.

Because color is so subjective, based on the lighting and surrounding colors, when selecting a color from the Pantone Matching System or evaluating a color proof, study it under several kinds of light. If the color is to be used in an office environment, look at it under fluorescent lights. Take it out in the sun and review it. Then look at it under the color-balanced lights at the print shop. You will be surprised how different it will look in the three places.

---

### ✎  TIP: COLOR-BALANCED LIGHTS MAY NOT BE

Most print shops will have a booth or room with a bank of color-balanced fluorescent lights installed for studying proofs. You can use these lights as a guide to color but they may not be that accurate. Many printers spend the money to install the lights but then replace the bulbs only when they burn out. Some shops don't even keep the dust off the bulbs. For the lights to be color-balanced the bulbs must be replaced regularly and kept clean.

---

## Special Print Processes

There are several other "effects" that you may encounter in design and printing. These include the following:

- **Foil stamping.**   A shiny foil is applied with heat by a die to the surface of a page. This foil may be used to create a logo or make a headline stand out. Though foil in the right design can be elegant and tasteful, foil stamping is overused in some pieces and although it is an expensive process, too much use of foil can be garish.

- **Blind embossing.**   Embossing is a process in which the paper is pushed up by a die. Embossing can be quite effective, but like foil stamping it is an expensive process. Some papers take embossing much better than others. Ask your printer for advice on which paper to choose.

- **Varnishes.**   Varnishes are used to add subtle contrast to a design element. Varnishes may be either glossy or matte and may have a hint of color added to make them more noticeable. Varnish is applied by a regular press.

- **Die cutting.**   Some jobs may need to be cut into special shapes after the print run. Examples of jobs that have been die cut are ones with rounded corners and business card holders cut into literature holders. All kinds of shapes are possible, but the dies used to make elaborate cuts can be expensive.

- **Mar coating.**   Mar coating consists of applying a plastic layer to a printed piece. It is used to protect the printed surface of documents that suffer frequent handling.

---

## TIP: TEST YOUR MATERIALS TO SEE IF THEY PHOTOCOPY!

When ordering letterhead or other materials that may be run through a copier, it's tempting to add a design element such as embossing or foil stamping to add a touch of class. Keep in mind that most embossed elements will get crushed during copying and foil that is applied through heat will come off in the copier's heated rollers. In extreme cases, damage will result to the copier from the letterhead. Some kinds of raised print processes do not work either.

In addition to these potential problems, some color schemes do not copy well. Most copiers turn red into black and light blue into white. Some may drop out yellow. Silver foil will not copy well. If your materials will be frequently copied, test the colors before going into print.

---

### Printing Terminology

There are several printing terms that you will hear frequently. Some of these terms will raise the price of your job, so you need to know what the designers and printers are talking about. Here are some of the most common terms:

- **Solids.**   Solids are solid areas of color. Depending on the paper and the size of the solid, they can be quite troublesome because pin holes may appear in the ink coverage or the colors may come out looking uneven. Printers charge extra for printing pieces that make extensive use of solids because of the headaches involved. They may also have to move the job to a more expensive press than would be required without the use of a solid.

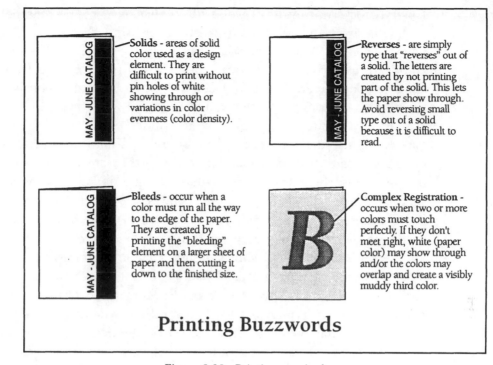

**Printing Buzzwords**

Figure 8.22. Printing terminology.

- **Reverses.** Reverses are simply solids with type reversed out of them, allowing the paper to show through. The type looks white or paper-colored on a colored background.

- **Bleeds.** Bleeds are necessary when ink is required all the way to the edge of the paper. Since no press can actually print all the way to the edge without causing a massive ink build-up on the rollers, bleeds are produced by printing on a larger sheet of paper than necessary and then chopping off the edge to create the bleed. This may raise the price because larger sheets of paper are required and trimming adds an extra charge.

- **Complex registration.** Wherever one color *abuts* (touches) another, the registration becomes critical. Printers charge extra for this because it makes the job more complicated and may require a more expensive press to run the project than had otherwise been required. Never hand a quick printer a job that involves complex registration!

## Printing and Papers

There are a number of papers available for all kinds of jobs—everything from six-part NCR forms for bureaucracies to papers made of plastic that are completely waterproof. Most kinds of paper (also called *stock* as in *paper stock*) you will use fall into two categories—coated and uncoated.

Coated stocks are made of wood fibers that have been combined with clay, adhesives, and additives to create a very smooth surface. Uncoated papers lack this smooth surface, instead being processed to add color and texture. Paper starts out as ground wood pulp or pulp from recycling existing paper. The only exception is a new and expensive paper actually made from plastic that requires special inks for printing.

From a printer's point of view, it is much easier to print on coated papers because the surface is smoother and less ink is absorbed into the paper. Uncoated stocks, depending on how they are manufactured, can be highly absorbent and printed colors become darker than on a coated sheet. Uncoated paper on the other hand offers a wide variety of colors and textures and it is generally less expensive than the best coated papers (although there are some very expensive uncoated sheets available).

Paper is usually selected by a designer in conjunction with the printer. Your designer may have a particular paper in mind that takes color a certain way or has a special texture. Printers often have a say in the matter too. Every printer has likes and dislikes when it comes to paper. Your printer may be able to buy a sheet of identical quality and appearance at a price substantially less than the paper your designer specified. Or the paper specified may be available only in an unsuitable size for your job—printing on it would mean trimming off and throwing away a large piece of each sheet.

There are more families of paper available than possible to cover in this book, but here are the kinds you will encounter when printing marketing communications projects:

- **Newsprint.** The least expensive paper stock used for printing is newsprint. Most familiar in the form of the morning newspaper, it is low cost and offers excellent opacity because of the lack of refinement of the wood pulp used to produce it. On the negative side, newsprint takes ink in a manner that prevents complex control of color and it is quite fragile to environmental elements. Wet, it quickly reverts to little more than pulp and newspapers printed on standard newsprint turn yellow after just a few hours in the sun. That's why most libraries convert important newspapers to microfiche for preservation. Use newsprint only for very short-lived projects where quantity and price are more important than quality.

- **Uncoated options.** Uncoated papers are available in a variety of colors and they may also be run through pressurized rollers to add textures and patterns. Use uncoated stocks for letterhead (you can't type on coated stocks and stamps fall off envelopes!) and for projects where colored paper and texture are important. If your project includes large areas of embossing, consider an uncoated stock because the fibers in this kind of paper are much more flexible than in coated stocks.

- **Coated options.** Coated papers come in colors ranging from bright-white to creme. There are also different kinds of coated finishes, ranging from dull mattes to shiny gloss. Generally matte-coated sheets take inks best, but they are also the most expensive. Avoid printing on glossy sheets unless you are working with a specialty printer who can get the ink to lay down evenly on the surface. Glossy and semigloss papers make for difficult reading, but often make attractive packaging and covers.

Most quality coated stocks are rated by a number between one and three. A number three sheet is the cheapest, least opaque, and takes ink inconsistently. A number one sheet is the most expensive because it has the most perfect surface and therefore takes ink and color best. Use these papers for high-quality printing that involves process color and/or careful control of spot colors and for jobs where color registration is critical.

---

## PAPER, THE ENVIRONMENT, AND YOU

One of the few global issues that almost everyone agrees on is that preserving the world's environment is important. You can do your part in saving trees by considering environmental issues when printing collateral materials, direct mail pieces, and other marketing communications. First limit print runs to what you will actually use plus a small percentage of extras for unforeseen contingency requirements.

Second, recycle unused collateral. Most print shops already have bins provided by outside companies for recycling their waste paper. Since this service costs the printer nothing (in most cases), they will willingly recycle your paper along with theirs at no charge.

Third, consider using recycled papers for your projects. Although currently there are no recycled sheets available that replace the best dull-coated number one sheets, the technology for producing improved recycled papers is evolving rapidly. For many jobs, there are a variety of handsome new recycled sheets available and by choosing these papers, you will help support the recycling industry.

Today recycled papers still cost more than conventional paper so let your customers know that you are doing your bit to help the environment by adding a line, "Printed on Recycled Paper" prominently on all collateral materials that use this approach. If you do choose to use recycled paper, select a printer who has a lot of experience printing on these stocks because some of them hold a few surprises for the press operator unfamiliar with their texture and absorbency.

## The Weights of Paper

Paper is manufactured in different weights for different purposes. A paper's weight rating refers to the paper's actual weight for 500 sheets of a given size (different categories of paper use different sizes for measuring the weight). This weight is used as a method for specifying and ordering paper. Heavier papers are more expensive papers.

At the low end of the scale are *writing weights* such as 20-pound bond. This paper is most familiar as the limp sheets used in the office photocopier. As weight increases so does the opacity and the stiffness of the paper. If you are printing both sides of a sheet of paper, you want it to be quite opaque so readers can't see through the page to the printing on the other side. Stiffness is the degree of rigidity in the paper and a given paper may have different thicknesses available that affect rigidity.

Most printing-grade paper is available in both text and cover weights. Cover weight is a heavier, stiffer stock that is intended for use as the outside of a brochure or as business card stock. Lighter text-weight paper is used for the inside of a brochure or as letterhead. Cover weight costs more than text weight.

At this point you have a basic knowledge and vocabulary to get you started in the world of communications. There are more terms, jargon, and production procedures involved with video production and multimedia presentations, but they are beyond the scope of the book. Most libraries have excellent resources on these topics if you want to get into the jargon even deeper. For now, you have enough knowledge to keep from being snowed.

# 9 | The Best Vendors for a Project: Matching Personalities and Capabilities to Your Needs

As previously discussed, the first challenge in marketing communications is to effectively communicate the desired message. The second, and often more difficult problem, is controlling escalating costs while meeting deadlines and ensuring quality. Doing both things well starts with hiring the right people at the right price to work on your communications project.

In marketing communications the people who work on projects are *vendors*. Selecting the best people for a project is as simple as matching vendor skills to your objectives and budget. Unfortunately, it sounds easier than it is. Choosing vendors is often the most daunting aspect of managing marketing communications projects. A poor choice can mean lost time, wasted money, and even failure of a product in the marketplace. The skills required to choose the right talent are a mystery to even the best managers. Managers are often "gun-shy" because they have had bad experiences with vendors in the past. Still, the skills can be learned, and if the guidelines presented in this chapter are followed, any manager can successfully choose marketing communications vendors.

## THE PERSONALITIES INVOLVED

Marketing communications projects may employ one or more people to write, design, schedule, budget, and ultimately print or otherwise bring a project to its final form. Whether it's an ad, direct mail piece, public relations program, or brochure—ideas must go through a series of predictable steps to be translated into final production. Though there are many specific skills involved in completing the transition from idea to implementation, marketing communications professionals come in two broad categories—creative talent (designers, illustrators, creative directors) and production talent (paste-up artists, printers, project coordinators). Both creative and production skills are required to execute any marketing communications project. Sometimes the creative and the production talents are available from one person—but more often the people involved in a project will be better at one skillset than the other.

The people in marketing considered to be *creative talent* are endowed with a mental gift of inventiveness—a gift that helps them translate last year's ideas, humdrum facts, boring figures, and ordinary features into fresh, exciting concepts. Good creatives are often eccentric, may be hypersensitive, and can be egotistical, though not all creative people fall into these stereotypes.

The craftspeople capable of completing the detailed work of transforming ideas into their final form are the production specialists. Production specialists are typically less eccentric—but not usually as creative. Good production vendors are detail-oriented, are adept time managers, and are comfortable working with pressure and deadlines.

Although both creative and production services can be purchased from a wide range of suppliers, most communications work is done by two broad categories of vendors—agencies and freelancers.

## DO YOU NEED A FREELANCER OR AN AGENCY?

Talent is priced according to the size of the vendor's organization and level of expertise, whether real or perceived. That means that big agencies typically cost more than small ones and freelancers can be a comparative bargain. However, there are pros and cons to every choice.

On the ground floor are *freelancers*—the individuals who work for themselves on a job and contract basis, often working at home with no support staff. This low-overhead arrangement means less cost to you and fast turnaround on projects if the freelancer has not already overcommitted his or her time. On the downside, any problems or conflicts must be ironed out directly. Freelancers will usually take on any kind of project, even if they lack the specific skills to complete it. And if your freelancer decides to spend your first installment check in the Bahamas before starting work on the project, there's little you can do about it.

Freelancers may not have the resources to provide a full range of services and that means you will have to hire and manage multiple individuals. This can be more difficult than working with a full-service agency if you are not experienced.

Higher on the cost scale is the *agency* or *design firm,* consisting of several principals and a staff. Agencies may employ from three to hundreds of people. Sometimes agencies hire the same freelancers you would to actually do the work. The agency "marks-up" the outside services to make a profit.

The polished approach of an agency may be reassuring to people unaccustomed to dealing with the diverse personalities of freelancers. The disadvantages of agencies are mostly the higher prices and typically slower turnaround. Also, you may not be able to select the creative people on your own account—and as a result you may be paying high prices for inexperienced talent. Your dollars must support larger offices and more people; however, it is often easier and less time consuming

---

## HELP WANTED: EXPERIENCED ONLY NEED APPLY

When attempting to hire a designer and desktop publisher for the marketing communications group of a large company, we ran two ads. The first one asked for "an experienced designer/desktop publisher with strong writing skills." The ad demanded samples of work and a resume.

A review of the arm-load of resumes and samples revealed 42 applicants mostly from the same local design college—none of whom had any credible samples. One used a form letter where he filled in blanks. (I am looking for a job as a _____.) In his resume he stated his career goal was to work in an advertising ajency (sic).

We reran the ad the following week with a higher salary and the words, "MUST HAVE TWO YEARS CREDIBLE EXPERIENCE" in bold. This brought most of the same would-be applicants. Also applying were a priest in charge of his church's newsletter and someone who had typeset meat ads for a local supermarket.

---

personally to have the agency do the coordination and it provides a *one-stop solution* for the busy manager.

Creative service vendors and production service vendors (whether agency or freelancer) vary considerably in both communications talent and project management ability. This means that the buyer must beware— or at least be well informed. The right vendors bring fresh thinking to a project and endeavor to deliver quality work on time and within budget. Poor talent produces work of varying quality with little regard for a project's budget or schedule—and often with little regard for the message and market you want to reach.

Unless you are on a shoestring budget and until you are practiced at selecting new talent, hire only experienced vendors with plenty of demonstrated project experience. Seasoned professionals provide more accurate cost estimates and practical advice on project problems that inevitably crop up. Fortunately, the most inept estimators usually get forced out of business because they get few return customers. Generally speaking, talented individuals survive if they provide good service and are careful when managing a client's money. Although experience costs more, it may ultimately prove to be more economical.

Sometimes you can get someone highly talented but less experienced to create their Magnum Opus for less than the going rate. There are plenty of freelancers looking for a "break." You pay less for the work and they get a chance to produce a portfolio piece. As you grow more experienced in vendor evaluation you will develop an eye for the occasional "diamond in the rough." Even the communications pros had to get a break somewhere.

By saving money with less experienced talent you can use the remaining budget for more expensive implementation or to keep expenses

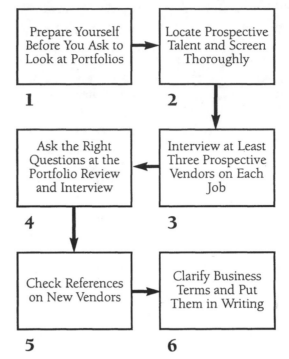

Figure 9.1. The six steps for evaluating and selecting communications vendors.

in line. However, you will need the skills and organization yourself to effectively manage inexperienced vendors. That is why we recommend that you hire only proven vendors until you gain experience.

## SELECTING TALENT: THE GOOD, THE BAD, AND THE UGLY

Experience aside, in our years of trials the selection process for vendors has been narrowed to six steps. If you use them, your chances of selecting the right talent will improve immeasurably. These steps apply equally well to hiring freelancers for a one-time project or to hiring an advertising agency for a long-term relationship.

**Step 1. Prepare yourself before you ask to look at portfolios.**   The first step in hiring any vendor, or in starting any project for that matter, is knowing what you want to do. What is the goal of the project? What is the target market? What is the message? Do you have a budget in mind? The steps to answer these questions are covered in other chapters. If you don't know the market, message, and purpose of your communications, no vendor, no matter how talented, will be able to give you what you want. Vendors may help you refine your messages and may even suggest ways to improve your ideas, but you cannot expect them to do all the groundwork for you.

If you have completed your basic marketing background, then you need to prepare yourself to evaluate the portfolios of the people you will be interviewing. It's important that you do your homework to know what you like and dislike and get a feeling for the possibilities. Visit the art and graphic design supply stores in any city and look through the design annuals. The most useful ones, such as *Communications Arts,* use juried competitions to select the work that is published. By studying the best work available, you will have a yardstick with which to measure prospective vendors.

---

## TIP: CREATE SAMPLE FILES OF BOTH GOOD AND BAD WORK

To aid you in your vendor selections, start two files—one for samples of your favorite ads and brochures and another for horrendous ones. Review them periodically and weed out materials that don't meet your current "standards." If you keep these files up to date you can use them to show vendors what you like and what you don't.

---

Begin to collect ads, brochures, and other print materials you find pleasing as well as ads and materials that are truly awful. Record TV commercials and radio spots you like if your communications projects include these media. Try to identify what you like about the materials you select—the look, the message, an unexpectedly cute idea, or the twist of something ordinary into extraordinary. Ask yourself if such an approach is appropriate for your project.

The next thing to do is to collect your competitor's materials and sort them into two piles—the ones you like and the ones you dislike or find inappropriate for your market. Study the competitive materials carefully—identify what's good about them and what could have been improved. Make notes on what you particularly like about each piece. Is the use of color or type compelling? Are the features and the benefits of the products clear? Now look at the rejects and weigh their merits. Do they look sloppy and unprofessional? Is the message muddled or are they simply bland and uninteresting? Ask other people in your organization what they think.

Put the materials away for a week or two and then go through the exercise again—you will be surprised how much more you can see the second or third time you look at the work. This gathering and review process should become part of your general operating routine as a manager responsible for marketing communications materials.

**Step 2. Locate prospective vendors and screen them thoroughly.** Use your networking skills, the *Yellow Pages,* or magazines to locate the appropriate kind of vendors for your job. We have included a section later in this chapter that gives you some advice and sources for finding appropriate people and agencies. Screen the candidates over the telephone. When you locate someone who sounds right, ask for samples or background information to be mailed to you for review before setting up an interview. Any vendor who insists on showing his work in person is probably planning to pressure you into a hiring decision or is low on samples because of a limited portfolio. Beware.

Carefully review the samples, cover letter, resume, and mailing envelope. These all provide valuable clues to that vendor's skills. Poorly written letters or ones with typographical errors or a photocopied form letter say something about the vendor's judgment and attention to detail.

**Step 3. Set up interviews with three prospective vendors.** After the telephone interviews and review of the sample materials, you should be able to narrow your search down to three possible vendors. Schedule an interview and portfolio review with each of the three, preferably within the same week.

Until you have a group of proven vendors to work with, always interview at least three writers, designers, or agencies before making a decision. You may see significantly different levels of quality and ability in the work. If you feel undecided or have not liked anything you have seen, keep looking. It's easy to interview three mediocre ad agencies (there are plenty of them) and conclude that you are not experienced enough to see the merit in the work. Avoid the opposite mistake of interviewing so many people that your head swims.

**Step 4. Ask the right questions at the portfolio review and interview.** All communications vendors keep samples of their best work for evaluation by prospective clients. This assemblage of work is called a *portfolio.* Printers show their most ornate brochures. Ad agencies will display their best ads. Radio and TV people carry around a briefcase full of recorded tapes.

When the vendors meet you for the first time they will show you their portfolios. A portfolio may be presented in a number of ways. Some portfolio presentations consist of going through a pile of printed materials or slides. Other portfolios are carefully mounted into books. Large agencies may present themselves with elaborate, multimedia presentations. One photographer we know uses mounted color transparencies and a miniature light table contained in a small briefcase. Portfolio presentations are as diverse as the materials you will see.

Study each portfolio carefully. Take notes—it will help you remember details later. Do the sample pieces draw your attention? Are you so mesmerized by the piece that you are unaware of the design? If so, it is probably good stuff. After reviewing the visual content and writing of each piece, ask questions: What was the purpose of the project? How much involvement did the client have in the ideas and message? Who was the photographer and designer? Who wrote the piece? What was the most difficult aspect of this project? How long did the project take? What was the project's budget? Did the project get finished on time? No? Why not? What was the project's intended benefit (i.e., to increase awareness, build quick sales, develop long-term credibility)? Were the results measurable?

If the answers seem unclear or if the vendor is unsure about any of the specifics, you may be looking at a piece that this vendor did not produce—or the vendor's actual involvement may have been minimal. Claiming a larger share of credit for a project than is due or outright plagiarism are unfortunate realities in the communications business.

---

### ✎ TIP: THE INTERVIEW EXPOSES PROBLEMS

A key giveaway for disorganized creative talent is poor judgment. A designer or writer who presents and explains 50 dusty brochures during an interview probably lacks the ability to prioritize and manage time. If they can't do it on a portfolio review, they surely won't be able to do it on a project.

---

Before or after the portfolio has been reviewed, depending on the meeting, you will need to ask each vendor specific, standard questions, including: How long have you been doing this? Who else have you worked for? What special qualities do you have that will allow you to complete this project better than anyone else? You should feel comfortable with the vendor. You should be made to feel that you are an important client and that the vendor is interested in your company and products.

If you like what you see and hear up to then, ask "the killer question:" *"If we hired you for this project today, off the top of your head, what would you do?"*

This question requires quick thinking by the applicant. Since creative people are trained to "think on their feet," they will usually provide a good answer. An inadequate response or waffling usually indicates serious inexperience and you should look elsewhere. Fast, pat, superficial, or incompetent replies are equally suspect.

If you are still interested after hearing their initial ideas, ask the obvious questions: How much will it cost and how long will it take? If they give you an immediate date and price, without taking time to scope out the job in further detail, be forewarned. Although a ballpark estimate at this point is okay, anyone who quotes a price and schedule without first reviewing your requirements and expectations in more detail is either so expensive that it doesn't matter or not experienced enough to know better.

---

✎      **TIP: SOMETIMES WHAT YOU SEE IS NOT WHAT YOU GET**

Business attire is one standard tool for evaluating conventional job applicants that may not apply to all creative service vendors. So, if you simply choose the best dressed vendor you may not be hiring the best talent.

---

**Step 5. Check references on new vendors.** Many single communications projects have budgets of more than a $100,000. The annual budget for advertising may be multiple millions of dollars. That is a lot of money to risk on an unknown vendor. Check out each new vendor you hire—whether agency or individual. The best con men are always remembered by their victims for their kindly, persuasive manner. Advertising people are experts at presenting the product (themselves) in a positive light. At the interview, ask the vendor for references. Then make a few polite phone calls to find out what the references thought about the work and the working relationship. Do some digging if you feel the reference answers are too contrived and practiced. A few minutes on the phone now could save your budget later.

**Step 6. Verify the business terms and put them in writing.** Before you make your final selection, be sure to verify the prices and business terms. Ask if the vendor charges by the hour or a flat fee for the project. Both ways are standard, though by the hour has more risk attached. If a flat fee, what exactly is included? How many drafts or changes can be made for the same fee? You should always agree on a fee schedule for changes and additional revisions, whatever the cause.

If other subcontractors will be working on the project, who pays for their services? When are payments due? What status reports will be provided? Are travel, telephone, and materials charges included in the estimates? You get the idea. If you don't ask in advance, you may be in for surprises you didn't budget for. And be sure to put the answers and final agreements in writing. True hell is a vendor who thinks the job is finished when you think it has just begun: you can quickly get caught in a battle over time and expenses. We have been there and it isn't fun. To avoid this, make everything clear in advance and the entire project and relationship with the vendor will go better.

# A BRIEF GUIDE TO THE VENDORS YOU WILL MEET

As stated before, the task in choosing vendors is to carefully match the right people to the work at hand. If you follow the six steps just detailed you will always have a reasonably good idea whether a vendor will be able to handle the job. But since the purveyors of creative and production services come in all shapes and sizes, it is also helpful to know a little about the various suppliers and how they operate.

In the following pages the key vendors you need to be familiar with are reviewed, with hints on what to look for when hiring each kind. These include advertising agencies, public relations agencies, design firms and designers, promotional writers, photographers, illustrators, printers, and commercial production companies. There are a number of specialty vendors not included; some of these are discussed in other chapters, but most of them fall generally under the headings presented here. Highly technical services, such as color separation, photo retouching, audio dubbing, and advertising research can be purchased directly, but these services are usually coordinated by the agencies or freelancers as part of their work.

## Advertising Agencies

> She hung up and I set out the chessboard. I filled a pipe, paraded the chessmen and inspected them for French shaves and loose buttons, and played a championship tournament game between Gortchakoff and Meninkin, seventy-two moves to a draw, a prize specimen of the irresistible force meeting the immovable object, a battle without armor, a war without blood, and as elaborate a waste of human intelligence as you could find outside an advertising agency.
>
> Raymond Chandler
> *The Long Goodbye*

In large or complex projects or extended advertising campaigns, you will need multiple people to complete the project; this is why companies hire agencies. The belief is that the agency has already selected the talent—all you have to do is select the agency.

Large, well-equipped agencies handle most aspects of a project inhouse, going outside only for special services. Ad agencies also plan and budget for clients and buy advertising space (media). Some agencies specialize in one type of advertising such as television, print, consumer goods, or technical products, although they may not tell you that directly. Most

| Vendor | Price per Hour | Business Terms | Best for: |
|---|---|---|---|
| Advertising Agencies | $65 - $180+ (Agencies also take a percentage of all media placed for clients. ) | Long term retainer or contract w/ extra charges for special projects. | Ad agencies are best at creating and placing media advertising. Most agencies will take on a variety of projects by buying services from subcontractors. |
| Public Relations Agencies | $65 - $145+ | Long term retainer or contract w/ extra charges for special projects. | PR agencies are best at writing and placing PR product and company releases with the press. Most PR groups will also handle special events such as seminars and press conference arrangements. |
| Designer /Design Groups | $50 - $150+ | Charges on a per project basis. | Best at design-intensive projects including brochures, annual reports and corporate identity programs. |
| Writers | $45 - $220+ | Charges on a per project basis unless handling a long term ad program. | Freelance writers may write only copy for a project or they may take the entire project from concept to finish, buying services from designers, photographers, etc. |

Figure 9.2. Four key vendors and what they are best at.

large advertising agencies will produce brochures and annual reports for clients, though this is rarely their forte.

Small agencies, consisting of a handful of people, abound. These may provide a wide range of services or specialize in servicing one kind of business, often local retail stores or small manufacturers. Some of these agencies specialize in collateral material or direct mail or even tradeshows. You may also run into "agencies" consisting of only one or two people. These firms have more in common with freelance talent and should be considered such.

Agencies are built up around the creative ability and industrious efforts of a principal or two. The agency is then grown into a business over a period of years. Some large agencies are the result of mergers and purchases, complete with employees and clients. Most advertising agencies consist of a creative team to develop the concept and carry out the work, a management team to oversee the development of the business, and a sales team to search out new accounts and coordinate existing ones. There is also a section of media buyers who purchase space in newspapers and magazines and time on TV and radio for their clients. Larger agencies may also offer a research department for assessing industry trends and buying habits based on advertising.

Most agencies will provide you with an account manager, also commonly called an account executive. The account manager is essentially a salesperson who serves as diplomat between a client, the agency management, and agency creative group. Because the account manager is responsible for coordinating the work on your projects, the person assigned to you is critical and an evaluation of their ability and personality should be part of your decision when you hire an agency. If your account is quite large or the agency small, you may deal directly with the principals.

Unlike writers and all but the most aggressive designers, agencies actively solicit clients and work. Most large agencies advertise their services in major publications. Agencies will arrange a *dog and pony show* to demonstrate their capabilities and willingness to take you on as a client. These shows can be deceptively compelling (just like the advertising these agencies produce).

The selection of an ad agency is a major event in most companies, involving multiple managers and even top executives in the decision, so the selection process can fall prey to compromise and politics. Don't let politics and theatrics cloud the decision. The most important thing is to hire an agency that fits your budget and creative needs and one that meets your schedules. If you are a small account and you hire an agency that is too large, they will put junior staff on your projects and generally ignore you. If an agency is too small or too new, you may not get work of the right caliber or the best placement of your ads because the agency has little leverage when purchasing media.

A recent trend in major companies is to give their most important work to small, highly creative agencies while handing out the long-term campaigns and on-going projects and media placement to a larger, established agency.

It is also important to locate an agency that has worked in your market. A good choice is an agency that formerly worked for a direct competitor. You will be pleased with the zealous treatment your projects receive and you will not have to educate the agency about the competition.

If the agency looks and feels right, identify the senior members on your account team and interview them individually (traditionally over lunch). Ask the standard interview questions with an emphasis on understanding the relationships back at the agency. Evaluate the account personnel based on your answers to these three questions:

1. Can I work with this person and communicate with him or her effectively?
2. Does this person have a positive relationship with the agency?
3. Are there political problems within the agency as evidenced by this person's answers and attitudes (common with the egos involved)?

The fancy song and dance put on by major agencies with expensive dinners and elaborate presentations sometimes demonstrates their interest in signing you as a client. Assuming that you are considering three or more possible candidate agencies, wait two or three days after the hoopla has subsided and then coldly rate each agency on its own merits. Rate an agency based on the criteria listed below. Combine the scores, based on a scale of 1–10, for each person involved in the decision and then total up the scores for each candidate agency. (A checklist has been provided you can use for this.)

1. **Knowledge of your products and marketplace.** Have they worked with clients in similar industries? Do they know your markets and distribution channels?
2. **Obvious creative ability as evidenced in the portfolio review and presentation.** Are their ideas good? Are the ideas appropriate for the market? Are they well executed? Does the portfolio show a range of capabilities and projects suitable for your industry?
3. **Results produced for other clients.** Can the agency demonstrate tangible successes in terms of increased sales and expanded customer awareness? Most agencies will loudly proclaim these successes; if they don't, it may be for good reason.
4. **The account manager.** Is the person knowledgeable and easy to work with?

5. **The principals.**   What are their backgrounds, strengths, and talents? Will they be involved in your account? Are they accessible? What is the reputation of the agency as a whole?

6. **Review of sample ideas for your account.**   If you have the time, give each agency a test. Have them take your input and produce simple sketches of their preliminary ideas for you to rate. If your account is worth the effort, an agency really interested in your business will do this free. If your account is small, however, you shouldn't expect an agency to do this unless you are prepared to pay for the work.

Before you make your final decision, bring the top scoring agency in one more time and discuss general business relationships. What is their discount structure for retained accounts? What level of retainer is required and what work will be completed for this retainer? How will schedules and status reports be handled? Do they have a sample contract to review?

---

✎   **TIP: REVIEW AGENCY PERFORMANCE REGULARLY**

Because agencies often lose their edge if they lose key employees or principals, you must continually assess their performance. Conduct a formal agency review every six months, or at least once a year. Even if the agency is doing a good job, it keeps them on their toes. Since larger agencies often demand a long-term contract, ensure that the relationship can be amicably terminated with a 30-day notice.

---

If the business terms seem agreeable, then you have found yourself an advertising agency! Many company/agency relationships last for decades. Typically these loyal companies ask for the account managers to be changed only when things start going awry. But be forewarned: many companies replace their agencies (or agencies resign) on a regular basis. Agencies are replaced because the relationship is always highly political and usually fraught with egos on both sides, because some agencies don't deliver what they promise, and because managers feel a change of agency is good for stirring up the market with fresh ideas. For whatever reason, your first agency selection may not be your last. However, if you do a good job the first time, you have a better chance of avoiding having to select another agency soon.

## Public Relations Agencies

Public Relations (PR) agencies handle all phases of public relations and publicity, including research and planning, writing of press releases and

Agency Name _____ Date _____

**Rating**
**1-10**

☐ Knowledge of your products and marketplace.

☐ Obvious creative ability as evidenced in the portfolio review and presentation.

☐ Results produced for other clients.

☐ The account manager.

☐ The principals and/or general agency reputation.

☐ Quality of sample ideas for your account.

☐ **Total**

**Ratings:**
- **50 to 60** - Probably a good choice.
- **40 to 49** - Okay, consider choosing this agency if you are in a market where no other
      affordable and available agency has adequate experience to handle
      your product.
- **0 to 39** -  Keep looking!

**Agency Notes and Comments:**

_____

_____

Figure 9.3.  Hiring an ad agency checklist.

related articles, and, most importantly, making editorial contacts. A good PR agency makes its money because of its contacts with the press and financial community.

Like advertising agencies, public relations agencies also come in various sizes. In fact, many small public relations firms consist of only one or two exceptional individuals and these small agencies may provide services of equal quality to the larger firms. In the larger agencies, a central core of managers works with clients and sales representatives to plan public relations strategies for their clients. A large PR agency usually has a brilliant PR tactician in the center, but if you're not a major client, you'll never see this person.

Larger PR agencies will almost always provide you with both a senior account executive (a senior member of the firm) for strategy and planning and an account manager for the routine, day-to-day activities. You should be able to communicate effectively with both of these people and you should feel confident in their ability to represent your company.

Though both PR agencies and ad agencies use account managers to service their clients, the role of the account manager in most PR agencies is different than in an ad agency. PR account managers are more active contributors and may do a lot of the writing and editorial contact directly. Again, this means that the account manager is a critical component in your choice of an agency.

Unlike advertising, which may immediately improve sales performance with a single ad, PR work may take longer to reap significant results. It may take months or even a year or more in some industries to get significant benefits from public relations efforts. Because of this, you should expect a long-term relationship with your PR firm before seeing results and you should take your time finding the right agency for your company. The better the match, the better the results. And, like choosing an ad agency, your PR agency must fit the size of your company and budget.

When selecting a PR agency pay particular attention to the key members of the team that calls on you. That person or persons must be intimately familiar with your industry and the newspapers and magazines that influence your customers. Never hire an agency on the premise that they will learn about your market—it takes too long and wastes your budget on useless hours of billable time.

Use the checklist provided to evaluate the PR agency (refer to the advertising agency section for more detail on the questions). Like hiring an ad agency, you can ask the prospective agencies to prepare sample press releases to evaluate their writing ability. Unfortunately, where the ad samples demonstrate most of the agency's capabilities, writing samples show little about a PR agency's total capabilities, so it's been left off the checklist.

Your team should contain one or more excellent writers. Ask for samples of their writing and review them carefully. Your account people must be able to communicate effectively in writing and then influence editors to print what they write. Your best indicators of PR accomplishment are the clippings from newspapers and magazines that the agency will show you as part of its portfolio. Compare their press releases to what actually made it into print. If they don't have quality clippings, the agency is of little value to you.

Agency Name _____ Date _____

Rating
**1-10**

☐  Knowledge of your products and marketplace.

☐  Obvious writing ability as evidenced in the portfolio review and presentation.

☐  Results produced for other clients.

☐  The account manager.

☐  The principals and/or general agency reputation.

☐  **Total**

**Ratings:**
- **40 to 50** - Probably a good choice.
- **30 to 39** - Okay, consider choosing this agency if no other agency has adequate experience in your market.
- **0 to 29** - Keep looking!

**Agency Notes and Comments:**

_____

_____

_____

_____

Figure 9.4.  Hiring a PR agency checklist.

If you can't find the right kind of talent locally, use an agency in another city. PR can be effectively handled with phone and FAX along with occasional fly-in meetings. If you are located in a major market, PR services can get quite expensive. Try interviewing firms in smaller, less expensive cities.

Some PR firms have high turnover rates. Others expand very quickly. In either case, the people assigned to your account may leave or become overburdened with too many other clients. Ask some pointed questions to make sure the people on your account will be able to handle your work effectively.

As always, before you make a final decision, clarify the PR firm's business terms. They vary considerably from agency to agency. PR firms typically work on a retainer or hourly basis. Some have different rates for clipping services, research, planning, and article placement. It is also important to establish some performance goals with your PR agency so both you and the agency are clear on the criteria for measuring success.

## Combination Agencies: One-Stop Shopping for Services

There are some agencies that have multiple divisions for advertising, public relations, and design. They are a one-stop solution and for this reason they are sometimes easier to use. However, in practice, these agencies are usually better at one aspect of communications than the others. It's best to evaluate each aspect of the agency as if you were hiring separate vendors for each service. In this way you will know if the agency really has the ability to meet all your needs under one roof.

## Designers and Design Firms

Design firms specialize in creating the look and feel of communications. Some design firms dabble in advertising strategy and placement as a sideline, although their main strength is graphic design. Designers are a must in most projects—but do not let them substitute for good writing and marketing talent. All advertising agencies have their own designers on staff, but they may still go outside for designers who specialize in a certain area such as packaging, tradeshows, or identity development. Note that ad agency designers are rarely as skilled in collateral projects as those found in a competent design firm. That's why the award-winning brochures and annual reports are rarely done by ad agencies.

Designers usually work alone or in small groups, sometimes employing or sharing a paste-up person. Most designers will accept any kind of visual project, although some successful ones specialize in one product area or type of design—such as brochures or displays or logos. Designers usually have a strong reputation in an area if they have been around a while—and it is easier to find an expensive one than a good, reasonably priced one, though these do exist.

As individuals, designers often have a degree in graphic design or fine art from a university or private art school. After graduating, many serve an informal apprenticeship with an experienced designer, working first as paste-up artist and "gofer." On showing promise, they may be promoted to the rank of junior designers and begin a journey up the design firm's ladder. After becoming frustrated with slow career growth and gaining enough practical experience and an adequate portfolio, most designers attempt to set up a freelance business. With success as a free-lancer, a designer will quit the day job and set up shop, hiring other people as the business grows.

Choosing design talent is done on the basis of the "Two Ps"—*Port-folio* and *Personality*. For personality, look for a designer who provides straightforward answers to your questions and makes at least a token attempt at being congenial. As far as the portfolio, attempt to select a designer who has produced work for your market. The work should look at least as good as some of the best samples you have collected.

If your current project requires the services of a writer, include the writer in the interview process along with the designer and seriously consider any objections or concerns the writer may have. If you are new to marketing communications, it's usually advisable to spend your energy selecting a writer capable of managing complete projects and let the writer choose the designer. A practiced eye is required to understand the complexity of visual design and to identify the right kind of personality for the project. This is an ideal opportunity to watch someone with more experience interview and select the right person for the job.

There are four types of designers who should be avoided if possible:

1. Designers with snobbish or condescending personalities. Although some of these people may be considered the best in the business, they are impossible to manage.
2. Freelancers with day jobs, unless you are on a tight budget and loose schedule.
3. Designers who absolutely insist on charging you by the hour and will not provide a budget for the project. The design budget is difficult to control even with a fixed quote.
4. Designers with portfolios in which everything looks the same. Unless this is the exact look you want for your company, these "one look" designers often lack the motivation, creativity, or both to create a unique and appropriate look tailored to your needs and market.

## Promotional Writers

For marketing communications you almost always need a promotional writer, a writer very different from technical writers or novelists. Promotional writers often specialize in particular product areas such as consumer goods or technology—although some are quite versatile. Writers may also specialize in certain kinds of projects—such as brochures, ads, radio/TV spots, or product articles. Even if the writer claims to be

Vendor Name _____ Date _____

Kind of Services Offered: _____

### Rating
### 1-10

☐  Knowledge of your products and marketplace.

☐  Obvious talent and experience as evidenced in the portfolio review and presentation.

☐  Results produced for other clients.

☐  The vendor's personality: Can I communicate effectively with this person?

☐  Total

**Ratings:**
- **30 to 40**  - Probably a good choice.
- **20 to 29**  - Okay, consider this vendor if the price is right and your schedule is not too tight.
- **0 to 19**   - Keep looking!

**Notes and Comments:**

_____

_____

_____

_____

_____

Figure 9.5. Hiring freelance vendors.

multifaceted, a review of the portfolio will usually give you an idea of the writer's strengths, weaknesses, and preferences.

Promotional writers usually work alone (unless they work inside an advertising or PR agency) and typically have strong contacts with designers and agencies in the area. Some writing agencies exist, but these usually handle technical manuals or foreign language translations and are not of use to you for marketing communications.

Most promotional writers have formal training in journalism or English. Some come from a technical field, such as computer science, engineering, or medicine. After leaving school, the prospective advertising writer usually takes a position that provides an opportunity to hone writing skills and build a portfolio. Some writers start out writing technical materials or in account management for an agency. After gaining experience and building an adequate portfolio, they pick up freelance business while continuing their full-time employment. If business is brisk, the writer quits the regular job and writes full time. Many good promotional writers become principals in agencies.

In your search for good promotional writers you will find writers who are experienced and inexperienced, brilliant and pedestrian, organized and scatterbrained. The most innovative writers are idea oriented and very creative—but not always meticulous. They depend on *proofreaders* to keep tabs on grammar and spelling. On the other hand, some meticulous writers are great at spelling and constructing orthodox English structures, but write boring copy. Most promotional writers fall somewhere between these extremes.

The six basic steps for finding a writer are the same as for any communications vendor. When you get to the portfolio review, you will be evaluating both the writing quality and the appropriateness of the writing for the target market. Evaluating strong writing takes a while to learn, though most poor promotional writing suffers from two basic problems: the *fog factor* and the *too much hype syndrome.*

Writing with a high fog factor (bad) requires too much concentration to get through. Are you yawning after skimming a couple of paragraphs? Do you have to force yourself to concentrate on the writing because it is vague or uninteresting. (If watching a portfolio of videotaped TV ads, do you stayed glued to the screen or is your brain subconsciously tuning out?) If so, the fog factor is unacceptable.

Writing with too much hype is easier to spot; it has lots of unbelievable statements and not much substance. This is usually an indication of a writer following a well-worn formula or one who really didn't understand the market or the product before writing about it. By using the fog factor and the hype syndrome you can evaluate most promotional writing without analyzing complexities such as sentence structure and style.

Strong, concise promotional writing is clear, often creative, and always stylistically appropriate and consistent for the market. Look for samples in your piles that you can't put down once you begin reading. Look for a clear message. Do you know what is being sold and why you would want to buy it? Are the benefits of buying the product or service clear or does the writer mindlessly list only the product's features?

Like any communications professional, an experienced writer will present you with a portfolio of projects to demonstrate skill and achievement. A very inexperienced writer may show you several well-executed college papers or work from a university newspaper. Most pros will show you one or two kinds of work that they consider their specialty. Some writers may show samples as diverse as ad campaigns, speeches, complete books, brochures, and even television scripts in one portfolio.

Match writing talent to your needs. A writer with a strong portfolio of car ads may be perfect for consumer goods advertising, but if you sell boards for computers, may stumble over the technology. Writing scripts for television ad spots is very different than producing effective copy for print advertising, although some writers can handle both. Look for direct experience with the kind of project you have at hand.

Most writers quote an hourly rate, with the very best ones charging as much as $300 an hour in major markets. You can find excellent writing services for $50 and up in most cities. Some writers quote by the job, studying the situation to see what the market will bear.

Depending on your level of experience and available time, you can hire writers to work on projects in one of three ways:

1. Spend a little extra money and have the writer handle the entire project. The writer will be the primary source for ideas and will hire and direct the designers and production people to bring the project to conclusion.
2. Manage the writer and the other project elements yourself. This will increase your involvement, but will reduce billable hours and save money (if you know what you want).
3. Write a rough draft of the copy yourself and hire a writer to polish the draft into copy. At the very worst, the writer can use your draft as input notes.

If your writer handles the entire project you will need a more experienced and more expensive vendor. Doing it yourself depends on your capabilities. If your manuscript is a real mess it may take extra time to sort it out and ultimately cost you more in time and money. On the other hand, if you effectively organize the subject matter and get the words down on paper in near finished form, a capable $25 per hour editor/proofreader can be used to polish the copy.

As with designers, there are also writers to avoid. Here are the five types to stay away from:

1. Overly academic writers. Their academic writing style is inappropriate and they are often tough to manage.

2. Writers who still use typewriters or paper and pencil (instead of a word processor), especially if you are in a hurry. It takes them longer to make changes and you pay for the extra hours. There are still some top talents around who don't use computers, but their numbers are dwindling.

3. Writers who won't quote a price on a first and second draft. If they insist on charging by the hour, you will have real problems controlling costs.

4. Writers who have day jobs and write part time on the side. Between the day job and your project, these writers are too tired to think, let alone write compelling copy.

5. Technical writers or other writers attempting to work outside their area of expertise.

## Printers and Print Shops

Printers are hired on a job-by-job basis. As already discussed in Chapter 8, there are three basic kinds of printers—quick printers, commercial shops, and specialty printers. These three kinds of printers are different in the equipment they own, the caliber and experience of their employees, and the kinds of jobs they can successfully handle. Small shops may be run by Mom and Pop. Really big shops may have 10 presses running simultaneously and employ 150 people or more.

When selecting a printer, your task is to match the right shop in terms of employee experience, equipment, and price to your needs. The best way to select a printer is to use your designer's eyes to evaluate several shops' samples (a print shop's term for a portfolio) coupled with your evaluation of the prices quoted. It may also be informative to visit each shop and take a tour of their facilities. This will give you a more realistic understanding of how printers work and you will get to inspect their equipment and organization firsthand. This is an excellent educational opportunity. Any printer who won't provide you with a tour probably has a dirty shop or less equipment than claimed—reasons to reject the bid.

Most designers and writers will already have a relationship with several printers. Providing there is no hidden financial relationship (as discussed in Chapter 10), one of these shops may be a good choice. Because your vendor has already worked with these shops, they will have a good idea of the printer's capabilities and reliability. And since most designers want to see the design project look as perfect as possible when finished, they will recommend a good shop. They may, however, recommend too good a shop with higher than average prices—something you need to watch out for.

When selecting a printer, look for ease of communication with the shop's rep, be it the owner or a hired salesperson. You need someone you feel comfortable asking questions of, as well as a person fully trained in the printing business. A good rep can look your project over and save you money. This person should also be your first line of defense should the project run into trouble on press or if the postpress bills exceed your expectations.

Second, unless your project consists of a simple black-and-white job for a quick printer, look for a shop that has been in business under the same ownership for at least five years. Poorly run shops with inept management, poor internal communications, second-string presspeople, and broken-down equipment rarely survive five years because the business is extremely competitive.

Although you want a shop that has been in business for a while, don't make the error of going with a shop just because it has been around for 75 years. Old shops may have archaic equipment not capable of the reproduction standards of modern presses. Although the basics of the technology have changed little in the past 30 years, the refinements during that period have been substantial. In the case of four-color process printing, the quality that only a handful of shops could achieve in the 1950s has become routine in the 1990s. If you are considering an older shop, make sure that they have updated their equipment and either retrained or replaced their employees within the past decade.

Before you and your designer select a printer, read about the printing process in Chapter 8 if you have not already done so. And, when you get the bids, always get them in writing on any job more complex than a short-run, one-color quick print job. A printer's bid should spell out exactly what you ordered in terms of number of colors, number of images, number of pages, paper brand and weight, and print quantity. If there are additional bindery or other special processes such as foil stamping, those should be described in detail. Here are several shops and people to avoid in your search for a printer:

1. Shops with crusty owners or reps. The printing business is very competitive and it can be difficult to make money. Over the years many shop owners, and to a lesser degree salespeople, become bitter after losing money and dealing with problem jobs. They may have the troubles of the world on their shoulders, but you don't need to share them. Find another shop.

2. Printers who will take on any kind of job. When interviewing shops ask them what kind of work they do. Most shops will respond by saying they handle mostly multicolored jobs such as brochures and color packaging or, in the case of a quick printer, cards and letterhead and small brochures. Printers who

claim to do everything should raise an immediate red flag. No printer has the right equipment to do every kind of work cost-effectively. Printers who will take on anything are either desperate for work because of little repeat business or willing to take on jobs that they may not be able to complete satisfactorily. In addition, the shop may charge too much, as in the case of a fully equipped printer taking on a small black and white job. Sometimes these all-in-one printers broker jobs to a friend with the right equipment. All of these scenarios are bad news and you should pass on using this shop.

3. Printers that bid too low. Assuming you are asking for bids from at least three shops, be wary of a printer that substantially underbids the other two. This may point to a shop that has poor estimating capabilities and other serious management problems within the company. Or it may expose a shop that cuts corners to the point that your project will suffer. When this happens, the low bid is always attractive but it may spell trouble. Of course it's always possible that the other shops were bidding your job too high. As a further check, ask for a bid from a fourth printer and then reevaluate the pricing.

## Independent Video and Commercial Production Companies

Except in a few instances when advertising agencies have their own production teams and studios, most television and radio commercials are not directed, filmed, or edited within the agency. Instead, the agency creative people supervise the production of the commercial and an independent commercial production company is used for the actual work. Because supervising television and radio commercial production is complex, companies will usually use their advertising agency to supervise the production. The trick here is making sure the agency has experience with these media. However, some small companies or one-time projects may be best served by going to a video or production company directly.

Usually centered around a core of principals (like an advertising agency), most production companies provide a full range of video or sound production services. Currently production companies are proliferating. Video technology is becoming far less expensive and that means more small companies can more easily afford to put together sophisticated production facilities.

Hiring a commercial production company or specialist is much the same as hiring a full-service advertising agency. There are thousands of such production companies around, ranging from closet-sized to massive studios. A typical TV commercial uses the skills of a director, a production assistant (and/or producer), a script writer, actors, set designers, animators, production specialists, sound and camera crews, and a skilled editor to assemble the pieces into a ready-to-air tape. In a small production company these people will be hired on a project basis. In a large production company many of the talents will be on permanent staff. Unless you are very experienced in producing commercials, it is best to use your energy selecting an agency or production company and let the professionals choose the talent for the rest of the project.

Most producers and directors, who will be the principals in a production company responsible for coordinating production and directing the commercials, study cinematography at a university or film school. Many begin by making short, low-budget films as class projects. Unfortunately, on graduating there are few profitable feature film opportunities for new directors, and graduates end up working in a related field, such as assisting in making commercials or training films, or as assistant directors and producers, gradually working into positions of increasing creative responsibility—maybe even forming their own production companies. Other commercial spot producers and directors may be found working inside radio and TV stations, running independent studios, and inside advertising agencies that handle this kind of work. There are also freelance directors and producers who pick up whatever work is available and interesting—although until you are experienced in coordinating commercial production, stay away from the freelancers.

Radio commercials may be made by advertising agencies in their own sound rooms or handled by a professional recording studio. Many commercials are written by a freelance writer and produced by a radio personality—a person with a strong, practiced voice. The radio personality may use the station's equipment or a personal in-home studio.

Evaluating radio and TV commercials is easier for most people than print projects because they are exposed to so many spots on TV and radio. Look for talent with a portfolio of strong, compelling tapes that captivate the eye (and/or ear) while providing a clear, crisp message about the product. Some prospects may show you a portfolio consisting of storyboards—a presentation with sequenced sketches of each scene with dialogue and captions printed underneath. These are harder to evaluate and their use may point to an applicant company that has had little success breaking into film.

Particularly important when selecting a production company is to get an idea of how much the portfolio spots cost. TV commercials are the most expensive media to produce with some Fortune 500 companies spending *millions* on a single 60-second spot. You need a production company that has produced effective work in your price range, not a company with tapes that cost 10 times your total budget. Of course, if you need to get at the masses on a major network, don't hire a company that has worked only on the cheap. If you are on a budget, look for a company that looks for ways to save you money. Rented props are cheaper than new ones. Often a friend of a friend will do the acting and voice-overs for less than the going rate. Occasionally a location may be available that will work instead of creating an expensive set in the studio. A vendor who attempts to look after your budget can save you both time and money without sacrificing quality.

Some production companies to avoid include the following:

1. Companies in which the principals have obvious ego problems. Because these people demand the complete obedience of everyone on a set and usually get it, it sometimes goes to their head. If you hire self-centered producers or directors, they may soon be managing you.

2. Small companies working out of their usual specialty. An out-of-work rock video producer or a freelancer who films weddings may not understand the timing issues associated with making effective 30-second TV or radio commercials.

3. In-house radio or TV station producers. Unless your project is on a *very* tight budget, the "assembly-line" approach used by most in-house producers will not adequately showcase your product. To see this kind of work in action, watch some late night television on the UHF channels in your area.

4. Production companies that insist on working on a time and materials basis. The unpleasant experience of watching the design budget for a print ad or brochure spiral out of control is nothing compared to what can happen when a TV spot goes awry. Agree to a project budget and stick to it or find another production company.

## Photographers

Many otherwise strong promotional pieces suffer from the incorporation of poor quality photography. Only professional photographers should be used to take the photos of people and products used in your marketing pieces. Photographers work either indoors in the studio where they can carefully control setup and lighting or outdoors *(on location)*. Very successful photographers may specialize in shooting only food, people, products, or complex location shots, but most are generalists, shooting whatever pays the bills. Photography requires expensive equipment as well as a large studio for indoor work. As a result, to save money, photographers often share studio space and equipment, and occasionally share jobs with each other.

Most photographers study photography in college, although some come from backgrounds in journalism or design. Most get started as

## ON LOCATION WITH THE COWS

We came up with the headline, "Put your blue box out to pasture" for a company with a competitor that manufactured the "blue box," a large, unreliable, and expensive piece of equipment. This manufacturer's solution replaced the blue box and sold for a fraction of the price. The ad was to show a blue box sitting in a field of cows (really!).

After a scouting trip we identified a willing dairy farmer with a farm located about 40 miles north of San Francisco. Arriving there the next week with an expensive photographer and a borrowed $35,000 blue box that weighed 145 pounds, we looked for a suitable site. By late morning, the farm was still socked in with fog and our photo budget was evaporating by the minute.

Trudging through mud (and worse) and trying not to disturb the cows, we finally found a good site, plenty of sleepy cows, and pasture not entirely torn up by hooves. The next step was to get the blue box out into the pasture and hope for the fog to lift. At 4:00 p.m., now covered with mud and soaked, the fog began to dissipate and we shot some test shots without the blue box. We decided it was a go and went to get the blue box from the van. Suddenly the cows got up and left. It was milking time.

photographer's assistants—setting up equipment, loading film, and processing prints. After learning the basics of running a photography business and acquiring equipment and a few clients, assistants go out on their own as photographers and hire assistants for themselves.

## ✐ TIP: USE STOCK PHOTOS TO SAVE MONEY

Quality photography is expensive in most markets and can seriously tax small budgets. Depending on the project requirements, you may be able to use existing photography shot by the best names in the business through a stock photo house. These organizations have thousands of professional images that you can rent for a one-time usage fee—usually a fraction of the cost of hiring a professional.

Choosing a photographer requires a practiced eye to understand the aesthetic quality of the work. Unless your shots are basic tabletop black-and-white product photos for a simple catalog or small newspaper ad, you will want to rely on the services of a designer or writer to choose and manage the photographer. Photo sessions require considerable art direction and creativity to get the best shots. This demands productive collaboration between the designer and the person behind the camera— and that takes experience. You can, however, save the designer's markup on the photo budget by paying the photographer's bill directly.

---

✎   **TIP: USE THE ASSISTANT TO SAVE YOUR BUDGET**

If your photos are not too complicated, you can sometimes hire the photographer's assistant to take shots for a much lower rate than the primary photographer. The assistant uses the features of the studio without having to pay for all the equipment.

---

Photography is usually purchased by the hour or day. Photographers typically quote the time separately, and charges for film, props, and finished prints are added to this price. If the shoot is to be on location, charges will be added for transportation and lodging if required. Photo session charges start at about $50 a shot for simple tabletop photographs, but most pros won't do that kind of work. Anything else costs $1000 to $4000 a day. A good designer working with the right photographer can save you money by squeezing in as many shots as possible in a short period of time.

Avoid using photographers who fit the following descriptions:

1. Photographers who do not own equipment or have a studio. This usually points to lack of experience or success. A photographer who rents equipment does not have the familiarity with it that day-to-day contact develops.
2. Moonlighting portrait photographers. Steer clear unless you want glossies of the kids for grandma.
3. Photographers who work through representatives, unless your project is so big that one photo studio can't handle it all. Working through an agent almost always inflates the bill.

### Illustrators

Illustrations include any kind of drawings or charts used in communications. Designers can handle very basic drawings and charts, but complex or highly stylized drawings require the services of a person who specializes in illustrations. Most illustrators prefer to work in one or two media such as pastel, airbrush, watercolors, or even paper sculpture. Many employ a personalized style in their work such as poignant cartoons, flashy superrealistic airbrush renderings, or silhouettes. More recently, illustrators are beginning to use the power of computers to create complex renderings and unusual special effects.

A typical illustrator studies art or graphic design in college, working a day job until honing drawing skills and building a credible portfolio. Because work is often in limited supply and there are too many would-be illustrators, only the best stay with it and prosper. For many styles of professional illustration, it takes years to develop the hand–eye skills and meticulous working styles that produce clean, professional quality drawings. Professionals also have to learn the difficult skill of making client-requested changes and corrections to a drawing without having to start over. Illustrators working on computers have less of a problem, but the computer still cannot provide the wide range of effects and textures available by hand.

Many illustrators often work through a business manager called an illustrator's rep. These representatives or agents usually manage a stable of illustrators working in a variety of techniques and styles. Thus, a single rep can provide almost any kind of illustration for his or her clients.

As with photographers, unless you are extremely experienced, hiring and directly managing an illustrator is a task for your designer. If, however, you buy services through a good rep, you can sometimes use the rep's skills to manage the artist and ensure quality. Illustrations can be less expensive alternatives to photography, and almost anything can be created, limited only by imagination and technical skills.

Pricing for illustration is most often based on the hours required to produce a finished image, with 20% added for the rep. Simple charts drawn by a designer start at $150. Professional airbrush illustrations with lots of detail go for $1000 and up, depending on the artist and the complexity of the piece. Artists who become well known for a particular style may charge astronomical prices, based on the demand for their work. Buying illustrations in Tulsa will be less expensive than in New York, although Tulsa will have a smaller range of professional illustrators from which to choose.

Illustrators you will want to avoid include the following:

1. Moonlighting technical illustrators. Most of these people have limited skill and imagination. Of course, if it is a technical drawing you want, then these artists are appropriate.
2. Illustrators with obviously strident personalities. If they seem irksome during an interview, they'll be a lot more difficult when you need changes to a drawing.
3. Illustrators who insist on working on a time and materials basis. This arrangement allows massive price overruns and may show a lack of project management experience on the part of the vendor. Most illustrators will quote a fixed price for an illustration, though they will charge extra for excessive changes and corrections by the client.
4. Illustrators who show a portfolio that does not display anything remotely in the style you need for your piece. They may insist that they can produce what you need, but be careful—some are

better than others in their ability to work in more than one modality.

## WHERE CAN YOU FIND VENDORS FOR YOUR PROJECT?

Now that you know what kinds of vendors are out there, you are probably wondering how to find them. If you are new to marketing communications, start your search for vendors by asking for recommendations from people who have more experience. Networking is one of the best ways to find good (and learn about the bad) talent. Ask peers in other companies, or if you see a piece you particularly like, call the company and ask who did it for them. Most large cities have advertising or marketing clubs and their meetings are listed in the business section of the local newspaper. Attend one. If you let the members know you have projects planned you will be besieged with business cards from freelancers and agencies alike.

If your contacts are slim, agencies tend to be longer surviving than freelancers—at least appearing in the phonebook before moving on. Look for them in the *Yellow Pages*. Depending on the city, there may be dozens or even hundreds of legitimate agencies listed. Commercial production agencies are also listed under *Advertising* or *Advertising Production* and occasionally under *Video Production.*

Some writers are listed in the *Yellow Pages* under *Writers*, but you may call 20 before you find one with the right kind of experience. Word of mouth is the best tool for locating a competent writer in most markets.

Design firms may be listed with the advertising agencies or under *Desktop Publishers,* now also listed in the phone book. Freelance designers are harder to track down. They move, take jobs, or go into another line of work when business is slow. Referrals by business associates are the best way to locate skillful, appropriately priced designers.

Calling a local graphic design school will bring lots of referrals (probably more than you want). Raw talent is rarely a substitute for real-world experience but occasionally someone will meet your needs for a simple project on a tight budget. You must be willing to put time and effort into intensive hands-on management if you hire people straight out of school. If you are new to communications, this is a rocky road to travel.

Most large cities and states have a source book published annually listing local advertising and marketing communications resources. In California and the western United States this reference is called *The Workbook.* Other regions and states have their own similar catalogs. There is even a national source book, called *The Creative Black Book,* for top agencies and expensive freelance talent across the United States. Other possible sources of information on agencies include the industry peri odicals, such as *Advertising Age* and *AdWeek,* widely read weekly business papers for people in the communications industry. The periodicals are best for general information or if you are looking for a large agency to handle your company's promotions. The book sections of large art sup ply stores carry many of these references.

## HOW TO CUT THE TIES IF THINGS GO WRONG

Sometimes, no matter how carefully you select a vendor, it just doesn't work out. You are left with no choice but to hire a replacement to complete or redo the job. Your company's purchase orders, the carefully negotiated bid, and the vendor's contract are your front-line defenses in a situation in which you need to terminate a vendor's work on a project (see Chapter 10).

If a vendor does fail to deliver on time, it is relatively easy to cancel the job. However, it is more difficult emotionally to cancel a contract with a vendor who is working hard to satisfy you but lacks the ability to satisfactorily complete the work. Always avoid personal attacks of any kind, but be clear and firm. Don't say, "This is the worst piece of junk I've seen since high school English." A boorish approach will make it difficult to precipitate an equitable settlement over the bill, and if the vendor is furious enough, you may find yourself involved in a lawsuit. Instead, try something like, "I feel that this isn't quite what we wanted and I am going to ask someone else to take another stab at it. What would you consider a reasonable price for the material completed so far?"

The unfinished work you purchase will always have some value. There may be useful research that another vendor can use. At worst it's a good example of what you don't want and that has value in helping to clarify your desires for the next vendor. When hiring replacement talent, follow the six steps for selection, but show the prospects the failed work. (Don't disclose the name of the last vendor. If you used someone very expensive, your vendor may quote high, figuring the last party did and got away with it.) Ask the new prospects how they would do it differently and listen carefully to their ideas or lack thereof before making a hiring decision.

And last, try to avoid the word "fired" with an undesirable vendor. If you follow the six steps in the selection process this will not happen often.

# 10 | Planning and Budgeting: Managing the Time and the Cost in Marketing Communications

Nothing in marketing communications should be started until you have a plan. A marketing communications plan includes the objectives for your marketing communications, the schedules for production, and the budgets for controlling marketing communications costs. Planning is important because it's your chance to sit back and think about the best ways to promote your product while evaluating the financial impact of various approaches. One of our clients put it best when he said that the reason to plan is simply because things go a lot smoother with planning than without it.

In addition, bringing communications projects in consistently late and over budget can be hazardous to your business and your career. This chapter provides guidelines for planning, scheduling, and budgeting your marketing communications that will allow you to consistently deliver communications projects on time and within budget.

## THE STEPS FOR CREATING A MARKETING COMMUNICATIONS PLAN

Marketing communications planning is usually done annually and broken out by month and quarter. Depending on your company's products and organizational structure, you may need to write individual plans for each product and product line. In large or segmented organizations with very different kinds of products a single marketing communications plan is impractical because of the hundreds of individual elements involved. It would be impossible to get an overview of how the events work with each other for specific products. Individual products with different target markets can rarely share communications tools, except for high level corporate image pieces. The products may have separate goals and priorities for communications. Therefore, it is best to create separate marketing communications plans for each different type of product. The separate plans also provide an easier mechanism for controlling costs associated with a particular product or goal. In addition to individual brand or product plans, companies need a corporate communications plan that covers overall image goals promoting the entire company.

In some companies all these individual plans are summarized and integrated into one master plan so an overall level of activity can be reviewed and potential conflicts in promotional activities can be identified before the plans are implemented.

Plans can also be broken apart by category of communications tool. For example, many companies have advertising plans, public relations plans, and collateral plans produced by outside agencies or internal departments. The plans for individual components are then integrated into an overall marketing communications plan.

The following steps will allow you to create a general marketing communications plan that works for almost any company, product, division, or type of marketing communications tool.

**Step 1. Start by evaluating where you are today.**   Every plan must start from the present. This information is often referred to as the situation analysis. Begin to prepare your new marketing communications plan by reviewing what you have or have not accomplished yet. Answer the following questions:

- What products do you sell and what are your markets? (Details on answering this are covered in Chapter 2.)
- What promotions did you use last year and what were the results?
- What is your market share?
- What is your financial situation? What were your sales, profits, margins, costs of goods sold, and other key financial indicators?
- What are the current trends and attitudes toward your products?
- How are your products distributed? Which distribution channels had the best results?
- And of course, complete the analysis with a comprehensive description of the competition, its products, share of market, and their marketing activities.

**Step 2. Establish and document your company objectives.**   You can't write a plan without new goals and objectives. Your company and product objectives will establish a foundation for building a complete marketing communications plan, choosing the most effective tools, and deciding on the priorities for allocating funds from the budget. Use your background information as a starting point. What things did you do well? What things need improvement? What new opportunities are here now that were not there last year? Overall corporate objectives that will affect your communications strategy include statements such as the following:

- Establish ourselves as the quality leader in XXX products.
- Maintain a 45% annual growth rate and increase profitability by 20% over last year.
- Enhance our overall corporate image as a technology innovator.

Specific corporate communications goals can be written after you answer these questions:

- What are my company's image development goals? (These goals include improving the image of a product line or company or adjusting the perception of a company's role in the community or marketplace in the mind of the market and the public. For example, a chemical company might want to improve its environmental image or a political candidate might want to gradually back away from an unpopular stand.)
- Are the corporate information tools we currently have adequate?
- Do customers recognize our name and products? Why or why not? What is missing? What could be done to improve this?
- Which market segments need the most attention?
- What relative position do we want to maintain in the industry?

**Step 3. Establish specific marketing and marketing communications goals for each product.**   After developing overall corporate goals, product specific goals for marketing and communications should be developed. The following questions should be answered to develop specific communications goals for each product:

- What are the short- and long-term plans for the product?
- What is the relative importance of this product compared to other products in the company's portfolio?
- What are the image goals for this product?
- How is this product positioned in relationship to the competition? (Is it higher quality and lower priced? Is it equal quality but more flexible? Is it unique in some way?)
- How many units do we need to sell to make our sales forecast goals?
- What percentage of marketshare do we need to meet our sales goals?
- Is there a new distribution channel planned?
- How many dealers or salespeople do we need to sign up to sell the products?
- Which market segments need to learn more about our products?

- Which important product or program introductions are coming up?
- What fixed-date events are important to our sales cycle (Christmas selling season, annual Friends of the Zoo party, election day)?

After answering these questions, you will be able to establish specific marketing goals for each product. Goals will include objectives based on financial criteria, including sales, profit, marketshare, and growth. In addition there should be objectives that cover concepts such as market exposure, image and attitude development within specific market segments, distribution development, and specific communications goals. These goals might be to:

- Introduce an XYZ product at a major tradeshow in January and follow up with a media blitz with the objective of establishing 100 new dealers by mid-March.
- Increase sales of DFG product by 35% while maintaining current profit margins based on superiority of the technology and concentrating on repeat purchasers.
- Be acknowledged by a majority of college students aged 21 to 25 as the best night spot in town as evidenced by a 50% increase in sales by the end of the year.
- Become the recognized standard for XDF products, as evidenced by support from at least three major trade organizations.
- Continue promoting the ABC product based on last year's plan, emphasizing quality and price advantages.
- Carefully phase out XYZ product, to be replaced by ZYX product later in the year.

These specific marketing objectives should be prioritized. Which event is most important? Which product needs the most promotion? What goal will have the most impact on your company profitability?

**Step 4. Create a list of marketing communications activities and projects to help achieve each goal on the list.** Starting with your prioritized list of objectives, list all your ideas for supporting and accomplishing each objective through marketing communications. Use the information from each of the specific chapters in the book to help you identify appropriate media and tools for each objective. Review the effectiveness of what is being used already. If something has always worked, why change it now?

Put together a wish list of your ultimate promotional dreams and then later scale them back to workable approaches wherever possible.

By not limiting the possibilities at the onset, you will feel free to come up with fresh ideas and innovative approaches. Do a complete wish list before beginning any scaling back—you might see an approach or combination of communications you never considered before. When putting the wish list together consider questions such as the following:

- Where do the customers get their information about products such as ours?
- What are the best ways to reach our customers based on our experience and the experience of our competition?
- What communications tactics have worked well in the past for this product or company?
- What tools can I reproduce that worked last year?
- What is the most outrageous, creative, spectacular event or promotion I can think of that would promote this product or company? (List them all.)

**Step 5. Choose the most effective promotions from your wish list.**   Now, using your wish list as a starting point, determine the best media mix for meeting your specific goals. Which media have the best reach for the least amount of money? Which tools have worked best in the past? Choose the specific tools you will actually use to meet your goals.

Approximate prices for each idea can be gleaned from last year's plans or a few phone calls to potential providers. Last year's plan, if you have one, is also a good reminder of important dates, and you can study the plan to see what worked and what flopped.

When choosing specific marketing communications tools and strategies from your list, you must weigh the cost and risk of each communication tool against its potential merit and reward. Simply put, you want "the most bang for your buck." If placing nightly 30-second commercials on TV's Cable News Network (CNN) looks like a promising tactic but will bankrupt your company months before it pays off, then its cost and risk greatly exceed its merit and reward. Scrap it in favor of a more workable approach such as placing radio commercials on less expensive local stations combined with newspaper ads. When your company gets more cash it can reconsider the ads on CNN.

Prioritize the projects and make sure a specific goal is established for each tool on your list that supports the overall objectives. For example, if your overall objective is to increase marketshare by 35%, then a specific goal for the magazine advertisement you have decided to use should be to get a certain number of new leads from the ad. Determine a rough monthly schedule for completion of each communication or placement of each advertisement.

As appropriate determine the media, format, and message platform for each of the marketing communications tools you have decided to use. In addition, determine the suggested frequency for all the advertisements and recurring events in your marketing communications plan.

**Step 6. Establish an overall budget for marketing communications.** Now that you have a prioritized list of projects, let a little reality set in. You will have to set a realistic budget for your corporate communications and your product communications. There are a number of ways that companies do this.

One of the most popular techniques is to allocate a percentage of sales to marketing communications. This percentage is usually based on an industry standard or the company's experience in the past. Unfortunately, the percentage is usually arbitrary and if a static percentage is allocated year after year, it assumes that the marketplace remains unchanged. This is rarely the case. Marketing communications are supposed to stimulate sales—therefore limiting communications to a percentage of sales violates this principle. If sales decline in this model, less will be spent on marketing communications—exactly the opposite of what should happen in most cases.

Another popular way that companies use to establish a budget for marketing communications is to copy what the competition does. This is called budgeting based on competitive parity. This is a dangerous way to budget—because your objectives are probably not the same as your competitor's. You may miss opportunities to steal marketshare with this kind of thinking. Let them follow you instead.

A recommended budget approach is to look at the rough costs for the most important projects on your wish list. If the goals for these pieces can be met, then the cost of doing the pieces should be worthwhile. This will establish an overall budget. Another approach that is similar to this is the zero-based budgeting approach, which is useful if there are too many projects or not enough resources.

The *Zero-Based Budget,* called ZBB for short, is a simple budgeting technique that allows you to set priorities and get a real understanding of exactly what can and cannot be accomplished. Best of all, if your superiors are trying to push you into an impossible marketing communications plan—one short on money or people—the ZBB provides a difficult to dispute gauge of project overload. And unlike complicated spreadsheet or project management charts, it is easily understood by just about anyone.

The ZBB is easy to implement. On a large sheet of paper simply list all projects under consideration. This can take the form of your "wish

**Project List**

| Project | Cost |
|---|---|
| 1. Six Updated Product Brochures | $78,000 |
| 2. New Ad Program | $211,000 |
| 3. PR Agency Retainer | $110,000 |
| 4. Direct Mail Program | $96,000 |
| 5. Press Tour | $65,000 |
| 6. Ads for New Product | $111,000 |
| 7. New Corp Brochure | $78,000 |
| 8. Annual Report | $78,000 |
| 9. Customer Conference | $249,000 |
| 10. New Product Brochure | $66,000 |
| 11. Six Updated Datasheets | $26,000 |
| 12. New Logo Design | $11,000 |
| 13. Replace Letterhead | $9,500 |
| 14. New Signs with Logo | $46,000 |
| 16. Demonstration Video | $235,000 |
| 17. New Tradeshow Booth | $148,000 |
| 18. Attend Boston Show | $46,000 |
| 19. Attend Chicago Show | $48,000 |
| 20. Attend Las Vegas Show | $52,000 |
| 21. New Product Package | $23,000 |
| 22. Company Newsletter | $14,000 |

Make a list of all marketing communications possibilities for the year. List the approximate cost of each project next to it.

**Project Priority List**

| Project | Cost |
|---|---|
| 6. Ads for New Product | $111,000 |
| 2. New Ad Program | $211,000 |
| 3. PR Agency Retainer | $110,000 |
| 4. Direct Mail Program | $96,000 |
| 5. Press Tour | $65,000 |
| 18. Attend Boston Show | $46,000 |
| 19. Attend Chicago Show | $48,000 |
| 10. New Product Brochure | $66,000 |
| 20. Attend Las Vegas Show | $52,000 |
| 21. New Product Package | $23,000 |
| 22. Company Newsletter | $14,000 |
| 8. Annual Report | $78,000 |
| 9. Customer Conference | $249,000 |
| 16. Demonstration Video | $235,000 |
| 12. New Logo Design | $11,000 |
| 11. Six Updated Datasheets | $26,000 |
| 1. Six Updated Product Brochures | $78,000 |
| 14. New Signs with Logo | $46,000 |
| 17. New Tradeshow Booth | $148,000 |
| 13. Replace Letterhead | $9,500 |
| 7. New Corp Brochure | $78,000 |

On a fresh piece of paper, copy the list. This time list each project in order of importance, with the most important projects at the top and the least important at the bottom.

**Project Priority List**

| Project | Cost |
|---|---|
| 6. Ads for New Product | $111,000 |
| 2. New Ad Program | $211,000 |
| 3. PR Agency Retainer | $110,000 |
| 4. Direct Mail Program | $96,000 |
| 5. Press Tour | $65,000 |
| 18. Attend Boston Show | $46,000 |
| 19. Attend Chicago Show | $48,000 |
| 10. New Product Brochure | $66,000 |
| 20. Attend Las Vegas Show | $52,000 |
| 21. New Product Package | $23,000 |
| 22. Company Newsletter | $14,000 |
| 8. Annual Report | $78,000 |
| 9. Customer Conference | $249,000  = $1,169,000 |
| 16. Demonstration Video | $235,000 |
| 12. New Logo Design | $11,000 |
| 11. Six Updated Datasheets | $26,000 |
| 1. Six Updated Product Brochures | $78,000 |
| 14. New Signs with Logo | $46,000 |
| 17. New Tradeshow Booth | $148,000 |
| 13. Replace Letterhead | $9,500 |
| 7. New Corp Brochure | $78,000 |

Now add up the costs starting at the top and working down. When your entire budget is spent (in this case $1,200,000), draw a line. This is the zero base where the money available approximately equals the money spent.

**Revised Project List**

| Project | Cost |
|---|---|
| 1. Ads for New Product | $111,000 |
| 2. New Ad Program | $211,000 |
| 3. PR Agency Retainer | $110,000 |
| 4. Direct Mail Program | $96,000 |
| 5. Press Tour | $65,000 |
| 6. Attend Boston Show | $46,000 |
| 7. Attend Chicago Show | $48,000 |
| 8. New Product Brochure | $66,000 |
| 9. Attend Las Vegas Show | $52,000 |
| 10. New Product Package | $23,000 |
| 11. Company Newsletter | $14,000 |
| 12. Annual Report | $78,000 |
| 13. Customer Conference | $249,000 |

The projects that fall below the line are dropped for the year unless more money becomes available. This technique can also be used for time and resource availability. Simply substitute days or people for project cost that was used in this example.

Figure 10.1. The zero-based budget process.

list" if you are still early in the planning cycle or a list of projects already scheduled if overload is beginning to set in.

Next take a second sheet of paper and relist the same projects, this time in order of priority and importance to the company and its objectives. (Do this in pencil because you may want to switch projects around several times to arrive at the best use of available resources). Now, next to each project name add either the dollars required for implementation if you are comparing available budget dollars to project dollars or the number of man hours if evaluating resources. Then, starting at the top with the most important projects and working down the list, add these numbers together as a running total next to each project.

---

### ✏️ TIP: TWEAK YOUR ZBB TO GET THE MOST FOR YOUR MONEY

Two kinds of minor adjustments (tweaks) to the ZBB can be used to maximize communications budgets. First, after drawing the zero line, study the projects near it on both the do and the scrap sides. Is there a marginally important, but very expensive project just over the line on the do side? Are there several less expensive but nearly as important projects just below the line? If so consider swapping the less expensive projects for the single expensive one. This technique may allow you to get more exposure from your communications dollars. Look also for any large single project that is eating up a disproportionate share of money and consider scaling it back or scrapping it if it is impinging on other equally important programs. You can instantly recognize a ZBB with this problem because you will have drawn the zero line close to the top of the list with a much longer list of projects on the scrap side instead of the do side of the line. This swapping technique works for both man hours and dollars.

---

Then, when you reach the point on the list where you have run out of either money or time, draw a line underneath the last affordable project. This is the *zero line*. The line indicates the place where your available budget minus project costs equals zero or where your available people resources minus project hours equals zero. All projects above the line are doable. All projects below the line get scrapped, put off to next year, or done only if more resources are made available. If you don't have enough projects above the line to meet your marketing goals, then you need to get more money.

After your budget is reviewed and approved, keep the ZBB list handy for reference as the year goes on. Projects have a habit of getting put off for a number of reasons. If one slips to next quarter or next year, cross it off the list and adjust the zero line accordingly. This may move other projects above the line to take advantage of the resources freed by the delayed project.

**Step 7. Lay the plan out for final approval.**   In small organizations, marketing communications planning may be quite informal. A ledger page, such as those accountants use, completed with months at the top and projects down the side may suffice as a simple plan for the entire year. Write the events in pencil and include a column for putting in approximate costs and another column for actual costs, to be used as a tracking device as the year progresses. Along the bottom of each month the totals are written for that month and they are tallied by category along the right for the year. This gives you an overview of both monthly cash flow requirements and your expenses for each category of communication.

Larger organizations may handle communications at the division or departmental level with a wrap-up at the corporate level for each division's major activities and expenses. Summarizing the monthly plans on a spreadsheet or ledger and then studying it is a powerful tool for exposing cashflow humps and bumps and it will help you identify a period of too much or too little activity. If too many events happen at once, they may strain the budget and resources and confuse customers. Too few promotions may slow sales and negatively affect overall profitability.

## HOW TO GET THE MOST FROM YOUR LIMITED FUNDS

There are a variety of techniques you can use to get the most from your limited budget dollars. Here are some that may help you get more communications for less money.

### Getting the Best Price from Vendors

Project cost overruns are common to many kinds of projects, but in the case of marketing communications, they are inevitable if consistent controls are not put in place. Controlling a project budget starts with the vendor selection process. When interviewing vendors (both ones you have used previously as well as new ones), always let each candidate know that you are requesting multiple bids because this helps keep them competitive. In the chart of vendor prices (see Chapter 9), you will see that prices vary considerably. These variances are based on talent, location, size of the firm, and industry served.

The quotes you get at the beginning of a project may change if you hire inexperienced talent or people fully prepared to take advantage of any experience you may not have. Unethical vendors will quote their lowest bid up front to *buy* the job and then raise prices later. This is easy to get away with because unless you know exactly what you want, including how many colors, pages, actors, photos, illustrations, and other particulars, you can't ask for a fixed quote.

Deal with this by being as specific as possible about what you think you want. By having each vendor quote on the exact same job, even it's not exactly what you eventually order, you can compare apples to apples. Or ask several vendors for rough quotes to get an idea of how much the project should cost and then ask for bids. You can also look up last year's budget (if you have one) to see how much was spent for a similar project.

It helps to have some idea of how much money you have to spend and what it will buy you, because some vendors will ask you how much you have budgeted for a project before they complete an estimate. There are two schools of thought about letting vendors know the budget for a project. One says to keep the price a secret because when a vendor knows the budgeted amount up front, the project magically comes in just below that dollar figure. The vendor is simply meeting the price rather than doing an estimate. He may overcharge assuming you will not know the difference. The second says take advantage of the situation—reveal an adjusted budget. Take your estimate based on experience and reduce the figure by one third. Reveal this "budget" to the vendor. You may get the reduced price or the vendor may logically explain why more money is required. If the final bid after haggling is still lower than your estimate, you have either overestimated the original price or you've saved money!

Because prices in communications are often negotiable, especially during off season or when business is slow, you will find it relatively easy to squeeze the estimates. Be careful that you do not squeeze the budget too much or you may reduce the motivation of your vendor and in turn their creativity and drive to get the project completed. Don't be a Scrooge, but do try to get the best quality for the least money that is fair to all parties.

Be aware that your vendors may hire other vendors as subcontractors to help complete your job. The designer or writer may hire a typesetter, illustrators or photographers, and printers. In these arrangements, the primary vendor pays these people directly and then marks up their services 10 to 100%. In some cases, especially with freelancers or small agencies, you can save that money by agreeing to pay these subcontractors directly.

## Get a Detailed Bid for Every Project

To better understand the charges from each vendor, ask for and get a detailed bid. Instead of settling for a bid that says "Ad services—$10,211.00," require an itemized estimate from all vendors. Go through the bid thoroughly and ask the vendor about things you do not see in the estimates. It is better to ask before the project starts than afterward. This itemization is important for several reasons:

1. A detailed bid explains how your money is being spent and you may see a line item that you could do without or handle yourself.

2. An itemized bid ensures that your vendor is going into the project with his or her eyes open. This helps you avoid using vendors that just pull a number out of a hat and then realize later that they underestimated the project. Underbidding dampens their enthusiasm for providing quality work delivered in a timely manner.

3. If an area of the project requires changes that justify extra charges, you can study the bid and identify exactly what charges should increase and which should remain as they are. The bid provides a focus for discussing charges with the vendor line by line. Otherwise, "Ad services—$10,211.00," may suddenly turn into a bill for, "Revised ad services—$30,612.00."

## Be Aware of Hidden Relationships

When hiring vendors be aware that it is common practice in the communications business to pay "commissions" on referrals. These commissions may consist of someone recommending someone else's services to you and then collecting a percentage for making the referral. These commissions cost you money in the form of higher bills and you may get referred to a vendor because they pay kickbacks not because of quality work or integrity. Fortunately, not all vendors do this.

The most common form of this practice is a writer or designer that pushes you into using a particular printer or video production house. Although everyone has favorite vendors, if they are overly adamant about selecting someone there may be more to the relationship than meets the eye. Remember a 5 to 15% commission (standard) can amount to a lot of money on a $200,000 production job.

Hopefully, in getting three bids, you will be able to immediately identify a bid that's out of range because a chunk of the money is going to someone else without your knowledge or consent. Watch out for vendors with substandard portfolios but impressive client lists—the vendor may not be up to snuff but gets lots of work through the commission scheme, not because of merit.

## Broker's Charges, Agent's Fees, and You

When choosing vendors there may be legitimate broker and agent fees for which you must budget. These fees are usually invisible, but if your job involves either a broker or agent, allow 5 to 25% more in your budget to cover the higher charges for their services.

When buying a variety of potentially expensive services such as photography, printing, video production, and advertising media, you may run into a broker. This is a person or company that makes the buying decisions for you and makes money by collecting a commission back from the money you pay to the selected parties. This is an entirely legitimate practice in many cases and a good broker can occasionally help you save money by selecting superior media or services that are cheaper than the going rate.

In the case of printing, a knowledgeable broker can help you match the right shop to your job and then manage and control the process to get the best from the printer. If you know little or nothing about printing, this is useful help and an excellent learning opportunity.

Unfortunately, there are also unethical brokers who choose services based on the percentage of commission paid rather than quality or effectiveness. If a broker recommends a little shop located in a small town five states away be wary unless the price and quality are really commendable. He may not only throw in airfare, he may take you for a ride as well.

## Look for Vendors Who Quote a Fixed Rate and Stick to It

A number of vendors will quote an estimated price up front and then bill you for actual hours used. The final figure is almost always higher than expected. Instead of working with this kind of open and loose arrangement, choose to work with vendors who are willing to quote and stick to a fixed price, even if they use more hours than expected. This should be carefully negotiated and spelled out in writing.

When working under one of these arrangements note that if you make rounds of changes or substantially alter the nature of the project, i.e., a 1/4-page black-and-white ad that becomes a two-page color ad, you can't expect the vendor to stick to the price. There are usually clauses in the contract that specify the limitations of the project. If there aren't, there should be.

## Be Aware of Hidden Charges

Vendors providing "per-unit" production services such as printers often have a contract clause that guarantees that you will pay extra for a print run that is 10% over the specified quantity. Although that may not seem like much, if you are printing a $200,000 annual report, an extra $20,000 charge for more reports than you ordered (or need) is a serious variance in your budget.

Another source of hidden charges is the inevitable *setup charges* that go along with certain kinds of projects. Setup charges are standard for projects quoted on a unit basis, such as silk screen printing, gee-gaws, and embossing. Don't just take the quote of $1.33 each and multiply it by the size of your order. There can and will be extra charges for screens, setup, dies, stencils, special colors, etc. Get the complete bid with setup and shipping charges included. When ordering these kinds of items in small quantities, the setup charges may exceed the cost of the finished goods. Be sure you plan for these charges in your budget.

## The Purchase Order: Your First Line of Defense

To control costs and vendor charges, there is a standard technique used by major corporations to control communications costs that works for almost anyone—the *Marketing Communications Purchase Authorization* (MCPA). This consists of a special purchase order that has a contract spelled out on the back pertaining to communications projects and their respective problems. This "fine print" contract is called *boilerplate* in the legal profession and you may have seen it on the back of invoices from car rental companies, major appliance retailers, and a variety of contracts of all kinds.

To implement a communications MCPA, have a contract attorney draw up the document. It should let you out of an agreement with a vendor for a variety of reasons and limit surprise charges. The best ones supersede all other contracts and allow you to cancel a job with a vendor for any reason. "If a red car drives by our offices between the hours of 8:00 a.m. and 6:00 p.m., we have the right to cancel and refuse payment." Use it to control your budget by enforcing the written extra charges authorization demand made on vendors. It is also useful for nullifying hidden charges such as the printer's 10% overage clause and for demanding that your money not be used to pay referral commissions (difficult to enforce because the process is so invisible).

If, on the other hand, you are dealing with a vendor who asks you to sign a contract and the dollars involved are large (such as producing a complex TV commercial), have your attorney study their document before you sign. The terms of the MCPA may not be enough to counteract a contract. This may cost you $1000 in attorney's fees but if the stakes are large and the risk great, that fee may be a bargain compared to what might happen if you sign the contract and the project goes awry.

## Managing the Costs as the Project Progresses

A marketing communications project that starts off on the right foot with carefully selected vendors has a much better chance of finishing within budget, but things can still go wrong without on going watchdogging. In addition to the common problems we've already documented, communications projects can suffer from outlandish overages, rivaling those of the Pentagon's weapons systems projects. Communications projects are creatively oriented and require putting something new together from scratch—leaving the possibility that a key cost element may be forgotten and left out of the estimate. There are other standard problems that blow the budget:

• **Trouble.** If the project runs into problems (not uncommon), extra money will have to be spent to either fix the problem or redo the work. Trouble includes things such as designers making a mistake in the production that is not caught until the job is on press, typographical errors that render a job useless, loss of master film by someone reviewing it within the company, or dumping a cup of coffee on master art boards. These problems are your responsibility, not the vendor's. The way to stay out of trouble is to be careful and to take your time reviewing all the elements on which you sign off before they go into production.

• **New ideas.** It is common in creative endeavors to have the really good ideas arise after the project is already well into production. In many cases it makes sense to incorporate these brainstorms. Other times, it is better to go with the current approach and save the ideas for the next project. It all depends on cost and impact.

• **Financial mismanagement.** People with strong creative skills are often not good at managing money and may have little regard for your budget. If you find this to be the case, it becomes your responsibility to watch the budget. Do this by having the vendor provide regular reports on the financial aspects of the project and hold frequent review meetings to go over both the production schedule and the status of the budget.

• **Rush charges.** Because vendors may overcommit their time just to get the job, one vendor may come in late, affecting other vendors. These other vendors may charge rush charges to get you back on schedule. Or you may have started a project too late and allowed it to bog down in the approval cycle. Rush charges are extra charges tacked on to a bill for turning a job around quickly. They are usually calculated as a percentage of the standard charges and then added to that figure. Rush charges vary from 25 to 200%. So 200% rush charges tacked onto a $35,000 design and production bill will total a scary $105,000! The vendor's contract usually specifies the terms and conditions when rush charges apply.

Rush charges should always be treated as a path of last resort. Not only are projects that incur these costs needlessly expensive, but if a project is that hurried, then there is a lot that can go wrong because of the frantic schedule. In most cases the vendors deserve the extra fees because they may work weekends, holidays, or all night just to finish your job. You can, however, attempt to get a reduced rate. Ask that the charges not apply to the entire bill—but only to the part that was rushed. Ask that a 100% rush charge be reduced to 50%. Get more time if possible. In some cases just a few extra hours will reduce or negate rush charges completely.

- **Changes.**    Most important in maintaining budget integrity is keeping changes to a minimum. (See the *100% Perfect Problem* in Chapter 11 for details.) Multiple rounds of changes not only frustrate vendors but in severe cases can blow both your project budget as well as your company's budget. Deal with this by either preselling the job politically and working at keeping changes to a minimum, or by adding extra money to the project budget during planning if you know that changes are inevitable because of the personalities involved.

- **Unauthorized or unexpected extra charges.**    As soon as the final bills arrive, discuss any unexpected charges with the vendor. If the charges really are inaccurate or superfluous, they will usually be removed and an apology presented. If the charges resulted from changes on your part, or additions to the project, then you are responsible for them if you failed to demand that all extras be authorized in writing in advance. One technique that works wonders for unauthorized charges is to refuse to pay the entire bill until an adjustment is made. Most vendors become quite reasonable if the check they were expecting is not going to arrive. It may be time to see an attorney if the amount is large or if the vendor is unusually nasty or threatening (rare, but not unheard of).

One word of warning for trusting souls: never, never pay a vendor in full before the finished work is delivered to your satisfaction. This saps motivation and you lose the leverage required to get the work done properly or completed on time. It is standard practice for vendors to ask for one-quarter to one-third of a bid in advance, however. Most freelancers cannot or will not check your company's credit. Instead, they use this traditional advance payment as a guarantee and commitment from your company that the commissioned work will be paid for in a timely manner.

# A FOUR-WORD CHANGE THAT COST $9000

One project fiasco some agency friends in San Francisco got caught up in was an expensive product brochure that extoled the benefits of the client's product line to major universities. Knowing that this large company had a reputation as a retirement community for white-collar bureaucrats, the agency built substantial extra hours into their bid to accommodate multiple rounds of changes to the design, copy, and mechanical art.

Predictably, all of these extra hours were earned because the corporation's managers and internal communications personnel made numerous batches of both minor and major changes before allowing the job to go to press. Even the day it was to be shipped to a printer in another city, another round of word changes came through and delayed the job yet another week while new type was set and more changes were incorporated.

Finally the job went to print and the agency people flew to Los Angeles for the press check. On press, after more than an hour of adjustments, everything looked just right. The agency gave the approval to begin the actual print run. Suddenly a frantic plant manager ran in and told the agency people to pick up the phone. It was a call from the corporation's communications manager. Four words absolutely had to be changed in the brochure. The changes did not seem significant when the agency heard them, so they tried to talk the client out of the changes. But the manager insisted it was a matter of life or death! Pulling the job off the press immediately, the changes were made and the job was rerun the following week. The charge to change four not very important looking words? Almost $9000 for wasted press time, plates, transportation, paper, and other expenses! Perhaps it's not so surprising that the company recently filed for protection under the bankruptcy laws.

## HOW TO GET THE WORK DONE ON TIME

Beyond controlling the vendors estimates and invoices, the other half of keeping budgets in line and delivering projects on time is the project schedule. Project schedules often have "drop dead" dates that render projects useless if missed. And projects that run late may incur expensive rush charges. Thus, a clearly specified and frequently updated schedule is key to keeping marketing communications projects on track.

### Scheduling Projects Realistically

Your marketing communications plan should include a rough production schedule, probably penciled in on a separate piece of paper, for each project. After all the projects are listed, guesstimate the time required from the delivery date backward for project execution and draw a line to show the implementation period for each project. If you are unsure how long something will take, increase the length of the line to add a "margin of error." You can use the flowcharts provided in each of the communications chapters for a list of activities for each type of communication. Just assign a time period to each of the activities that is realistic. (If you don't know what is realistic, ask someone with experience who does.) Then list the dates on a calendar based on the estimated times for each task and voilà, you have a schedule for each communication.

All projects that require more than a day or two to complete should be planned on paper. When scheduling you must keep in mind the impact of other concurrent projects because these may eat into your *resources* (people and vendors) or otherwise impact the delivery date. When scheduling, unless you have absolutely no involvement in a project, make sure that you will also be available when needed for reviews and meetings.

The best way to get accurate advice when scheduling communications projects is to use the input of your *project team,* whether your team is only yourself and a printer, or a large group of people along with an outside agency. Do this well in advance of your projected start date. It could be that you have left out a major section of the work and it will take one of your team members to recognize the hole.

Before sitting down with the team, list all of the steps required for the project on paper. Then, use the following worksheet to list all the steps in approximate sequence. A step or task consists of any activity that takes a day or more such as typesetting or producing a draft of copy. It should also include brief but important events such as "final script approved for video." If two (or more) steps occur at the same time, list them in alphabetical order. Add the approximate duration of each step in days and then your "best guess" start and finish dates once you are satisfied that all of the steps are in place.

Always estimate from the start to the finish, never the other way around. Put the name(s) of each participant in the name column next to the step name. Then use this worksheet to create a flowchart for a team meeting. You may find that you require more time than is available. Unless it's obviously impossible to complete the project on time, discuss it with your team members before looking for recourse. They may know of a way to cut down the time required or how to better structure the sequence of steps.

For large projects, have a schedule review meeting and put up the project flowchart on a whiteboard for your project team to study. Go over the project from start to finish and ask your team if they see any missing steps. If so, add them to the chart. Reestimate the days to accomplish each step and then adjust the start and finish date for each step. Add the name of the person(s) or vendor(s) responsible for each step from your worksheet. Make sure that holidays, other projects, and

| Task Name | Duration | Start Date | Finish Date | Person(s) Responsible |
|-----------|----------|------------|-------------|-----------------------|
|           |          |            |             |                       |
|           |          |            |             |                       |
|           |          |            |             |                       |
|           |          |            |             |                       |
|           |          |            |             |                       |
|           |          |            |             |                       |
|           |          |            |             |                       |
|           |          |            |             |                       |

Figure 10.2. Project scheduling worksheet.

other events, such as vacations and tradeshows that will affect people's availability during the project, are accounted for.

Now consider your projected completion date. If the project finish date is before the required deadline—great! But if this date is later than the deadline, you must either get the deadline extended, add more people to get the project done faster, or reduce the scope of the project and accomplish less. Note that each time you double the resources to complete a step faster, you will get less than double throughput. Some

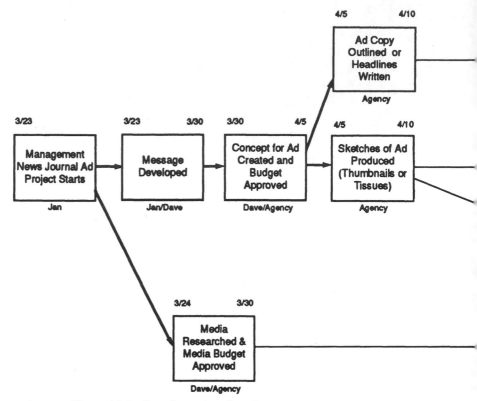

Figure 10.3. Sample project flowchart.

tasks that are creative such as writing and design may actually slow down if you add too many resources. Production-oriented tasks, however, such as typesetting, proofreading, or stripping, usually benefit from increased manpower. Another alternative is to agree to pay rush charges. This may blow your budget but if the project must get done, consider it a last-ditch alternative.

In addition to detailed production schedules, most planners like to create a plan timeline with projects listed down the side and months listed across the top. The purpose of creating a timeline, also known as a Gantt chart, is to give you a better idea of the year's project load to see if work can be shifted from an intensely busy period to a period of slack time. The second purpose is to provide you with a scheduling document so you know when to begin implementation of each project as the year progresses. This should be a "living" document—one that is regularly updated to reflect changes in marketing communications priorities.

## Always Communicate Your Schedule

Before signing on a vendor or beginning a project, make sure that all participants, both inside and outside your organization, buy in to your

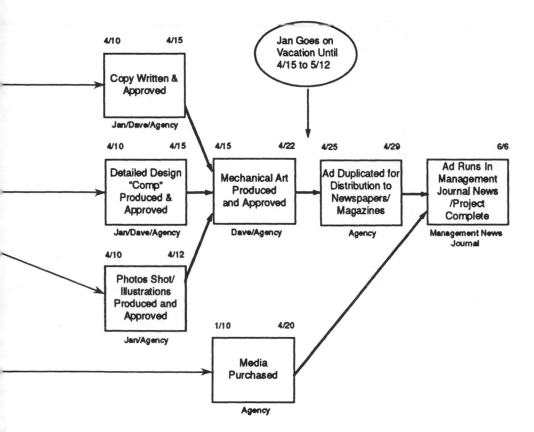

schedule. Go over it carefully and get it approved if necessary. Although some people's participation may be minimal, they can become a major roadblock by not turning their work around in a timely manner. Make sure everyone understands their schedule responsibility in advance. When issuing a purchase order or MCPA to an outside vendor make sure that the dates are clearly specified for their part of the project.

Should your project get rescheduled for any reason, assemble a new schedule and distribute it again to all those involved. If you don't create a revised schedule confusion on due dates can slow down work. Don't make the opposite mistake of producing a revised schedule on a daily basis as dates change—your project team will stop paying attention to so much paper flying around their work areas. Schedules that change more than weekly indicate a project out of control. If this is the case, gather all the people in a room and find out what is going wrong.

## Controlling Project Schedules Throughout a Project's Life Span

Just as selecting the right vendors is critical to your budget, selecting the right people for a project is also vital to keeping it on schedule. Some people work faster than others. Keep this in mind when selecting

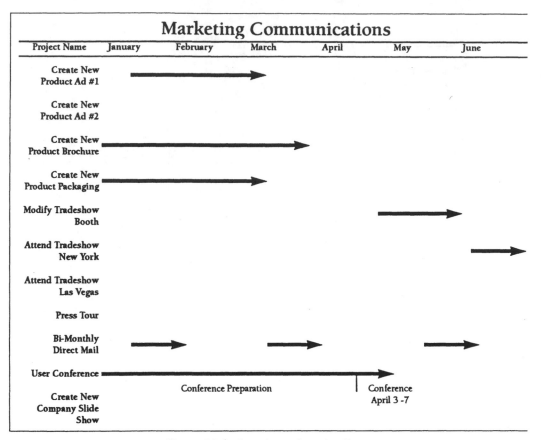

Figure 10.4. Sample project timeline.

people. Also, once you have worked with the same team members a few times, you will get a better idea of their working habits and what they do best.

Once a project is underway, your best system of control is to hold regular meetings with the entire project team to review your flowchart and establish actual progress as compared to the dates on your plan. If your project includes a large block of services from an outside agency, you should ask them for regular status reports both in writing and by phone. How often should you check on the project? If it is a long project on a comfortable schedule, have meetings every two weeks. If it is a brief-duration project with a short fuse, meet daily. Don't, however, allow overly lengthy meetings or reports to get in the way of progress. Have clear agendas and objectives for the meetings.

Remember that as each project progresses, you should also document how much was actually spent compared to the planned budget (actual expenditures vs. forecast expenditures). This technique allows better tracking of cashflow and quickly exposes an out-of-control plan. Occasionally a budget review may show the availability of unused funds that

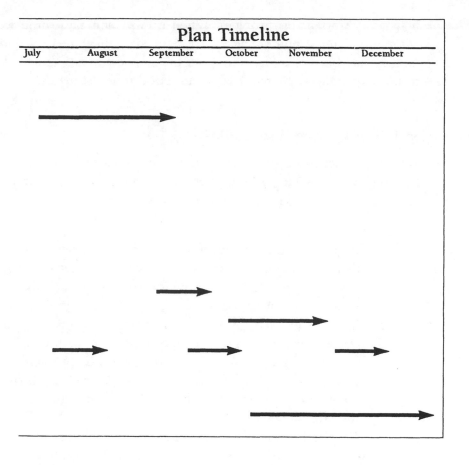

could be put to good use elsewhere. Often the same problems that cause projects to go over budget cause problems with schedules.

• **Changes.**   Rounds of changes blow schedules quickly. To avoid this, sell the project politically and really keep on top of the approvals and change cycle. Minimize these cycles wherever possible. If you know that a long cycle of changes will be inevitable, build it into the schedule up front.

• **Trouble.**   Problems occur in communications projects that can interfere with timely completion. The best recourse for this problem is to used seasoned people to handle potentially troublesome areas of projects. They may be able to completely avoid the problem through experience and foresight, or they may know of a quick fix that will avoid serious slowing of the project.

• **Inaccurate time estimates.**   Some members of your team are going to be better estimators than others. Using the team approach will hopefully help you through this problem. When one person says three weeks to complete a step, another more experienced participant may quote two months and be able to credibly back up their estimate. Your best bet is to use experienced people if you want good time estimates.

## If the Project Is Slipping, What Should I Do?

When your schedule starts slipping and it's apparent that you may not be able to meet your deadline, here are common problems to look for and solutions that will help you get back on track:

1. If the problem is nonperforming project participants either get them moving or replace them. If you can't get rid of a person because of their position in your company, do your best to work with or go around them.

2. Look for problems in your own organization including too many changes or people sitting on approvals. Get the project approved and moving again ASAP. Internal political problems can also be a prime source of project delays. Attempt to hammer out differences and operational procedures through meetings with the offending parties.

3. Poor estimating can result in serious problems. Depending on the severity of the problem, you can add resources, speed the project up by making it a higher priority, or get the end date pushed out.

4. Project priorities may shift and as a result your project gets backburnered. If this happens fine, but make sure everyone knows the completion date has changed.

5. Key people may get sick, take other jobs, or get buried in unexpected projects. If this happens and you have no replacement, consider using an experienced outsider on a temporary basis. Many experienced freelancers will come to work inside a company if the pay is right and you aren't asking for a permanent commitment. In the case of a person who is really impossible to replace (rare in communications projects, but common in other kinds of projects such as the design of technically oriented products), you may just have to shelve the project until the person becomes available or a replacement is found and trained.

6. Logistical failures such as the failure of paper stock to be delivered to a printer or a mistake at an early stage of a project that is not apparent until later can cause serious last-minute schedule havoc. If it is a simple matter such as the paper example,

print on a similar but readily available stock, or buy the paper elsewhere. If the mistake is severe, try to make the project work as a stopgap if possible and then replace or repair it as soon as possible. If the mistake is so severe that the finished product will be unusable, use what work isn't flawed and replace the rest.

### Computerize Your Planning for Better Tracking and Control

There are many easy-to-use project management programs available for personal computers that can simplify and improve your marketing communications planning and on-going project management efforts. Go to any computer store and the sales people can tell you about them. Most of these programs are easy to learn and can produce a variety of informative reports, graphs, and charts that can be used for tracking and controlling your communications projects as you go through the year. The programs can do things such as calculate schedules, produce timeline charts, integrate multiple projects into one plan, specify individual workloads, and much more. Some of the more sophisticated programs will also track your expenditures and produce variance reports so you can compare your planned schedules and costs with what really happens. If you have a large communications budget or many projects to control, the investment of a few hundred dollars and a few hours of your time to learn the program is definitely worthwhile.

## COMMUNICATIONS PLANS, BUDGETS, AND SCHEDULES ARE ALL SUBJECT TO CHANGE WITHOUT NOTICE

Remember that communications plans are subject to change and almost no one managing marketing communications projects makes it through a full year without revising some if not all of the plan. Why? Organizations change priorities midstream, product development finishes late, budgets get cut, today's "Godsend product that will change the course of history" gets the axe, and departmental people and prerogatives shift. When changes occur in the workflow or product plans in the company, it precipitates changes in the communications program. Also, as marketing communications projects and programs are completed, some will have better results than others. So future promotions based on a tactic that didn't work are expected to be scrapped. Thus, the plan must be changed to emphasize new types of communications and new ideas.

If you have anticipated changes in advance, you can simply pull out your wish list or your ZBB and decide on the next logical communication to produce to meet your new goals.

# 11 | Common Marketing Communications Problems: Recognizing Them and Bailing Yourself Out before It's Too Late

There are a variety of things that can and will go wrong with any marketing communications project. Mistakes get made, new processes do not work, or it takes longer than expected to complete a draft of copy or a comp of the design. These problems are normal and with careful management you can minimize run-of-the-mill mishaps. Hopefully the mistakes will be so minor that you can quickly correct them with a minimum of project delays and extra charges.

But, in addition to these ordinary and inevitable setbacks, there are numerous bugbears that continue to dog marketing communications projects of all sizes and kinds. These problems are pervasive and occur in all organizations from small family-run retail stores to giant megacorporations. Some of them occur because of politics or difficult people within your company. Others are the result of work habits and attitudes on the part of vendors hired to work on projects. Almost all of these problems are avoidable but companies continue to fall into the traps.

This chapter provides you with a representative example of these common problems that will allow you to identify trouble spots in your own project and organization. In addition, advice is provided for fixing or improving each situation when you find yourself caught in the middle.

Remember, the longer a problem goes on, the harder it will be to solve or eliminate. And, as time goes, solutions get more expensive.

## THE 100% PERFECT PROBLEM (OR THE 90% DONE PROBLEM)

Your job is to get a 35-mm slide presentation written and designed that showcases the community work in which your not-for-profit organization is engaged. The purpose of the show is to encourage donation commitments from local companies and corporations. You know that the presentation must look professional, because these groups are accustomed to seeing strong, colorful presentations and yours must look as credible.

After finishing the presentation and getting it approved, you drop the copy and charts off at the slide design house. After picking up the "finished" presentation and showing it to your bosses, they make numerous changes. After implementing all of the changes again, you show the presentation to your bosses once more and receive changes to more than half the images. And so it goes again one more time. There seems to be no end in sight.

## What's the Problem?

The *100% Perfect Problem* is a very common hurdle that affects marketing communications projects everywhere—in small businesses and in large corporations. It stems from the erroneous idea that if you continue to work on an ad, brochure, plan, PR release, or other marketing communications project long enough, eventually you will get it perfect. The reality is that no communications project is ever more than 90% perfect—there's always something that could be tweaked or improved, but in the course of reaching the unattainable 100%, the change cycles often dilute the original creative ideas that made the project strong and interesting. It is better to accept a 90% perfect project and finish it so it can begin to do its work, rather than keeping it caged while chasing the elusive 100% perfect goal.

The problem usually starts with a "committee" of managers reviewing a project and making changes and suggestions during endless rounds of meetings. A slightly more skewed version of the same problem is the old bosses' proverb, "it's not right until I've sent it back at least five times." In actual practice, the tiny details that you may spend months mending are rarely noticeable by your market.

## The Problems It Creates

The 100% Perfect Problem causes massive project cost overages and missed completion dates; sometimes a year or more can be spent on revisions. It also frustrates all parties concerned with a project, because no one, particularly a creative vendor, wants to keep redoing the same job over and over.

## How to Recognize It

Any project that goes through more than four major review cycles, such as copy/script rewrites, major layout changes, retakes with new actors, or other multiple sets of other changes, suffers from this problem.

## What to Do about It

This is a tough one. Either you, if you are the decision maker, or your bosses are guilty of not being able to make a decision—common when managers are not sure what kind of decision should be made and how to make it. The best way around it is to put the brakes on the project and do a "sanity check." That means sitting down with the work completed to date and carefully reviewing all aspects of the job—then making only those changes that are mandatory, such as fixing misspelled words, retaking flubbed lines in a script, or replacing out-of-focus photographs. If you still have a nagging suspicion that something is wrong or missing, review the work with an outside third party, carefully considering their biases as well as their comments.

# THE AGENCY MUST BE RIGHT PROBLEM

Receiving the advertising plan from your agency, you are stunned with the media charges. Paging through the plan you find expensive placements in several magazines that produced poor results last year. A call to your account representative brings you little justification for the ads, instead the representative is short with you and takes a condescending approach to the conversation. You finally okay the plan because the agency must know what it is doing, otherwise it would not be in the business. . . right?

## What's the Problem?

Because few people have direct or extensive experience with managing advertising or PR programs, clients are forced to take what their agencies tell them at face value, even when this results in serious cost overruns or ineffective promotional programs. Many agency people including account managers and principals have very dominant personalities and adopt an arrogant air when dealing with "uninitiated" clients. This attitude of superiority and condescending tolerance can lead clients to accept a diminutive role when faced with an intolerant agency know-it-all.

## The Problems It Creates

The *Agency Must Be Right* problem creates an environment of friction between client and agency and makes you, the client, feel insecure about your knowledge, judgment, and experience, however shallow or deep it may be. It can also tie you into a long, expensive program of ads, PR, or collateral materials that you can ill afford or don't really need.

## How to Recognize It

If you cannot justify in *your own words* each project and program you and your agency are currently engaged in or planning, then the *Agency Must Be Right* problem may be at hand.

## What to Do about It

The best way to deal with this problem is to quietly interview several other agencies and ask them what they think of your current programs. You may hear engaging criticisms you never dreamed existed. Of course if these ring true then it's time to change agencies or go back to the existing one and let them know your feelings (best done with a principal rather than an account manager). If the agency continues its uncooperative or condescending approach, then definitely go elsewhere and let them know why you've gone.

# THE CREEPING DESIGNERISMS PROBLEM

You just received the design and printing bills after completing a new catalog and the bottom line on the invoices is twice what was estimated at the beginning of the project. A phone call to the printer confirms the amounts. The reasons for the overage are the project bid did not include two kinds of varnishes or seven extra screen tints used on the print run. A call to the designer also confirms the charges. When asked why you weren't told, the designer responds, "I asked you about each change and you said you thought it was a good idea."

## What's the Problem?

Designers love design and are visually oriented. They love to create attractive ads, brochures, tradeshow booths, direct mail pieces, and signs that reflect their creative prowess and technical ability. This helps them build a strong design portfolio and get higher paying jobs. It may also win them a prestigious design competition.

Unfortunately, to achieve these ends, your designer may agree to a fee up front and then inflate the budget as the project progresses with expensive design, photos, illustrations, or print treatments. In practice, your design budget may incrementally double or triple. A two-color, eight-page brochure may balloon into a six-color piece with a hefty increase in design and print charges.

## The Problems It Creates

Massive cost overruns are the major problem with *Creeping Designerisms,* and with the additional work required to finish and print the piece, the delivery date may slip too.

### How to Recognize It

If you designer has lots of great ideas and is always asking questions such as "What if we did it this way?" or making suggestions for improving the looks of the piece, then you might have a problem. A nod of interest on your part may be taken as agreement from the vendor's point of view. Really arrogant designers (there are plenty of these out there) will just go ahead and add anything they see fit and bill you for it later.

### What to Do about It

Always get quotes in writing before starting a project and provide vendors with a purchase order that plainly states that all additional charges over and above the quoted price must be approved in writing or they will not be paid. Also when your designer makes suggestions, additions, or changes to the project, listen carefully and then ask, "How much will that cost?" Take notes on all such conversations.

## THE EVERYONE'S AN EXPERT PROBLEM

When discussing direct mail ideas with your writer and designer, the meetings must be scheduled for the big conference room, because so many people insist on attending. There are all seven marketing people including the secretary, four managers from sales, all your department, a representative from product development, and even the company president. Most of these meetings turn into a free-for-all arguing session because everyone from secretary to president has ideas about what needs to be done and how to do it.

### What's the Problem?

For reasons known only to the gods of advertising (in the unlikely event there are any), everyone in every organization is a self-proclaimed advertising and marketing communications expert. They, their friends, relatives, and next-door neighbors will freely criticize your communications efforts without being asked. It may be because the projects are visually oriented and since people have two eyes, this qualifies them as experts in this area. It may also be because communications is considered a "fun" job—one far more interesting than accounting or sales. Unfortunately, communications is complex and demands special skills and experience. However, although no one goes and tells the engineering or accounting departments how to do their jobs, they will certainly come over and tell you how to do yours.

Additionally, this takes a more insidious form when senior company managers and/or owners constantly comment on projects. Since these people may have a real say on a project and rarely know enough to provide valid advice, it makes it tough to finish projects on time and still maintain a semblance of creative integrity.

## The Problems It Creates

The *Everyone's an Expert* problem blows dates and budgets, and transforms strong promotional programs into toothless committee-designed projects lacking impact. It also leads to scrabbling that creates odd political polarizations. These political manifestations may outlast the project at hand and go on to undermine the next project and sometimes the company.

## How to Recognize It

Depending on the visibility and perceived importance of a project, you will notice that a number of people will involve themselves in it for no particularly good reason. They may comment on design, budgets, writing, and printing quality and quantity. They will also state the credentials that make them experts in the communications field—"When I printed that two-color price list back in 1958, I made sure that. . . ." They will present their views and advice (ranging from ludicrous to useful) and attempt to insert themselves into the approval process. In really serious cases, the meddlers will actually visit the agency's or vendor's place of business and make changes without your presence or knowledge.

## What to Do about It

The best technique for limiting interference from others is to handle all aspects of every project yourself. Unfortunately, this is rarely possible, so a second-best solution is to limit the number of people in the approval loop before a project commences. The reviewers and schedules should be documented in advance, and people's roles in the project should be clearly specified as part of the overall plan. It is also important that responsible parties be as far up the ladder of an organization as possible. Because people at a high level will become involved anyway, this technique at least removes layers of lower level decision makers from the sign-off sheet. Try, wherever possible, to assign ultimate no/go authority to one person. That way if another committee member insists on something unworkable, the power of veto is available if necessary.

If the "experts" are all part of an approval committee, present the issues or artwork at a meeting with all responsible parties in attendance.

That way if they disagree on a point, it can be hammered out right there. Otherwise you will be forced to run around in circles trying to get consensus and possibly get caught in the middle. Make sure someone takes notes at these meetings for later reference.

The most difficult "expert" arrangement to manage is the "progressive" young company that believes that everyone in the organization should have a say or vote on major marketing communications issues. We saw one start-up company that actually had the entire company vote on every marketing communications concept—including the logo, ads, brochure concepts, and colors. Four agencies resigned in the first year and the company never did figure out the problem. If you find yourself having to work with this unworkable arrangement, either dissuade company officials from using this approach or update your resume.

---

## TURN OVER ANY ROCK AND THERE WILL BE AN EXPERT HIDING UNDER IT

*The Angry Natives.* When working as marketing communications manager for a major Silicon Valley corporation, a friend arrived earlier than usual for work one morning, only to find an angry group of engineers crowded into his cubical. They were pawing through a series of proofs for a new ad and collateral program. Since these proofs had been stored in a drawer, they had apparently gone through private cupboards and drawers in search of the materials. Obviously angry at the way marketing had "sugar-coated" the engineering breakthroughs (or at least they considered them such), this bunch was last sighted heading off to the vice president's office for a confrontation with the proofs in hand. No changes were made to the program although a couple of the more abrasive engineers suddenly found themselves unemployed.

*In the Heat of the Night.* When working in a now deservedly defunct company, the corporate communications manager discovered a series of notes attached to proofs for an ad left on top of her desk. The notes pointed out flaws in the proofs that needed correcting and one commented on the quality of the copy used. The unsigned notes remained a mystery, although the comments were surprisingly right on the money. In fact, they were downright insightful.

Several days later, a young man showed up at the manager's office cubical late in the afternoon to empty the trash receptacle. He explained that he was the new night janitor who had once worked in a print shop and he had left the notes because he wanted to abandon his janitorial career and break into marketing communications. We hope he did.

---

## THE MORE MONEY THAN SENSE PROBLEM

A flashy new start-up company with an exciting new technology is well funded by a venture capital group. With all the money available the brash young executives do everything "right." They travel first-class, drive corporation-purchased Mercedes Benz automobiles, and want you to run a series of expensive ads in *Fortune* touting the company's success. Fine, but these ads will use up every dollar you have to work with. No problem they say, they will just give you another chunk of the investor's cash when you need it. You wonder just how long the company will survive at this rate.

## What's the Problem?

Particularly common to new ventures with a lot of investment capital is the *More Money than Sense Problem.* It happens in new operations ranging from small specialty stores to richly funded start-up companies—only the scale of the mistake is different. It consists of spending excessive capital on prestige communications tools, often at the expense of more necessary projects. Although all companies want to look good through their promotional activities, sometimes these programs are simply inappropriate. Common boondoggles include fancy corporate brochures, expensive ads in prestigious magazines not read by the target market, and tradeshow booths that resemble the Taj Mahal.

## The Problems It Creates

This kind of spending causes serious problems because it diverts large chunks of cash from business-building activities to ones that satisfy the owner's or chief executive officer's ego. While they are sitting in first-class and proudly pointing out their new ad in *Forbes* to a seatmate, awareness is not being built for the company or the products among real-world customers. If the company is investor funded, too much of this problem may result in a new team of cost-conscious execs being brought in to replace the high-flyers.

## How to Recognize It

Look for single projects that use more than 10% of a total communications budget and scrutinize each one. If your budget is particularly well endowed, check out projects above the 5 to 8% threshold for superfluous spending.

## What to Do about It

A frank talk with the people who want to blow the wad will usually buy you little more than a place in the unemployment line. It's best to quietly start job hunting because if this is a frequent occurrence the company has a dim future. To look on the bright side, these megaprojects will make great portfolio samples for you.

# THE I'VE GOT A FRIEND IN THE BUSINESS PROBLEM

On taking a position responsible for product marketing and marketing communications, the company's president tells you to print a series of color datasheets with his friend Joe who has a print shop. Bidding the job through Joe and two other printers reveals that Joe is substantially more expensive. The president says go ahead and use Joe anyway because he is a friend and he does great work.

Two weeks later, Joe's assistant drops off the finished datasheets. Before you see them the people in shipping are distributing them and laughing at the printing quality. An angry salesperson shows up at your office, throws a datasheet down on the desk, and asks you why you do such sloppy work. One look at the piece and you realize the guy is right. The colors are misregistered and the ink is blotchy and uneven. By now an angry company president has seen the mess and comes storming into your office wanting to know why you can't do your job right.

Later, while looking for a new job, you visit Joe's print shop, curious to lay eyes on the guy that "always does great work." You find the shop in a old strip mall and upon entering discover that the shop consists of a messy quick print press and piles of old ink cans and rags. With this equipment, Joe could not have done a good job even if he had tried.

## What's the Problem?

This person may actually be a friend or a relative. Another explanation is that because communications projects often go awry without proper management, when someone finds a vendor that does adequate work, they often stick with the vendor rather than taking a risk trying out a new face. Over the years, this person may end up managing more complicated projects but still use the same vendor. So the next time they need a project handled they call their "friend in the business"—even if this person lacks the expertise to carry out the work at hand.

In its most insidious form, this person may accept a commission from the vendor for sending him or her work. This is usually limited to dinner "with an old friend." As a worst case, a sizable monetary kickback is a possibility.

## The Problems It Creates

This kind of problem results in delivery of substandard work, or the forced acceptance of a bid that is noncompetitive using a vendor ill equipped for the job. It is also difficult to fire a vendor who is a friend or relative of someone you work with, especially if the someone is the boss.

## How to Recognize It

You will be approached with recommendations from a variety of people when managing any communications project. Watch out for the ones that are particularly solicitous or persistent.

## What to Do about It

Keep such suggestions and vendors at arm's distance. Always insist on portfolio reviews and competitive bidding as a "matter of policy." Put the policy in writing. However, if your boss dictates a vendor then you may have no choice in the matter. Sometimes you may be able to talk the person out of such a decision if other competent vendors will perform the work for substantially less money.

A variation on this problem is the *Approved Vendors List,* common in many corporations. There is no graceful political maneuver around this list except to pretend that you do not know it exists (a tactic used successfully by the authors). Another approach is to hire a specialized type of vendor not on the list. Although most lists will have many printers to choose from, few will have a "lithographic image-to-paper transfer specialist"!

If (in rare cases) someone you work with is taking money or other tangible perks (nights in a vacation condo, frequent fancy lunches, or a supply of expensive liquor) from a vendor and then forces you to work with the person or company, bring it to the attention of senior management. If you are senior management, a long talk is in order. This is an illegal practice and you want no part of it.

# THE TOO MANY EGOS PROBLEM

A new tradeshow booth is in the works and you are in charge of the project. It is already March 3 and the booth must ship on April 1 in order to make the show. Suddenly the booth designer quits in a huff leaving you holding the bag. A "postmortem" discussion with him reveals that what he told you about the photographer trying to change the direction of the project was all true. He won't come back unless the photographer is replaced with someone willing to take his directions.

## What's the Problem?

All people have an ego. Groups of two or more people constitute a political entity with the potential for ego problems. All individuals need to feel that their contributions are both valuable and appreciated. This goes double (or triple) for creative personalities. Putting two creative people together on a project can precipitate ego conflicts, with one undermining the efforts of the other.

## The Problems It Creates

This kind of problem may result in delivery of substandard work, or a project may be delivered late if one party suddenly quits in a huff. In the case of a serious conflict, one party may deliberately sabotage the project to make another party look bad.

## How to Recognize It

It usually starts with a missed deadline or offhand comments and sarcasm concerning another member of the project team. Individually ask each person working on a project how it is going and then discreetly inquire what they think of so and so's contribution. If you get a sudden torrent of complaints or criticisms, then you most likely have a problem. In the case of television advertising production or other complex projects in which large groups of creative people are attempting to work as a team, actual fights may be the ultimate indicator of this problem.

## What to Do about It

The best way around it is to use teams of people who have successfully worked together in the past. Talking it out sometimes helps.

# THE IT'S IMPORTANT TO US SO IT MUST BE IMPORTANT TO OUR CUSTOMERS PROBLEM

After working on an elaborate set of expensive product brochures for several months and finally nearing the mechanical stage, the company's marketing chief calls you in for a meeting. The marketing chief wants to add a section to each brochure that explains how hard the company has worked to produce each piece and how expensive they were to create. Further, along with the table of contents in each one, a photo of the executive committee and a paragraph full of superlatives about each person's contributions to the brochures are to be added.

After a brief but futile discussion on the merits of these question-able additions, you leave to get estimates for these changes and quietly look over the classified ads for any job openings.

## What's the Problem?

The *It's Important to Us So It Must Be Important to Our Customers Problem* involves self-centered perceptions by company personnel. They think that because issues are important within an organization they automati-cally have relevance to customers. It is a by-product of fuzzy thinking and the problem points to management that lacks experience. It is also standard in organizations where the most senior person is surrounded by yes-people who ignore reality and feed this person's ego.

Although some company activities that are not directly product oriented are important to customers, such as profitability pointing to success and stability, many internal matters should remain just that—internal.

Another variation on this problem is harder to identify and pin down. This occurs when a company believes that its customers are interested in its products for one reason, but customers actually purchase the prod-ucts for reasons that are completely different. For example, your com-pany sells hand tools and kitchen knives made out of a new, superhard alloy that is really cheap to manufacture, allowing these goods to be sold at very low retail prices. Your internal marketing people are convinced that the new technology is really exciting and they spend a lot of money promoting it. They "know" that the goods are selling because customers are thrilled with this invention. But, in the minds of the customers, what is really selling the line of tools and knives are the low prices! They see the new alloy technology as secondary to being able to purchase a really solid, well-made hammer or kitchen knife for half the price of the com-petition's models.

## The Problems It Creates

In really serious cases of promoting internal priorities to the outside world, purchasers become confused. They may buy elsewhere because they are unable to separate what is important from the internal matters that obscure the key message. In the case of a promoter or manager who is featured prominently and with lavish praise in communications proj-ects, customers tend to sneer.

In the case of misguided promotion, where the company percep-tions about what is important are different than what customers believe, substantial sums of money may be spent on ineffective promotions. In the hand tool example above, if the company had included the price message along with the superior technology message, they would have had a strong promotion at their disposal.

## How to Recognize It

In the case of ego-oriented managers and owners, the problem is painfully simple to identify. In the case of mispositioned products, if you ask questions and do your research in advance and during the promotions, you will usually recognize this problem quickly.

## What to Do about It

This is also a tough one. Fixing the problem starts with changing the thinking of the people who are responsible for it. If the problem is extremely deep seated in the company, often the case with an arrogant manager surrounded by yes-people again, there is little you can do. You will have a tough time containing this ego without insulting its owner. Worse, the "yes-brigade" will close ranks to protect their leader.

In the case of mispositioned products, if the company management is open minded, focus research (see Chapter 3) is a powerful tool for effectively understanding and changing this behavior.

When communications professionals get together, they love to swap war stories on communications projects that went wrong. (There's never any shortage of tales to be told!) These stories bring chuckles, although at the time most of these horrors occurred, few people—client, agency, vendor, or project manager—were laughing. As you work in communications, it's likely you'll pick up a few tales of your own. For reasons unknown, some projects move from initiation to completion with nary a scratch, whereas others have problems from start to finish. But, by using the advice given in this chapter, you will be able to deal with many of the problems you will likely encounter and, more importantly, recognize them before they become chronic or serious.

There's one last problem that doesn't quite fit in above because it's so easy to avoid: never make the mistake of assuming that because a project is small, simple, unimportant, or has been done before, that it will be a piece of cake. It's these *easy* projects that can run off the rails and cause headaches for years to come. You may bring in 20 complex projects on time and within budget that people are completely pleased with, but that one little, dumb project that got messed up will be the one they remember. Avoid this trap by exercising equal care with *all* projects and treat them with the respect they deserve. A little extra care and personal supervision will allow you to escape this trap and you will always get the word out with impact.

# 12 | On the Cheap and on the Fly: Getting More Results for Less Money

There are often economical alternatives to expensive communications projects. These alternatives can be used to save money, or test questionable or risky concepts, or as an inexpensive extra project to add to the standard communications repertoire on short notice. This chapter covers a variety of tactics we've learned or seen others use effectively to get communications done with limited funds or limited resources. These suggestions, combined with do-it-yourself PR, can help provide a less costly communications program that is still quite effective.

## WHEN TO SPEND AND WHEN TO SAVE

The most powerful tool for saving money in communications is to not spend funds on projects that will not help sell products or build image. Just because your company has always mailed out a new brochure every June does not mean the brochure has any positive effect or is even getting noticed by customers. We are not suggesting not spending money on marketing communications. Just the opposite. But you should evaluate each of your projects and make sure you are spending money only on marketing communications that are making a positive difference to your bottom line.

Here are some basic guidelines for using your budget effectively:

- Unless your company obtains most of its revenue from one selling season (Christmas, summer camping trips, skiing in winter), spread dollars and programs over the entire year. Avoid the *big blowout* approach that cripples your budget for the remaining months.
- Study your promotional mix to get the most from less expensive communications tools such as public relations and direct mail.
- Wherever possible look at expensive projects and ask yourself, "Am I doing this more to suit my ego (or the bosses) and show off to the competition, or is this really necessary and appropriate?"
- When considering complex projects such as multicolor brochures, ask yourself, "Do we really need an eight-color

brochure, or would a well-designed two-color piece work just as well?"

- Use the *zero-based budget* described in Chapter 10. This is a powerful tool for setting priorities when the budget is limited and/or time is in short supply.

- When planning communications activities, the usual tactic is to take the budget dollars and spread them evenly throughout the months of the year. Look at programs and events occurring during your organization's off-season (summer for many markets). Analyze each activity and decide whether the money and the promotion could be more effective if implemented at a more opportune time of year. In the case of retained accounts such as advertising and PR agencies, consider asking them to take reduced retainers during periods of little activity.

- Look at retained accounts and find out if you are consistently using all the hours the retainer is buying. If not, consider adjusting the contract hours to save money.

- Eliminate pet projects and organizational sacred cows. Many companies have special projects and events that really mean more to the organization than to customers. Suspect line items include expensive corporate brochures, customer conferences at swanky resorts, and image campaigns with a focus on corporate quality. They may be justifiable, but make sure before you spend a bundle.

## Don't Scrimp Just to Scrimp

An obvious tactic for saving money is to cut the quality of the communications, but in some cases this may nullify their effectiveness. Excessive scrimping can cause problems. And there are two expensive types of products that should almost never be promoted on the cheap—luxury goods and technology-based products.

Luxury goods require high-class promotion and packaging. For example, an expensive perfume would suffer serious image problems if the product was packaged in plastic eye-dropper bottles—sales would fall off as soon as the product hit the retail shelves. (No matter that the perfume probably costs less than $2.00 to manufacture.) Likewise, cheap, quick-printed brochures for a tract of $875,000 executive-style houses would cause similar image problems.

In the case of technology-oriented products such as computer hardware and software or expensive machinery, photocopied brochures point to a lack of product or company stability. Banks of the past built massive stone buildings to suggest their permanence and legitimacy. Purchasers of products that depend on the continued support and existence of the manufacturer also need to feel that the company will be around to handle problems and repairs.

A minimum standard of communications quality should be set by all companies. This may involve a watchful company president who personally inspects all projects before they are submitted for print or run in media. Or it may be you, the person producing the communications, who personally inspects all projects to maintain the quality standard.

## IF YOU SIMPLY DON'T HAVE ENOUGH MONEY . . .

A common problem in marketing communications is having too many projects or too many products to promote and not enough money. As just mentioned, don't stretch what you do by cheapening individual projects to the point that the results are embarrassingly inadequate or ineffective. Stretching an ad budget too far will result in poorly executed ads, or placements lacking adequate frequency. Low-budget, poorly executed collateral programs or direct mail pieces negatively affect your image and do not help promote sales.

If your budget is extremely tight there are several approaches to consider to be as effective as possible:

- Focus existing dollars on products most likely to generate income. With a successful sales year, you can approach next year with a larger promotional budget and support more activities.
- Get more money. If you are responsible for managing communications in a single department of a large company, money can often be reappropriated from another division, group, or project.
- Focus dollars on advertising and direct mail—proven awareness generators. Then do the publicity work yourself, which costs nothing more than postage and phone calls (see Chapter 4).
- Cancel retained agencies and look for less expensive services elsewhere. Many times busy agencies get neglectful of retained accounts that produce regular income and may not give good value for your money on a monthly basis.
- Telemarketing (outside the scope of this book) is an inexpensive approach for generating leads in certain markets. Telemarketing has been used successfully in many markets that you wouldn't consider likely candidates for this technique, such as large equipment manufacturers and software companies. Look into it.
- Consider advertising in the classified section of the local paper. A large classified ad for a car dealer, for example, is much less expensive than a display ad and may produce just as many leads.

## SAVE MONEY WITH DESKTOP PUBLISHING

Though the technology was nearly unheard of in 1984, desktop publishing (DTP) has revolutionized graphic design and publishing. Beginning with the introduction of the Apple Macintosh computer and Hewlett Packard's first inexpensive laser printer, DTP offers enormous savings over traditional methods. It's also great for projects "on the fly" because time from concept to print can be as little as two days for simple jobs.

An accomplished desktop publisher can write, design, and set type for an entire project—all without leaving his or her chair. Where type used to be set by an outside typesetter requiring several days for turnaround and corrections, with DTP methods an entire project can be handled by one person, start to finish. You'll save money with desktop publishing by getting jobs done faster and by having type changes and corrections made on the spot. In addition to basic design and typesetting, a well-equipped DTP shop or designer can process photos and illustrations and then insert the resulting halftones or color separations into the art right on the desktop computer.

For many projects, laser printer output from the computer is adequate for producing a variety of simple publications. For more complex projects, the finished design is shipped to a *service bureau* for output on an *imagesetter* (a *very* high-resolution printer). The imagesetter produces mechanical art on either *resin-coated paper* or film, ready for the printer. Film is better than paper because although it costs a little more to output, the image is ready for direct transfer to metal plates. Film is also capable of much higher resolution than paper.

DTP systems can also create flashy slide and overhead presentations. Choosing from a number of packages, a designer can assemble a presentation for you to review right on the computer screen. Changes can be made immediately and the presentation output at a service bureau or on the designer's *film recorder* (an output device that makes color 35-mm transparences).

## SAVING MONEY AT THE PRINTERS

Much like costly advertising media charges, printing is an expensive line item on the marketing communications budget. There are ways to save money, however, that few designers or printers will think to suggest. Here are several that have saved money for others.

- **If you are printing an expensive color piece, ask the printer to quote the job on both the designer's choice of paper and the printer's *house sheet*.** A house sheet is a brand and kind of paper that the printer buys in volume and keeps on hand for printing the bulk of the shop's work. Assuming that your four-color job is going to a first-class specialty printer, the shop will usually use a first class paper as the house sheet. Because the printer buys this paper in great volume, his price for it will be substantially less than for a small order of paper used only for your job. All printers will gladly pass this savings on to you and you may get better results because the press people are intimately familiar with the properties of the house sheet and how it takes ink and color.

• **Consider printing your job out of state.** Printing is more expensive in most major cities because labor and property costs are substantially higher. Smaller cities and those located in states experiencing economic downturns can provide excellent printing services at prices considerably lower than those charged in New York, Los Angeles, San Francisco, or Chicago. For example, a four-color job quoted in both Los Angeles and Phoenix revealed that the Los Angeles-based printer's price was more than 25% higher than in Phoenix, because of Arizona's lower overhead.

• **Consider *gang separation* for breaking photos and transparencies down into film for the stripping process.** Gang separation means that multiple color images will be separated at the same time, often considerably reducing expensive prepress separation charges. On the downside, there is a loss of quality and color control because the darkest image may affect the lightest. The bluest colors may shift the yellows with gang separation, but in the case of a catalog, this may be acceptable.

• **Ask the printer for money-saving suggestions.** The pros know the business and have a real knack for identifying minor project changes that can save considerable money. For example, one job required die cutting to create a cardboard product package. The original quote was nearly twice the client's budget, but by asking the printer for advice, the box tabs were shortened by an unnoticeable 1/2 inch allowing the die cutting to be handled through a much cheaper shop capable of using only smaller dies. This cut the quote by 50% !

• **In the case of a brochure or manual that requires frequent updating, consider printing a fancy outside cover and less expensive inside pages.** This allows you to replace the contents as needed without incurring the charges to reprint the more expensive covers each time. To do this, print enough extra covers to last for the project's entire life span and print just enough inside pages for immediate needs. Have the printer store the extra covers and use them to bind successive runs of the piece.

## SAVING MONEY WHEN BUYING MEDIA

For many organizations, advertising media charges are one of the largest expenses in the budget. There are ways to keep prices in line by asking for the agency's share of the commission (assuming you are not working with an agency) or using an agency to locate more effective, but less expensive media (see Chapter 3). In addition, there is another tactic used with substantial success by the authors—just ask for a discount. Yes, just ask!

Depending on the media supplier, there may be unsold pages in a publication or available airtime on radio and TV. Rather than produce a thin publication or stretch programming to cover the nonexistent commercial breaks, many newspapers, magazines, and radio and television channels will give advertisers a deal on unsold space (this is true of billboards and transit ads too). Although it may mean waiting until the last minute to see if anything is available, the savings can be significant, often as much as 50% or more. A really desperate media supplier may give you one or more free placements for each full-price placement. This is even more likely if you are a regular advertiser or buy expensive placements in prime space or prime time.

The obvious exception to this scenario is a media supplier that regularly sells out all placements. Some media channels actually have a backlog of advertisers waiting for space, so asking for a deal will rarely buy you anything. The following are some of the best opportunities for media deals:

- New media channels such as newly launched magazines, new cable-only TV channels, and radio stations that have just changed formats—for example, a country and western station that has recently changed to a top-forty pop format. While the demographic profile may be shaky, the price is right.
- Media channels with declining influence. For example, most afternoon daily newspapers are losing readership to morning papers and offer lower rates to attract advertisers. Even with this tactic they are still losing major accounts to the morning papers. Keeping this in mind and remembering that such a media supplier still has thousands of readers, you might get a deal.
- Offer to place an ad in a prime space if a cancellation occurs. For a variety of reasons, advertisers cancel at the last minute and pull their ads, often paying a penalty in the process. It may be because something material effects the ad's content such as a new product that doesn't work or a key sale item that has unexpectedly become unavailable. Or it may be as simple as an ad that isn't finished in time for placement. A magazine near final production at the printer would rather fill the page with your ad at a cut rate than lay out the entire publication again. By contacting media suppliers at the last minute and asking if they have

any cancelled space that will physically accommodate your ad, you can get a great placement at a fraction of the regular price.

Another kind of tactic workable for companies that regularly place large volumes of ads through a particular media channel is to commit to placing a substantial number of ads in advance if the media supplier will cut the price. Don't confuse this with the frequency discounts that are already automatically available for repeat placements. In this case you get the frequency discount and then ask for an even better deal. For example, a local television station accustomed to the regular revenue from your three-times-daily ad will usually cut their price rather than risk losing you to a competitor. Although this may require a long-term commitment, if you were planning on placing ads that far into the future anyway, this may save you money over the regular frequency-discount price. Again, it doesn't hurt to ask!

## USING A LOW-COST INTERIM PIECE

Quality collateral materials are usually quite expensive to produce. The design, production, and printing costs can run into tens of thousands of dollars surprisingly fast. In the case of a new product where the details may change or the target market may need to be shifted slightly, today's hot new brochure may suddenly turn into tomorrow's pile of trash.

A way around this is to create a test version of the finished piece. Create the piece and have it taken into mechanical and then photocopy the mechanical for distribution. Stamp each copy with a large red stamp that says "NEW" or "PRELIMINARY" or a similar statement announcing it as unfinished, but timely. If there are multiple pages and panels, copy it double-sided on heavy paper and staple the pages together. In the case of a really new product, customers don't mind reading copied literature—in fact, it reminds them that the product is new and fresh. Best of all, this gives you extra time to find typos, refine a wavering message, and sell a few products to pay the upcoming printing bill. As an alternative, you can now use a color copier that provides excellent results for short runs at a fraction of the cost of printing a full run of the final brochure.

In conclusion, the tips and techniques suggested in this chapter can save you a substantial amount of money. But don't limit yourself to these ideas—keep a notebook or card file of tips and techniques that you hear about or that are suggested to you by a helpful vendor. Then, when the budget gets tight, look through your card entries for money-saving suggestions and ideas that will provide you with a dynamite promotion on a shoestring budget!

# The Marketing Communications Glossary

Rather than being just another glossary of general advertising terms that can be found in standard books on the subject, this glossary provides frequently used technical terminology and standard English words that have taken on new meanings in the world of communications. Understanding this jargon will help you work better with vendors and agencies and make you appear more experienced. If you need a more comprehensive glossary of advertising and marketing communications terms, one standard reference is the *Ayer Glossary of Advertising and Related Terms* available from IMS Press. Your local bookstore can order one for you.

**Actual versus Forecast.** A standard accounting tool for tracking how much was spent on a project or category of projects (actual) compared to how much was planned (forecast).

**Agate Lines.** A form of measurement used for newspaper and some column-based magazine advertising. One agate line equals 1/14 inch of depth by one column wide.

**Agency Commission.** The percentage paid to agencies by the media for their services planning and placing media. Usually 15% of the total media bill after discounts.

**Art Director.** The agency person responsible for the design of ads and other print projects. An art director often supervises a staff of designers and production personnel.

**Backgrounder.** A document that provides the press with general information on a product or company to be used to supplement the information in news releases.

**Bingo Leads.** Leads that come from readers circling numbers on a postage-paid business reply card found in many magazines. By circling a number, the company whose ad references that number can respond with literature or a sales call. Bingo lead systems are in the process of being replaced with telephone and FAX-based systems that provide faster response.

**Blitz.** An intense promotional campaign used to build strong awareness of a product and company in a short period of time.

**Blueline.** Paper-based proofs that are usually light blue in color. They are used to show mechanical problems and missing elements before materials go to print. Blueline proofs must be kept out of direct sunlight or they will fade quickly.

**Body Copy.** Copy (text) in an ad or brochure that expands on the main message conveyed by the headline and subheads.

**Business Reply Card (BRC).** A postage-paid postcard used frequently by companies to get responses from ads and direct mail campaigns.

**Cable-Only.** Television stations that can be received only by households that subscribe to cable. These are different from *premium cable* stations and *public access cable stations* because cable-only stations carry paid advertising.

**Cheshire Labels.** Labels produced in solid sheets for mailings that are computer generated. They must be separated and applied by a special kind of machine. Cheshire labels are much less expensive than adhesive labels.

**Chrome.** Short for Chromalin, a color proofing process developed by Dupont that uses dry powder instead of ink.

**Clipping Service.** Outside reading companies that page through publications, watch for articles or editorials that mention the client company or competitors, and clip or copy these to track press coverage.

**Collateral.** All nonmedia print items that a company creates to assist in the sales process. Typical collateral materials include brochures, datasheets, and catalogs.

**Color Separation.** Color photos and illustrations are separated with special photographic equipment into cyan, magenta, yellow, and black layers to print them on a four-color lithographic press.

**Comp.** Short for comprehensive. Designers assemble comps of print designs to show clients what the finished project will look like. In the case of video, the comp takes the form of a storyboard.

**Co-Op Program.** Product manufacturers may pay a portion of a retailer's charges for advertising their products. In most co-op programs, the retailer places an ad for the product, sometimes advertising several products from different manufacturers at once. After the ad runs, the retailer sends the manufacturer a copy of the bill and tearsheet of the ad and the manufacturer then reimburses a percentage of the bill.

**Corpcom.** A euphemism for corporate communications, a name for the communications or advertising department inside companies and corporations.

**Cost per Thousand (CPM).** The cost of reaching 1000 people or prospective customers. CPM rates are used to compare the relative cost of various media options.

**Creative Director.** The person responsible for coming up with ideas for communications programs and seeing them through. The creative director usually manages the art director and the writing team. Sometimes the creative director will also do the writing or part of the design on a project.

**Creatives.** The idea people inside an agency. Good creatives are much sought after and protected by other agency personnel.

**Cross-Promotion.** Several departments in the same large company making products that can be sold together may cross-promote them by advertising them together in the same ad or promotion. Effective cross-promotion delivers a "complete solution" message and saves money at the same time.

**Damage Control.** Used to describe public relations and to a lesser extent advertising efforts used to quell corporation-caused disasters and mishaps. Many companies have damage control plans secretly in place to cover a wide range of market catastrophes.

**Decoding.** A term used to describe how an ad's words and images are perceived by a reader or listener. For example, a TV ad that shows an unattractive man suddenly being noticed by an attractive young woman after using the advertised product is decoded by watchers as "use this product and no matter how you look, you will become instantly desirable to the opposite sex."

**Demographic.** A specific piece of profile information on the kind of people likely to pay attention to a particular media source. For example, a radio station may have demographics emphasizing 35- to 45-year old males, making $25,000 to $45,000 per year, and living in single-family homes in the suburbs.

**Drive Time.** The time of day when radio listeners are likely to be in their cars commuting to or from work. For many radio stations this is the most effective and therefore highest priced time for commercials.

**Editorial.** The news or story content of magazines and newspapers. Not all news in some publications is really news. It may be *advertorial*—paid for articles that masquerade as editorial.

**Encoding.** The process of converting a marketing message into a format suitable to persuade a target audience.

**Eyebrow Head.** A small secondary headline at the top of a page consisting of as few as one word that suggests the topic or subject for a page in a brochure or occasionally in an ad.

**Feedback.** The process of collecting or receiving data on the success (or failure) of a promotional program. This feedback may be as simple as "we sold fourteen extra lawn mowers last week," or as complex as "8% more respondents showed a positive response to the corporate logo than did last week in random testing."

**Four-Color Process.** A system for breaking down continuous tone photographs and illustrations into a format suitable for lithographic reproduction. It allows (in theory) any color to be reproduced as a composite of different levels of the colors cyan, magenta, yellow, and black.

**Freelancer.** A person who provides creative or production services without an agency or corporate affiliation. Occasionally a person with a watch, a Pantone swatch book, and a portfolio, but without a job.

**Frequency.** The number of times an ad is run or seen in a specific media. In direct mail, frequency is the number of times people on a list have ordered products similar to yours from a direct mail promotion.

**Gee-Gaws.** A sarcastic term for advertising specialty items such as imprinted ballpoint pens and other equally imaginative give-away items.

**Glitches.** Tiny, undesirable marks that creep into printed jobs. Often caused by minor sloppiness on the drawing board or dust in the stripping room, the advent of computer-based publishing is reducing this problem significantly.

**Goal or Objective.** A purpose and desired result for a promotional program. Goals are often defined by desired revenue, number of items sold, or new customers acquired.

**Greeking.** A way of representing unwritten copy in layouts, comps, and sketches. It may consist of lines that represent sentences, old copy from another project, or actual Greek or Latin text set in the desired typeface and size. The purpose of greeking is to show a client what a design will look like even though the copy isn't yet written.

**Halftoning.** A technique for breaking continuous tone photographs and illustrations down into dot patterns using screens that can be then reproduced by lithographic presses.

**Headline.** The main attention getting sentence or words in an ad or brochure spread. Also the main idea or message behind a radio or TV commercial.

**Hickies.** Donut-shaped marks printed on paper by offset presses. They are called hickies because of their shape. They are removed by having the pressperson clean the rollers before the final printing is completed.

**Image.** The perceived identity of a company or organization in the minds of the outside world. Image can be both acquired accidently or built deliberately through communications activities.

**Imagesetter.** Specialized print machines that can take a computer-created design or illustration, and typeset and output it at high resolution on paper, negatives, or plates. Charges for imagesetter output are based on the number of dots per inch and the time it takes to output a complex image.

**Infomercial.** A euphemism for a program-length commercial. Infomercials sometimes go to great lengths to look like regular programming and that deliberate deception may eventually get them regulated or banned.

**Insertion Order.** Written confirmations to buy space or media from a media supplier. Insertion orders are contractual and an attorney should review your form before you put it into widespread use.

**Itals.** Short for italics, a modified subset of many typefaces used for expression or to delineate the proper names of books and other publications.

**Joint Promotion.** Several companies joining together to promote products that work together. This, if properly handled, creates powerful communications and saves money.

**Lines per Inch (LPI).** A common way of describing the resolution to be used in halftoning, screening, or printing images.

**Listenership.** A radio station's audience.

**Lit Kit.** Short for literature kit. Many companies have kits consisting of a complete line of literature, testimonials, and maybe even a video that is automatically sent as a package to enquiring customers.

**Litho.** Short for offset lithography, a printing process used for most quality printing in the Western world.

**Logo.** A mark or special type design of a company's name. The logo is used in all communications to create part of the visual identity for a company or organization.

**Mailing List.** A list of addresses (preferably with names but not always) that have identifiable and desirable demographics. These lists are compiled, rented, or sold for addressing direct mail pieces.

**Marcom.** Short for marketing communications, a name given communications and advertising departments in companies and corporations.

**Masthead.** The main identifying symbols of newspapers and newsletters appearing at the top of the first page or near the front of a magazine. The masthead takes the place of a logo for these publications. The information below the masthead provides names and addresses of offices, editors, and sales representatives.

**Matchprint.** A dry color proofing system developed by 3M Corporation.

**Mechanical.** White-faced cardboard (illustration board) with the type and other elements mounted down on it ready for the printer to take into final production. The mechanical may have clear acetate overlays with masks showing where colors should go. A designer, working with a production person, assembles these elements as the final phase of the design job.

**Media Buyer.** Advertising agencies have a specialist on staff who plans and purchases media space for clients. In the case of a large agency, they may have an entire department dedicated to selecting media.

**Media List.** A list of media contacts important to a company or PR agency. These contacts are regularly sent press materials and releases. Also, a list of media useful to a company, usually prepared by an advertising agency as part of a media plan.

**Message.** The central purpose of advertising and other promotional activities is to communicate a clearly defined message.

**Mix.** Refers to a media mix or promotional mix or a marketing mix, which are all different but related things. A media mix is the combination of media that will reach the most prospective customers at the lowest price. A promotional mix is a combination of promotional activities chosen to reach and persuade a maximum number of prospects to buy a product. The marketing mix is the combination of the 4 Ps— product, price, promotion, and place (distribution)—implemented by a company to sell a product.

**Motivate.** To move a prospective customer into action. Motivation may result from the persuasion of advertising or through incentives such as coupons or special pricing.

**News Release.** A document that explains a newsworthy event or happening. The release is mailed to a list of editors and press contacts. Also called a press release.

**Optical Character Recognition (OCR).** A computer-based tool for translating pictures of text into actual text that can then be edited and manipulated within a word processing or page layout program. OCR provides an efficient alternative to retyping lengthy documents.

**Outdoor.** Refers to billboard and transit advertising. Large agencies may have an entire outdoor division.

**Pantone Matching System (PMS).** Colors within the system are called by their PMS numbers. For example, PMS 423 is a medium warm gray. You can buy a Pantone color chart at most art supply stores.

**Place.** One of the four Ps of marketing. Place is where a product is sold, be it in a store, through the mail, or elsewhere. Place is also referred to as distribution by some marketing professionals.

**Placement.** The commitment to run an ad in a specific media at a specific time or location. If you are lucky, an advertising space rep may offer you three placements for the price of two.

**Point.** A typesetter's measurement of type size; there are 72.27 points to an inch. So a character that is 36 points in vertical size is about 1/2 inch tall.

**Portfolio.** An individual's or agency's samples of work done in the past for other clients. Creative people show a portfolio of their best work to get more jobs. Portfolios may consist of samples mounted in a book, slides, photographs, and many other formats depending on the nature of the work.

**Postproduction.** After a commercial is shot either on film or video, a number of tasks must be completed before the commercial is ready to run. These tasks are called postproduction.

**Preproduction.** Before a commercial is shot either on film or video, a number of tasks must be completed and in place. This is referred to as preproduction.

**Press Kit.** Most organizations assemble press kits that contain their backgrounder, recent news releases, and product literature. These kits are sent or given to enquiring editors.

**Price.** One of the four Ps of mar-keting. Price refers to the price of the product. Factors including product value, competitor's pricing, cost of manufacturing, distribution cost, and many other issues must be considered when setting price.

**Prime Time.** In television, prime time is the period from 7:00 p.m. to 11:00 p.m. It is considered the time of day when the largest number of people are likely to be watching TV. As a result, it's the most expensive time to run commercials with the exception of placements during megaevents such as the Super Bowl.

**Product.** One of the four Ps of marketing. Product is what you have to sell. It may consist of goods or services. From the viewpoint of this book, products also include soliciting votes for politicians and donations for not-for-profit organizations.

**Promotion.** One of the four Ps of marketing. Promotion consists of variety of activities to generate awareness and interest in the product that ultimately leads to a purchase commitment. Promotion is largely what this book is about.

**Proofs.** Copies, samples, or tests that show how a completed job or parts of a job will look before the production run is started. The purpose of a proof is to catch mistakes as early in the process as possible.

**Readership.** The people who read a specific magazine or newspaper.

**Registration.** When printing more than one color, the colors must line up with each other or images will look out of focus and white space may appear between colors that touch. If the printing is in registration, the colors will not overlap or have white space between colors. Misregistration occurs when one station of a press is laying colored ink down in the wrong place in comparison to the other station or stations. Misregistration can be cured on press by adjusting the station that is out of register or in extreme cases by making a new plate.

**Rush Charges.** Extra charges applied to jobs where the required turnaround time is less than can normally be expected from a vendor. Rush charges can be substantial. Often, reduced rush charges can be negotiated.

**Sans Serif.** A large family of type faces that do not have serifs (lines or strokes that cap the end of each letter). Most sans serif fonts are also distinguished by the use of equal line widths throughout each character.

**Segment.** Refers to a market segment. A market segment is a portion of the complete set of potential customers for a product. For example, a luxury car with a reputation for extreme reliability and durability make sell to one segment of people concerned with prestige. It may sell to another segment concerned with purchasing a safe and durable car. These segments combined with all the others make up the complete market. Because most markets are segmented, promotional programs often have to be designed with separate marketing communications to reach each segment.

**Serif.** A large family of typefaces characterized by a small stroke at the end of each line that makes up each letter. Serif fonts often have varying line weights throughout each character to add visual interest.

**Service Bureau.** A growing number of small businesses that rent time on expensive equipment used to output computer-designed layouts, illustrations, and color separations at high resolution.

**Share of Mind.** Because potential customers are constantly bombarded with promotions, share of mind refers to the amount of attention they are paying to a particular product or company. One of the goals of advertising is to increase share of mind about a product.

**Shelf Appeal.** In the case of consumer goods sold through retail stores, shelf appeal is important to getting noticed. Attractive packaging is a key aspect of creating a product that has adequate shelf appeal.

**Showings.** The number of billboard or transit ads placed for one ad.

**Signature.** A set of pages to be bound into a book, catalog, or magazine. Lengthy documents are printed in signatures (small groups of pages) and then these groups are bound together to make the finished book. Also, a logo and tagline that appears in all of an advertiser's ads regardless of media. Radio and TV commercials may have audio signatures in the form of snippets of music or sounds that are always used in an advertiser's commercials.

**Spot Color.** Solid colors usually chosen with the Pantone Matching System and laid down as colored type, solids, or as decorative elements.

**Stock Photography.** Existing photographs can be rented from a house that handles stock photos. Many of these houses have thousands to choose from and it is a less expensive alternative to a photo session with a professional photographer.

**Storyboard.** Used to illustrate a television commercial concept. Consisting of a board with several windows cut into it, each window has a drawing of one scene from a commercial with the script written underneath. The purpose of a storyboard is to explain the continuity of the commercial to a client before it goes into production.

**Stripping.** The process of compositing the art for a print job into plates ready for the press. Usually handled by print shops inside their stripping room.

**Subhead.** A secondary headline(s) that helps support or augment the main headline's message. Subheads may also emphasize secondary messages and are used to help draw readers into and through body copy.

**Tape.** Video or audio tape (never adhesive tape).

**Target.** As in target market—the intended audience for an ad or other promotional activity.

**Tearsheets.** Duplicate pages of ads from magazines and newspapers given to the client placing the ad. Tearsheets are used as proof that the ad ran and was reproduced properly.

**Thumbnail.** A miniature drawing of a prospective print layout. Thumbnails illustrate a proposed layout before any of the headlines or images are complete or even defined. Designers often use thumbnails to enhance and refine a

design before moving into tissues or comps.

**Tissues.** Drawings of a layout usually completed early in the design cycle. They are called tissues because they are produced on vellum or other see-through paper. The purpose of using transparent paper is to allow the designer to trace a series of earlier tissue drawings, gradually refining a design.

**Web Press.** A (usually) large press that takes paper from a roll rather than by the sheet. They are called webs because the paper must run through a series of rollers and switchbacks before reaching the printing area of the press. The paper moving through the rollers resembles a spider's web and hence their name. Webs are used for long runs where perfect quality isn't as important as keeping the press time to a minimum.

**Wish List.** Used frequently in communications to list all the projects useful to promoting a product if money and time were no object. Using a wish list sometimes brings out new and fresh ideas that otherwise would never have been considered. Wish lists are subsequently scaled back to fit time and budget realities.

**Zero-Based Budget (ZBB).** A powerful tool for evaluating exactly those projects that should be implemented and those that must be put off or scrapped due to time and/or budget constraints.

# Useful References

## WHERE TO LOCATE AGENCY AND CREATIVE TALENT

Many of following publications can be found in the book section of a large art supply store.

*A.R. 5—The Complete Annual Report and Corporate Image Planning Book,* Macmillan Creative Services Group, 115 5th Avenue, New York, NY 10003.

*Adweek Portfolios,* A/S/M Communications, Inc., 49 E. 21 Street, New York, NY 10010.

*Agency Book, The,* Gavin Brackenridge & Company, Inc., 307 E. 37th Street, New York, NY 10016.

*American Showcase,* American Showcase, Inc., 724 5th Avenue, 10th Floor, New York, NY 10019.

*Communication Arts,* Communication Arts, 410 Sherman Avenue, PO Box 10300, Palo Alto, CA 94303.

*Creative Black Book, The,* Macmillan Information Company, 115 5th Avenue, New York, NY 10003.

*Graphis,* Graphis Press Corporation, Dufourstrasse 107, 8008 Zurich, Switzerland.

*N.Y. Gold,* N.Y. Gold, Inc., 150 5th Avenue, New York, NY 10011.

*O'Dwyer's Directory of Public Relations Firms,* J. R. O'Dwyer Company, 271 Madison Avenue, New York, NY 10016.

*Standard Directory of Advertising Agencies,* National Register Publications Company, Inc., 5201 Old Orchard Road, Skokie, IL 60076.

*Stock Photo and Assignment Source Book,* The Photographic Arts Center, 127 E. 59th Street, New York, NY 10022.

*Workbook, The,* Scott and Daughters Publishing, Inc., 940 N. Highland Avenue, Los Angeles, CA 90038.

## ADVERTISING RESEARCH ORGANIZATIONS

A. C. Nielson Company, 1290 Avenue of the Americas, New York, NY 10019.

Advertising Research Foundation, 3 East 54th Street, New York, NY 10022.

Arbitron Company, 1350 Avenue of the Americas, New York, NY 10019.

Audit Bureau of Circulation, 123 N. Wacker Drive, Chicago, IL 60606.

Gale Research Inc., 2200 Book Tower, Detroit, MI 48226.

Gallup & Robinson, Marketing and Advertising Research, 575 Ewing Street, Princeton, NJ 08540.

Statistical Research, Inc. 111 Prospect Street, Westfield, NJ 07090.

## USEFUL PUBLICATIONS AND DIRECTORIES ON MEDIA AND RESEARCH

*Ayer Glossary of Advertising and Related Terms,* 2nd ed., IMS Press, 426 Pennsylvania Avenue, Fort Washington, PA 19034.

*Bacon's Publicity Checker,* Bacon's Publishing Co., Inc., 332 S. Michigan Avenue, Chicago, IL 60604.

*Gale Directory of Publications and Broadcast Media,* Gale Research Inc., Dept. 77748, Detroit, MI 48277–0748.

*Guide to Advertising Research Services,* Advertising Research Foundation, Inc., 3 East 54th Street, New York, NY 10022.

*Journal of Advertising Research,* Advertising Research Foundation, Inc., 3 East 54th Street, New York, NY 10022.

*Standard Rate and Data Service,* Standard Rate and Data Service, Inc., National Register Publication Company, 5201 Old Orchard Road, Skokie, IL 60076.

## HOW AND WHERE TO PLACE PROMOTIONAL ARTICLES AND BOOKS

*Writer's Market,* Writer's Digest Books, 1507 Dana Avenue, Cincinnati, Ohio 45207.

## USEFUL ASSOCIATIONS AND ORGANIZATIONS

American Management Association, Marketing Division, 135 West 50th Street, New York, NY 10020.

American Marketing Association, 222 South Riverside Plaza, Chicago, IL 60606.

Business and Professional Advertising Association (BPAA), 41 East 42nd Street, New York, NY 10017.

US Small Business Administration (SBA), PO Box 15434, Fort Worth, TX 76119.

# Bibliography

Aldrich-Ruenzel, Nancy, ed., *Designer's Guide to Print Production*, Watson-Guptill Publications, New York, 1990.

Bovée, Courtland L., and Arens, William F., *Contemporary Advertising*, 2nd ed., Richard D. Irwin, Homewood, IL, 1986.

Denton, Keith, "Improving Community Relations," *Small Business Reports*, August 1990, pp. 33–41.

Gray, Ernest, *Profitable Methods for Small Business Advertising*, John Wiley, New York, 1984.

Haberman, David A., and Dolphin, Harry A., *Public Relations: The Necessary Art*, Iowa State University Press, Ames, IA, 1988.

Higgins, Denis (interviewer), *The Art of Writing Advertising: Conversations with William Bernbach, Leo Burnett, George Gribbin, David Ogilvy and Rosser Reeves*, NTC Business Books, Lincolnwood, IL, 1987.

Nash, Edward L., *Direct Marketing: Strategy, Planning, Execution*, 2nd ed., McGraw-Hill, New York, 1986.

White, Hooper, *How to Produce Effective TV Commercials*, NTC Business Books, Lincolnwood, IL, 1986.

# Index

Printed in the United States
By Bookmasters